Super Easy

Mediterranean Diet Cookbook

for Beginners

2000 Days Quick & Delicious Mediterranean Recipes for Living and Eating Well
Every Day | Along with A No-Stress 30-Day Meal Plan

Bethany O. Morgan

Table of Contents

INTRODUCTION

The Mediterranean Diet: A Path to Health and Well-being

The Mediterranean diet has emerged as a powerful and proven approach to eating that not only promotes physical health but also contributes to overall well-being. With its roots in the traditional dietary patterns of countries bordering the Mediterranean Sea, this way of eating has garnered significant attention and recognition for its numerous health benefits.

At its core, the Mediterranean diet is more than just a meal plan – it represents a lifestyle characterized by balance, moderation, and an appreciation for wholesome, natural foods. The diet emphasizes a high consumption of fruits, vegetables, whole grains, legumes, nuts, and seeds, which are rich in essential nutrients, antioxidants, and dietary fiber. These plant-based foods provide a solid foundation for overall health, promoting optimal functioning of the body's systems and reducing the risk of chronic diseases such as heart disease, diabetes, and certain types of cancer.

Central to the Mediterranean diet is the liberal use of olive oil as the primary source of dietary fat. Olive oil, a staple in Mediterranean cuisine, is abundant in monounsaturated fats, which have been shown to have numerous health benefits, including reducing inflammation, improving heart health, and supporting brain function. The inclusion of healthy fats in the diet not only contributes to satiety and flavor but also aids in the absorption of fat-soluble vitamins.

Another defining feature of the Mediterranean diet is the moderate intake of fish, poultry, eggs, and dairy products. These protein sources provide essential amino acids, vitamins, and minerals that support muscle growth, repair, and overall health. Fish, in particular, such as salmon, sardines, and mackerel, is rich in omega-3 fatty acids, which are beneficial for heart health, brain function, and reducing inflammation. The diet also allows for moderate consumption of red wine, which is enjoyed in moderation and provides antioxidants like resveratrol.

On the other hand, the Mediterranean diet encourages limited consumption of red meat and sweets. Red meat is typically reserved for special occasions, while sweets and sugary beverages are enjoyed sparingly. By minimizing the intake of these foods, the Mediterranean diet reduces the risk of weight gain, high cholesterol levels, and other negative health outcomes associated with excessive sugar and saturated fat consumption.

Portion control is also an essential component of the Mediterranean diet. This mindful approach to eating allows individuals to savor their meals, tune in to their body's hunger and fullness cues, and avoid overeating. The diet promotes a slower pace of eating, providing ample time to enjoy the flavors and textures of each dish and fostering a sense of satisfaction and contentment after a meal.

Beyond the physical health benefits, the Mediterranean diet is also associated with improved mental well-being. The diet's emphasis on fresh, whole foods, rich in nutrients and antioxidants, supports brain health and cognitive function. Additionally, the Mediterranean lifestyle encourages social connections and a sense of community, as meals are often shared with family and friends, fostering a positive impact on mental health and overall happiness.

The Mediterranean diet's impact extends beyond the individual level to the environment and sustainability. With its focus on locally sourced, seasonal ingredients, the diet promotes a more sustainable food system, reducing the carbon footprint associated with long-distance transportation and supporting local farmers and producers. By embracing the Mediterranean diet, individuals can contribute to a healthier planet and a more resilient and interconnected food system.

In conclusion, the Mediterranean diet offers a holistic approach to health and well-being, encompassing not only the nourishment of the body but also the enjoyment of meals, social connections, and sustainable living. By adopting this lifestyle, individuals can unlock the benefits of wholesome, flavorful foods while embracing a balanced and mindful way of eating. The Mediterranean diet is not just a path to physical health; it is a journey towards overall vitality and happiness.

Chapter ①
Mediterranean Diet Essentials

Understanding the Mediterranean Diet

To truly embrace the Mediterranean diet and reap its numerous benefits, it is essential to develop a comprehensive understanding of its principles and foundations. This section will delve into the core elements of the Mediterranean diet, allowing you to grasp the essence of this time-honored way of eating.

At its heart, the Mediterranean diet is a plant-based dietary pattern inspired by the traditional eating habits of countries surrounding the Mediterranean Sea. It emphasizes the consumption of fruits, vegetables, whole grains, legumes, nuts, and seeds as the foundation of daily meals. These plant-based foods are not only rich in vitamins, minerals, and antioxidants, but they also provide dietary fiber, which plays a vital role in supporting digestive health and maintaining a healthy weight.

Olive oil is a cornerstone of the Mediterranean diet, serving as the primary source of fat. This golden elixir, derived from the pressing of olives, is packed with monounsaturated fats, which are known for their heart-healthy properties. Olive oil not only adds flavor and richness to dishes but also provides anti-inflammatory benefits and helps lower "bad" cholesterol levels. It is used liberally in cooking, dressings, and marinades, further enhancing the flavors of Mediterranean cuisine.

Fish and seafood play a significant role in the Mediterranean diet, providing lean protein and essential omega-3 fatty acids. Fatty fish such as salmon, sardines, and mackerel are particularly prized for their omega-3 content, which supports heart health, brain function, and overall well-being. Poultry, eggs, and dairy products are also included in moderation, offering additional sources of protein and essential nutrients.

Red meat, on the other hand, is consumed sparingly in the Mediterranean diet, often reserved for special occasions. This approach aligns with research suggesting that excessive red meat consumption is linked to an increased risk of certain chronic diseases. By limiting the intake of red meat, the Mediterranean diet encourages a more plant-centric approach to eating, which has been associated with various health benefits.

The Mediterranean diet also encourages a generous intake of fruits and vegetables, showcasing the vibrant colors and flavors of the Mediterranean region. These antioxidant-rich foods provide a wide range of health-promoting compounds, supporting immune function, reducing inflammation, and protecting against chronic diseases. The diet encourages seasonal and local produce whenever possible, ensuring the freshness and nutritional integrity of the ingredients.

Another key aspect of the Mediterranean diet is the inclusion of whole grains, such as whole wheat, barley, and oats. These grains offer complex carbohydrates, fiber, and a host of essential nutrients. They provide sustained energy and help regulate blood sugar levels, promoting satiety and preventing spikes in insulin. Whole grains are a staple in Mediterranean cuisine, featuring in dishes like whole grain salads, pilafs, and bread.

In addition to its emphasis on wholesome foods, the Mediterranean diet places importance on the social and cultural aspects of eating. Meals are typically enjoyed in the company of others, fostering a sense of community and connection. This shared experience promotes a relaxed and enjoyable approach to eating, encouraging individuals to savor each bite and cultivate a mindful relationship with food.

Understanding the Mediterranean diet also involves recognizing its potential health benefits. Extensive research has shown that adhering to the Mediterranean diet can reduce the risk of heart disease, stroke, and certain cancers. It has also been associated with improved cognitive function, better weight management, and increased longevity. The combination of nutrient-rich foods, healthy fats, and an overall balanced approach contributes to these positive outcomes.

By embracing the Mediterranean diet, individuals have the opportunity to transform their relationship with food and embrace a lifestyle that promotes well-being, longevity, and a greater appreciation for the pleasures of the table. With its abundance of delicious flavors and diverse culinary traditions, the Mediterranean diet offers a roadmap to a healthier and more vibrant way of life.

Exploring the Mediterranean Flavors

One of the most delightful aspects of the Mediterranean diet is the vast array of flavors it offers. From the sun-kissed fruits and vegetables to the aromatic herbs and spices, Mediterranean cuisine is a symphony of tastes that tantalize the palate and nourish the body. This section will take you on a flavorful journey, exploring the essential ingredients and spices that define the Mediterranean flavor profile.

Essential Ingredients:

a) Olive Oil: The Mediterranean's liquid gold, olive oil, is not only a healthy source of monounsaturated fats but also a flavor enhancer. Its smooth and fruity notes add richness to salads, sautés, and marinades, elevating dishes to new heights.

b) Fresh Herbs: The Mediterranean region is renowned for its abundant use of fresh herbs like basil, oregano, rosemary, thyme, and parsley. These aromatic herbs infuse dishes with a burst of freshness and add complexity to soups, stews, sauces, and roasted vegetables.

c) Citrus Fruits: Lemons, oranges, and grapefruits feature prominently in Mediterranean cuisine, providing a tangy brightness to both savory and sweet dishes. The zesty flavors of citrus fruits complement seafood, salads, and desserts, adding a refreshing twist to the meal.

d) Tomatoes: Juicy, ripe tomatoes are a staple ingredient in Mediterranean cooking. From fresh tomato salads to rich tomato-based sauces, they lend a vibrant, sweet-tart flavor to countless dishes.

e) Garlic and Onions: These aromatic ingredients form the foundation of many Mediterranean recipes, adding depth and complexity to sauces, soups, and marinades. Their pungent flavors create a savory base that enhances the overall taste of the dish.

Signature Spices and Seasonings:

a) Mediterranean Herb Blend: A combination of dried herbs like basil, oregano, thyme, and rosemary, this versatile blend infuses dishes with the earthy and fragrant notes of the Mediterranean region. It works well in marinades, roasted vegetables, and pasta sauces.

b) Cumin: This warm and earthy spice adds depth and a hint of smokiness to Mediterranean dishes, such as hummus, roasted vegetables, and grilled meats.

c) Paprika: Whether sweet, smoked, or spicy, paprika lends a vibrant red color and a mild, sweet pepper flavor to Mediterranean stews, soups, and meat dishes.

d) Cinnamon: While typically associated with sweet treats, cinnamon also plays a role in Mediterranean cuisine. Its warm and aromatic notes complement savory dishes, such as slow-cooked lamb, Moroccan tagines, and Greek moussaka.

e) Za'atar: A Middle Eastern spice blend, za'atar combines dried herbs like thyme, oregano, marjoram, sumac, and sesame seeds. It adds a tangy, herbal flavor to salads, roasted vegetables, and grilled meats.

Exploring Mediterranean flavors means embracing the unique taste profiles and experimenting with different combinations of ingredients and spices. It's about allowing the natural flavors of fresh, seasonal produce to shine and using herbs and spices to elevate and enhance the overall taste experience.

In addition to the key ingredients and spices, the Mediterranean diet celebrates the simplicity of preparation. It encourages cooking methods like grilling, roasting, and braising to bring out the natural flavors and textures of ingredients. It's about appreciating the beauty of a ripe tomato drizzled with olive oil and sprinkled with sea salt or savoring a grilled fish seasoned with fresh herbs and a squeeze of lemon.

As you embark on your culinary journey through Mediterranean flavors, don't be afraid to experiment, adapt, and personalize your dishes. The Mediterranean diet offers a treasure trove of taste sensations, allowing you to create meals that are both nourishing and utterly delicious. So gather your ingredients, fire up the stove, and let the Mediterranean flavors transport you to the sun-drenched shores of the

Mediterranean Sea.

Traditional Mediterranean Dishes

The culinary heritage of the Mediterranean region is rich with a diverse array of traditional dishes that have stood the test of time. These dishes not only reflect the unique flavors and ingredients of the region but also represent the cultural and historical significance of Mediterranean cuisine. In this section, we will explore some of the most beloved and iconic traditional Mediterranean dishes.

- **Greek Moussaka:** A beloved Greek dish, moussaka is a layered casserole consisting of eggplant, ground meat (often beef or lamb), and a rich tomato sauce. It is typically topped with a creamy béchamel sauce and baked until golden and bubbling. Moussaka showcases the harmonious combination of flavors, textures, and spices that define Greek cuisine.

- **Spanish Paella:** Hailing from the coastal regions of Spain, paella is a vibrant and aromatic rice dish cooked in a wide, shallow pan. Traditionally, paella features a variety of ingredients such as saffron-infused rice, chicken, seafood, and vegetables. It is a celebration of flavors and a testament to the bounty of the Mediterranean's land and sea.

- **Italian Caprese Salad:** Simple yet elegant, the Caprese salad is a classic Italian dish that epitomizes the essence of Mediterranean flavors. It consists of ripe tomatoes, fresh mozzarella cheese, and basil leaves, drizzled with extra-virgin olive oil and balsamic glaze. The combination of these ingredients creates a harmonious blend of colors, textures, and tastes.

- **Moroccan Tagine:** A staple in Moroccan cuisine, the tagine is a slow-cooked stew that takes its name from the clay pot in which it is traditionally cooked. It features a combination of tender meats, such as lamb or chicken, and an array of aromatic spices, dried fruits, and vegetables. The slow cooking method allows the flavors to meld together, resulting in a rich and fragrant dish.

- **Lebanese Hummus:** Hummus is a creamy and velvety dip made from cooked chickpeas, tahini (sesame seed paste), garlic, lemon juice, and olive oil. It is a staple in Lebanese cuisine and is often served with warm pita bread, fresh vegetables, or as part of a mezze platter. Hummus showcases the simplicity and versatility of Mediterranean ingredients, offering a delightful blend of flavors and textures.

- **Turkish Baklava:** Indulge your sweet tooth with the decadent delight of Turkish baklava. This pastry is made by layering thin sheets of phyllo dough with a mixture of finely chopped nuts, honey or syrup, and fragrant spices such as cinnamon and cardamom. The result is a flaky, sweet treat that perfectly balances richness and nuttiness.

- **French Ratatouille:** Ratatouille is a classic French vegetable stew originating from the Mediterranean region of Provence. It features a medley of fresh summer vegetables such as tomatoes, eggplant, zucchini, bell peppers, and herbs. Slow-cooked until the flavors meld together, ratatouille embodies the rustic charm and vibrant flavors of Mediterranean cooking.

These traditional Mediterranean dishes are just a glimpse into the vast culinary heritage of the region. They exemplify the use of fresh, seasonal ingredients, aromatic herbs and spices, and cooking techniques that bring out the natural flavors of each ingredient. Whether you're enjoying a comforting plate of moussaka, savoring the flavors of paella, or indulging in the sweetness of baklava, these dishes capture the essence of Mediterranean cuisine and offer a true taste of the Mediterranean way of life.

Adapting the Mediterranean Diet

While the Mediterranean diet is rooted in the traditional eating patterns of Mediterranean countries, it is also a flexible and adaptable approach to nutrition. This adaptability allows individuals from diverse cultural backgrounds and dietary preferences to embrace and benefit from the Mediterranean diet. In this section, we will explore how you can adapt the Mediterranean diet to suit your individual needs and lifestyle.

- **Incorporating Local Ingredients:** One of the key principles of the Mediterranean diet is the emphasis on fresh, seasonal, and locally sourced ingredients. By adapting the diet to your local environment, you can explore and incorporate regional produce that aligns with the Mediterranean diet's core principles. Whether it's incorporating local fruits, vegetables, or grains, embracing the flavors and nutritional benefits of your local food culture can enhance your Mediterranean diet experience.

- **Vegetarian and Vegan Adaptations:** The Mediterranean diet is inherently plant-based, making it well-suited for those following a vegetarian or vegan lifestyle. By focusing on legumes, whole grains, fruits, vegetables, nuts, and seeds, you can create a diverse range of delicious and nutritious vegetarian or vegan meals. Plant-based proteins such as tofu, tempeh, and legumes can be used as alternatives to animal-based proteins, ensuring that your diet remains balanced and rich in essential nutrients.

- **Gluten-Free Options:** For individuals with gluten sensitivities or celiac disease, adapting the Mediterranean diet to be gluten-free is entirely possible. Naturally gluten-free grains such as quinoa, brown rice, and buckwheat can be substituted for gluten-containing grains like wheat, barley, and rye. Fresh fruits, vegetables, lean proteins, and healthy fats continue to form the foundation of a gluten-free Mediterranean diet, allowing you to enjoy a wide range of flavors and dishes.

- **Customizing Portion Sizes:** Portion control is an essential aspect of the Mediterranean diet. While the diet encourages the consumption of wholesome foods, it also emphasizes moderation and mindful eating. Adapt the Mediterranean diet to your specific energy needs and lifestyle by customizing portion sizes. This ensures that you maintain a healthy balance between calorie intake and expenditure while still enjoying the rich flavors and variety of Mediterranean cuisine.

- **Fusion and Global Influences:** The beauty of the Mediterranean diet is its ability to embrace culinary influences from around the world. By incorporating elements of other cuisines and flavors, you can create unique and exciting Mediterranean-inspired fusion dishes. Experiment with herbs, spices, and cooking techniques from various cultures to infuse your meals with new dimensions of flavor while keeping the essence of the Mediterranean diet intact.

- **Meal Planning and Preparation:** Adapting the Mediterranean diet can be made easier by incorporating meal planning and preparation into your routine. Set aside time each week to plan your meals, create shopping lists, and prep ingredients in advance. This not only saves time but also ensures that you have nutritious and delicious Mediterranean-inspired meals readily available. By planning ahead, you can maintain consistency and make the Mediterranean diet a seamless part of your daily life.

Remember, the Mediterranean diet is not a rigid set of rules but rather a flexible and adaptable approach to healthy eating. It is about embracing the core principles of the diet while tailoring it to your individual preferences and needs. By adapting the Mediterranean diet to suit your lifestyle, cultural background, and dietary requirements, you can enjoy the countless health benefits and culinary delights that this vibrant way of eating has to offer.

Mediterranean-Inspired Fusion Cuisine

One of the exciting aspects of the Mediterranean diet is its versatility and adaptability to various culinary influences. Mediterranean-inspired fusion cuisine allows you to explore the vibrant flavors of the Mediterranean region while infusing them with elements from other culinary traditions. By combining the essence of the Mediterranean diet with ingredients, techniques, and spices from around the world, you can create unique and tantalizing dishes that showcase a fusion of cultures. In this section, we will delve into the world of Mediterranean-inspired fusion cuisine and how you can get creative in your kitchen.

- **Spice Blends and Seasonings:** Spices are the gateway to creating flavorful fusion dishes. Experiment with spice blends from different regions and cultures to add depth and complexity to your Mediterranean-inspired creations. For example, combine Mediterranean herbs like basil and oregano with North African spices like cumin and coriander to create a fusion of Mediterranean and Moroccan flavors. These spice blends can be used to season meats, vegetables, and sauces, infusing your dishes with a delightful fusion of aromas and tastes.

- **Ingredients from Other Cuisines:** Expand your culinary horizons by incorporating ingredients from other cuisines into your Mediterranean dishes. For instance, you can add Asian-inspired elements like ginger, soy sauce, and sesame oil to create a fusion of Mediterranean and Asian flavors. Consider using ingredients like coconut milk, curry paste, or lemongrass to infuse a touch of Southeast Asian flair into Mediterranean-inspired soups or stews.

- **Fusion Tapas and Small Plates:** The concept of tapas, popular in Mediterranean countries like Spain, lends itself well to fusion cuisine. Create a tapas-style menu featuring a variety of small plates that combine Mediterranean flavors with ingredients and techniques from other cuisines. For example, serve crispy falafel bites with a zesty Asian-inspired dipping sauce or top bruschetta with a fusion of Mediterranean and Mexican ingredients, such as fresh tomatoes, avocado, and a sprinkle of crumbled feta cheese.

- **Global Ingredient Substitutions:** Put a Mediterranean twist on traditional recipes from other cuisines by substituting Mediterranean ingredients for their counterparts. For instance, replace traditional pasta with zucchini noodles or spiralized sweet potatoes in an Italian-inspired dish. Swap out traditional bread for pita or lavash to create a Mediterranean-inspired wrap with fillings from different cuisines. These creative substitutions allow you to explore new flavor profiles while still incorporating the essence of the Mediterra-

nean diet.

- **Fusion Grilling and Roasting:** The Mediterranean diet's love for grilling and roasting can be taken to a whole new level with fusion cuisine. Experiment with different marinades, spice rubs, and glazes inspired by various cuisines to infuse your grilled or roasted meats, seafood, and vegetables with exciting flavors. Consider marinating chicken in a blend of Mediterranean herbs, lemon, and Middle Eastern spices like sumac and za'atar for a fusion of Mediterranean and Middle Eastern flavors.

- **Dessert Delights:** Don't forget to bring the fusion concept into your Mediterranean-inspired desserts. Incorporate exotic fruits, spices, or sweet ingredients from different cultures to create unique and delicious sweet treats. For example, infuse a classic Mediterranean yogurt parfait with tropical flavors by adding diced mango, coconut flakes, and a drizzle of honey. Or experiment with a fusion of Mediterranean and Latin American flavors by combining rich dark chocolate with spices like cinnamon and a sprinkle of chili powder.

Mediterranean-inspired fusion cuisine is a playground for culinary creativity. It allows you to combine the best of Mediterranean flavors with elements from other cuisines to create dishes that are truly one-of-a-kind. So unleash your imagination, experiment with different ingredients and techniques, and let the fusion of flavors transport you to new culinary realms where the Mediterranean meets the world.

Embracing the Mediterranean Lifestyle

Congratulations on embarking on a journey to embrace the Mediterranean lifestyle! By adopting the Mediterranean diet and incorporating its principles into your daily life, you are not only nourishing your body but also cultivating a holistic approach to health and well-being. The Mediterranean lifestyle goes beyond just the food on your plate—it encompasses a way of life that promotes balance, enjoyment, and connection with nature and community.

Throughout this cookbook, we have explored the origins and principles of the Mediterranean diet, its health benefits, and the diverse range of flavors and ingredients that make up its culinary tapestry. We have delved into traditional Mediterranean dishes, learned about the importance of seasonal eating and local produce, and discovered the art of mastering Mediterranean cooking techniques. We have also ventured into the realm of Mediterranean-inspired fusion cuisine, allowing our taste buds to explore new horizons while staying true to the essence of the Mediterranean diet.

By adopting the Mediterranean lifestyle, you are embracing a way of life that celebrates the simplicity and abundance of nature's offerings. It encourages you to savor each meal, relishing the flavors and textures of fresh, wholesome ingredients. It emphasizes the importance of social connections and gathering with loved ones around a shared table. It encourages regular physical activity, such as leisurely walks, gardening, or dancing, to keep your body active and energized. It promotes a mindful approach to eating, paying attention to hunger and fullness cues, and savoring each bite.

Not only does the Mediterranean lifestyle support your physical well-being, but it also nourishes your mental and emotional health. The focus on whole, nutrient-rich foods provides your body with the necessary nutrients to thrive, while the abundance of antioxidants and anti-inflammatory compounds in Mediterranean ingredients supports brain health and reduces the risk of chronic diseases. The act of preparing and sharing meals with others fosters a sense of connection and belonging, promoting positive mental well-being. The Mediterranean lifestyle encourages you to slow down, savor the present moment, and find joy in the simple pleasures of life.

As you embark on this Mediterranean journey, remember to be patient with yourself and allow for flexibility. The Mediterranean lifestyle is not about strict rules or perfection—it is about finding a sustainable and enjoyable approach to nourishing your body and soul. Embrace the diversity and adaptability of the Mediterranean diet, and feel free to modify and personalize it to suit your individual preferences, cultural background, and dietary needs.

In closing, I invite you to embrace the Mediterranean lifestyle with open arms and an open heart. Let the flavors of the Mediterranean nourish your body, delight your senses, and bring joy to your life. Explore the vast array of traditional dishes, get creative with Mediterranean-inspired fusion cuisine, and savor the benefits of seasonal eating and local produce. Embrace the Mediterranean lifestyle not just as a short-term diet but as a lifelong commitment to your health, happiness, and overall well-being. Bon appétit and cheers to a vibrant and fulfilling Mediterranean journey!

30 Days Mediterranean Diet Meal Plan

DAYS	BREAKFAST	LUNCH	DINNER	SNACK/DESSERT
1	Broccoli-Mushroom Frittata P13	Braised Radishes with Sugar Snap Peas and Dukkah P54	Red Pepper, Pomegranate, and Walnut Salad P86	Greek Yogurt with Honey and Pomegranates P93
2	Summer Day Fruit Salad P13	Stuffed Artichokes P54	Pipirrana (Spanish Summer Salad) P86	Lemon Coconut Cake P93
3	Avocado Toast with Smoked Trout P14	Herbed Shiitake Mushrooms P54	Arugula Spinach Salad with Shaved Parmesan P86	Chocolate-Dipped Fruit Bites P93
4	Savory Zucchini Muffins P13	Spicy Creamer Potatoes P55	Bacalhau and Black-Eyed Pea Salad P86	Fresh Figs with Chocolate Sauce P95
5	Italian Egg Cups P14	Sautéed Crunchy Greens P55	Arugula and Fennel Salad with Fresh Basil P87	Minty Watermelon Salad P95
6	Strawberry Basil Honey Ricotta Toast P16	Saffron Couscous with Almonds, Currants, and Scallions P55	Tossed Green Mediterranean Salad P87	Whipped Greek Yogurt with Chocolate P94
7	Spanish Tuna Tortilla with Roasted Peppers P14	Mushroom-Stuffed Zucchini P55	Caprese Salad with Fresh Mozzarella P87	Mascarpone and Fig Crostini P94
8	Golden Egg Skillet P15	Puréed Cauliflower Soup P56	Valencia-Inspired Salad P88	Grilled Fruit Kebabs with Honey Labneh P95
9	Peach Sunrise Smoothie P16	Roasted Broccolini with Garlic and Romano P56	Raw Zucchini Salad P88	Karithopita (Greek Juicy Walnut Cake) P94
10	Quick Low-Carb Avocado Toasts P14	Caponata (Sicilian Eggplant) P56	Sicilian Salad P88	Brown Betty Apple Dessert P98
11	Blueberry-Lemon Tea Cakes P16	Sea Salt Soybeans P26	Mediterranean Potato Salad P88	Grilled Stone Fruit P98
12	Morning Buzz Iced Coffee P16	Honey and Spice Glazed Carrots P57	Cauliflower Tabbouleh Salad P91	Baklava and Honey P95
13	Amaranth Breakfast Bowl with Chocolate and Almonds P16	Lemon-Rosemary Beets P60	Zucchini and Ricotta Salad P87	Peaches Poached in Rose Water P95
14	Almond Butter Ba-nana Chocolate Smoothie P16	Mediterranean Cauliflower Tabbouleh P58	Panzanella (Tuscan Tomato and Bread Salad) P89	Individual Apple Pockets P96
15	Baked Ricotta with Pears P17	White Beans with Rosemary, Sage, and Garlic P58	Powerhouse Arugula Salad P89	Roasted Orange Rice Pudding P96

DAYS	BREAKFAST	LUNCH	DINNER	SNACK/DESSERT
16	Power Peach Smoothie Bowl P15	Balsamic Beets P58	Asparagus Salad P89	Lemon Fool P96
17	Breakfast Panini with Eggs, Olives, and Tomatoes P18	Steamed Cauliflower with Olive Oil and Herbs P56	Tuscan Kale Salad with Anchovies P88	Pears with Blue Cheese and Walnuts P98
18	Berry Baked Oatmeal P18	Sautéed Mustard Greens and Red Peppers P59	Greek Black-Eyed Pea Salad P89	Vanilla-Poached Apricots P97
19	Spiced Antioxidant Granola Clusters P15	Fried Zucchini Salad P59	Citrus Fennel Salad P89	Orange–Olive Oil Cupcakes P97
20	Crunchy Vanilla Protein Bars P13	Zesty Fried Asparagus P60	Flank Steak Spinach Salad P91	Ricotta with Balsamic Cherries and Black Pepper P97
21	Greek Breakfast Power Bowl P17	Roasted Eggplant P60	Tuna Niçoise P91	Chocolate Turtle Hummus P93
22	Nuts and Fruit Oatmeal P18	Braised Fennel P58	Orange-Tarragon Chicken Salad Wrap P90	Red Grapefruit Granita P97
23	Enjoy-Your-Veggies Breakfast P17	Steamed Vegetables P60	Dakos (Cretan Salad) P90	Spanish Cream P98
24	Berry Breakfast Smoothie P18	Rustic Cauliflower and Carrot Hash P59	Traditional Greek Salad P90	Figs with Mascarpone and Honey P98
25	Mexican Breakfast Pepper Rings P18	Baba Ghanoush P61	Garlic-Asparagus Israeli Couscous P21	Cinnamon-Stewed Dried Plums with Greek Yogurt P99
26	Berry Warming Smoothie P18	Garlicky Sautéed Zucchini with Mint P61	Couscous with Apricots P21	Chocolate Lava Cakes P99
27	Breakfast Hash P19	Lemony Orzo	Chili-Spiced Beans P61	Italian Crepe with Herbs and Onion P71
28	Oat and Fruit Parfait P17	Ratatouille P60	Moroccan White Beans with Lamb P22	Fig-Pecan Energy Bites P72
29	Butternut Squash and Ricotta Frittat P19	Vegetable Terrine P59	Herbed Barley P22	Marinated Olives P73
30	Turkish Egg Bowl P15	Sesame-Ginger Broccoli P60	Chickpea Fritters P22	Sfougato P76

Chapter 2

Breakfasts

Broccoli-Mushroom Frittata

Prep time: 10 minutes | Cook time: 20 minutes | Serves 2

1 tablespoon olive oil	½ teaspoon salt
1½ cups broccoli florets, finely chopped	¼ teaspoon freshly ground black pepper
½ cup sliced brown mushrooms	6 eggs
¼ cup finely chopped onion	¼ cup Parmesan cheese

1. In a nonstick cake pan, combine the olive oil, broccoli, mushrooms, onion, salt, and pepper. Stir until the vegetables are thoroughly coated with oil. Place the cake pan in the air fryer basket and set the air fryer to 400ºF (204ºC). Air fry for 5 minutes until the vegetables soften. 2. Meanwhile, in a medium bowl, whisk the eggs and Parmesan until thoroughly combined. Pour the egg mixture into the pan and shake gently to distribute the vegetables. Air fry for another 15 minutes until the eggs are set. 3. Remove from the air fryer and let sit for 5 minutes to cool slightly. Use a silicone spatula to gently lift the frittata onto a plate before serving.

Per Serving:

calories: 329 | fat: 23g | protein: 24g | carbs: 6g | fiber: 0g | sodium: 793mg

Savory Zucchini Muffins

Prep time: 10 minutes | Cook time: 35 minutes | Serves 13

1 tablespoon extra virgin olive oil plus extra for brushing	parsley
2 medium zucchini, grated	1 tablespoon chopped fresh dill
⅛ teaspoon fine sea salt	1 tablespoon chopped fresh mint
1 large egg, lightly beaten	¼ teaspoon freshly ground black pepper
1½ ounces (43 g) crumbled feta	3 tablespoons unseasoned breadcrumbs
¼ medium onion (any variety), finely chopped	1 tablespoon grated Parmesan cheese
1 tablespoon chopped fresh	

1. Preheat the oven to 400°F (205°C), and line a medium muffin pan with 6 muffin liners. Lightly brush the bottoms of the liners with olive oil. 2. Place the grated zucchini in a colander and sprinkle with the sea salt. Set aside for 10 minutes to allow the salt to penetrate. 3. Remove the zucchini from the colander, and place it on a tea towel. Pull the edges of the towel in and then twist and squeeze the towel to remove as much of the water from the zucchini as possible. (This will prevent the muffins from becoming soggy.) 4. In a large bowl, combine the egg, feta, onions, parsley, dill, mint, pepper, and the remaining tablespoon of olive oil. Mix well, and add the zucchini to the bowl. Mix again, and add the breadcrumbs. Use a fork to mash the ingredients until well combined. 5. Divide the mixture among the prepared muffins liners and then sprinkle ½ teaspoon grated Parmesan over each muffin. Transfer to the oven, and bake for 35 minutes or until the muffins turn golden brown. 6. When the baking time is complete, remove the muffins from the oven and set aside to cool for 5 minutes before removing from the pan. Store in an airtight container in the refrigerator for 3 days, or tightly wrap individual muffins in plastic wrap and freeze for up to 3 months.

Per Serving:

calories: 39 | fat: 2g | protein: 2g | carbs: 3g | fiber: 1g | sodium: 80mg

Summer Day Fruit Salad

Prep time: 5 minutes | Cook time: 0 minutes | Serves 8

2 cups cubed honeydew melon	½ cup unsweetened toasted coconut flakes
2 cups cubed cantaloupe	¼ cup honey
2 cups red seedless grapes	¼ teaspoon sea salt
1 cup sliced fresh strawberries	½ cup extra-virgin olive oil
1 cup fresh blueberries	
Zest and juice of 1 large lime	

1. Combine all of the fruits, the lime zest, and the coconut flakes in a large bowl and stir well to blend. Set aside. 2. In a blender, combine the lime juice, honey, and salt and blend on low. Once the honey is incorporated, slowly add the olive oil and blend until opaque. 3. Pour the dressing over the fruit and mix well. Cover and refrigerate for at least 4 hours before serving, stirring a few times to distribute the dressing.

Per Serving:

calories: 249 | fat: 15g | protein: 1g | carbs: 30g | fiber: 3g | sodium: 104mg

Crunchy Vanilla Protein Bars

Prep time: 10 minutes | Cook time: 5 minutes | Serves 8

Topping:	tablespoon unsweetened vanilla extract
½ cup flaked coconut	¼ cup virgin coconut oil
2 tablespoons raw cacao nibs	½ cup coconut milk
Bars:	1½ teaspoons fresh lemon zest
1½ cups almond flour	⅓ cup macadamia nuts, halved
1 cup collagen powder	Optional: low-carb sweetener, to taste
2 tablespoons ground or whole chia seeds	
1 teaspoon vanilla powder or 1	

1. Preheat the oven to 350°F (180°C) fan assisted or 380°F (193°C) conventional. 2. To make the topping: Place the coconut flakes on a baking tray and bake for 2 to 3 minutes, until lightly golden. Set aside to cool. 3. To make the bars: In a bowl, combine all of the ingredients for the bars. Line a small baking tray with parchment paper or use a silicone baking tray. A square 8 × 8–inch (20 × 20 cm) or a rectangular tray of similar size will work best. 4. Press the dough into the pan and sprinkle with the cacao nibs, pressing them into the bars with your fingers. Add the toasted coconut and lightly press the flakes into the dough. Refrigerate until set, for about 1 hour. Slice to serve. Store in the refrigerator for up to 1 week.

Per Serving:

calories: 285 | fat: 27g | protein: 5g | carbs: 10g | fiber: 4g | sodium: 19mg

Avocado Toast with Smoked Trout

Prep time: 10 minutes | Cook time: 0 minutes | Serves 2

1 avocado, peeled and pitted	plus more for sprinkling
2 teaspoons lemon juice, plus more for serving	¼ teaspoon lemon zest
¾ teaspoon ground cumin	2 pieces whole-wheat bread, toasted
¼ teaspoon kosher salt	1 (3¾-ounce / 106-g) can
¼ teaspoon red pepper flakes,	smoked trout

1. In a medium bowl, mash together the avocado, lemon juice, cumin, salt, red pepper flakes, and lemon zest. 2. Spread half the avocado mixture on each piece of toast. Top each piece of toast with half the smoked trout. Garnish with a pinch of red pepper flakes (if desired), and/or a sprinkle of lemon juice (if desired).

Per Serving:

calories: 300 | fat: 20g | protein: 11g | carbs: 21g | fiber: 6g | sodium: 390mg

Quick Low-Carb Avocado Toasts

Prep time: 10 minutes | Cook time: 10 minutes | Makes 4 toasts

Quick Bread Base:	2 tablespoons water
¼ cup (28 g/1 ounce) flax meal	Avocado Topping:
2 tablespoons (16 g/0.6 ounce) coconut flour	1 large ripe avocado
2 teaspoons (2 g) psyllium powder	¼ small red onion or 1 spring onion, minced
⅛ teaspoon baking soda	1 tablespoon extra-virgin olive oil
Optional: ½ teaspoon dried herbs, ¼ teaspoon paprika or ground turmeric	1 tablespoon fresh lemon juice
Salt and black pepper, to taste	Salt, black pepper, and/or chile flakes, to taste
¼ teaspoon apple cider vinegar	2 teaspoons chopped fresh herbs, such as parsley or chives
1 teaspoon extra-virgin olive oil or ghee, plus more for greasing	Optional: 2 ounces (57 g) smoked salmon and/or poached egg
1 large egg	

Make The Bread Base: 1. Combine all the dry ingredients in a bowl. Add the wet ingredients. Combine and set aside for 5 minutes. 2.Divide the mixture between two wide ramekins lightly greased with the olive oil and microwave on high for about 2 minutes, checking every 30 to 60 seconds to avoid overcooking. (If the bread ends up too dry, you can "rehydrate" it: Pour 1 tablespoon [15 ml] of water evenly over it, then return it to the microwave for 30 seconds.) 3.Let it cool slightly, then cut widthwise. Place on a dry nonstick pan and toast for 1 to 2 minutes per side. Set aside. Make The Topping: 4. In a bowl, mash the avocado with the onion, oil, lemon juice, salt, pepper, and chile flakes. To serve, spread the avocado mixture on top of the sliced bread and add fresh herbs. Optionally, top with smoked salmon. 5.Store the bread separately from the topping at room temperature in a sealed container for 1 day, in the fridge for up to 5 days, or freeze for up to 3 months. 6.Refrigerate the topping in a sealed jar for up to 3 days.

Per Serving:

calories: 112 | fat: 10g | protein: 3g | carbs: 4g | fiber: 3g | sodium: 71mg

Italian Egg Cups

Prep time: 5 minutes | Cook time: 10 minutes | Serves 4

Olive oil	4 teaspoons grated Parmesan cheese
1 cup marinara sauce	Salt and freshly ground black pepper, to taste
4 eggs	
4 tablespoons shredded Mozzarella cheese	Chopped fresh basil, for garnish

1. Lightly spray 4 individual ramekins with olive oil. 2. Pour ¼ cup of marinara sauce into each ramekin. 3. Crack one egg into each ramekin on top of the marinara sauce. 4. Sprinkle 1 tablespoon of Mozzarella and 1 tablespoon of Parmesan on top of each egg. Season with salt and pepper. 5. Cover each ramekin with aluminum foil. Place two of the ramekins in the air fryer basket. 6. Air fry at 350°F (177°C) for 5 minutes and remove the aluminum foil. Air fry until the top is lightly browned and the egg white is cooked, another 2 to 4 minutes. If you prefer the yolk to be firmer, cook for 3 to 5 more minutes. 7. Repeat with the remaining two ramekins. Garnish with basil and serve.

Per Serving:

calories: 123 | fat: 7g | protein: 9g | carbs: 6g | fiber: 1g | sodium: 84mg

Spanish Tuna Tortilla with Roasted Peppers

Prep time: 15 minutes | Cook time: 15 minutes | Serves 4

6 large eggs	packed in water, drained well and flaked
¼ cup olive oil	2 plum tomatoes, seeded and diced
2 small russet potatoes, diced	
1 small onion, chopped	
1 roasted red bell pepper, sliced	1 teaspoon dried tarragon
1 (7-ounce / 198-g) can tuna	

1. Preheat the broiler on high. 2. Crack the eggs in a large bowl and whisk them together until just combined. Heat the olive oil in a large, oven-safe, nonstick or cast-iron skillet over medium-low heat. 3. Add the potatoes and cook until slightly soft, about 7 minutes. Add the onion and the peppers and cook until soft, 3–5 minutes. 4. Add the tuna, tomatoes, and tarragon to the skillet and stir to combine, then add the eggs. 5. Cook for 7–10 minutes until the eggs are bubbling from the bottom and the bottom is slightly brown. 6. Place the skillet into the oven on 1 of the first 2 racks, and cook until the middle is set and the top is slightly brown. 7. Slice into wedges and serve warm or at room temperature.

Per Serving:

calories: 247 | fat: 14g | protein: 12g | carbs: 19g | fiber: 2g | sodium: 130mg

Spiced Antioxidant Granola Clusters

Prep time: 10 minutes | Cook time: 1 hour 10 minutes | Serves 10

1 cup unsweetened fine coconut flakes	½ teaspoon ground nutmeg
1 cup unsweetened large coconut flakes	½ teaspoon ground cloves
¼ cup packed flax meal	1 tablespoon fresh lemon zest
¼ cup chia seeds	¼ teaspoon black pepper
½ cup pecans, chopped	¼ teaspoon salt
1 cup blanched almonds, roughly chopped, or flaked almonds	⅓ cup light tahini
	¼ cup virgin coconut oil
2 teaspoons cinnamon	2 large egg whites
1 teaspoon ground anise seed	Optional: unsweetened almond milk, coconut cream, coconut yogurt, or full-fat goat's yogurt, to serve

1. Preheat the oven to 265°F (130°C) conventional or 230°F (110°C) fan assisted convection. Line a baking tray with parchment paper. 2. Place all of the dry ingredients, including the lemon zest, in a large bowl. Stir to combine. In a small bowl, mix the tahini with the coconut oil, then add to the dry ingredients. Add the egg whites and mix to combine. 3. Spoon onto the lined baking tray and crumble all over. Bake for 1 hour and 10 minutes to 1 hour and 20 minutes, until golden. Remove from the oven and let cool completely; it will crisp up as it cools. Serve on its own or with almond milk, coconut cream or coconut yogurt, or full-fat goat's yogurt. Store in a jar at room temperature for up to 2 weeks or freeze for up to 3 months.

Per Serving:

calories: 291 | fat: 25g | protein: 6g | carbs: 15g | fiber: 6g | sodium: 128mg

Golden Egg Skillet

Prep time: 15 minutes | Cook time: 20 minutes | Serves 2

2 tablespoons extra-virgin avocado oil or ghee	1 teaspoon Dijon or yellow mustard
2 medium spring onions, white and green parts separated, sliced	½ teaspoon ground turmeric
1 clove garlic, minced	¼ teaspoon black pepper
3½ ounces (99 g) Swiss chard or collard greens, stalks and leaves separated, chopped	Salt, to taste
	4 large eggs
	¾ cup grated Manchego or Pecorino Romano cheese
1 medium zucchini, sliced into coins	2 tablespoons (30 ml) extra-virgin olive oil
2 tablespoons water	

1. Preheat the oven to 360°F (182°C) fan assisted or 400°F (205°C) conventional. 2. Grease a large, ovenproof skillet (with a lid) with the avocado oil. Cook the white parts of the spring onions and the garlic for about 1 minute, until just fragrant. Add the chard stalks, zucchini, and water. Stir, then cover with a lid. Cook over medium-low heat for about 10 minutes or until the zucchini is tender. Add the mustard, turmeric, pepper, and salt. Add the chard leaves and cook until just wilted. 3. Use a spatula to make 4 wells in the mixture. Crack an egg into each well and cook until the egg whites start to set while the yolks are still runny. Top with the cheese, transfer to the oven, and bake for 5 to 7 minutes. Remove from the oven and sprinkle with the reserved spring onions. Drizzle with the olive oil and serve warm.

Per Serving:

calories: 600 | fat: 49g | protein: 31g | carbs: 10g | fiber: 4g | sodium: 213mg

Turkish Egg Bowl

Prep time: 10 minutes | Cook time: 15 minutes | Serves 2

2 tablespoons ghee	1 tablespoon fresh lemon juice
½–1 teaspoon red chile flakes	Salt and black pepper, to taste
2 tablespoons extra-virgin olive oil	Dash of vinegar
	4 large eggs
1 cup full-fat goat's or sheep's milk yogurt	Optional: pinch of sumac
	2 tablespoons chopped fresh cilantro or parsley
1 clove garlic, minced	

1. In a skillet, melt the ghee over low heat. Add the chile flakes and let it infuse while you prepare the eggs. Remove from the heat and mix with the extra-virgin olive oil. Set aside. Combine the yogurt, garlic, lemon juice, salt, and pepper. 2. Poach the eggs. Fill a medium saucepan with water and a dash of vinegar. Bring to a boil over high heat. Crack each egg individually into a ramekin or a cup. Using a spoon, create a gentle whirlpool in the water; this will help the egg white wrap around the egg yolk. Slowly lower the egg into the water in the center of the whirlpool. Turn off the heat and cook for 3 to 4 minutes. Use a slotted spoon to remove the egg from the water and place it on a plate. Repeat for all remaining eggs. 3. To assemble, place the yogurt mixture in a bowl and add the poached eggs. Drizzle with the infused oil, and garnish with cilantro. Add a pinch of sumac, if using. Eat warm.

Per Serving:

calories: 576 | fat: 46g | protein: 27g | carbs: 17g | fiber: 4g | sodium: 150mg

Power Peach Smoothie Bowl

Prep time: 15 minutes | Cook time: 0 minutes | Serves 2

2 cups packed partially thawed frozen peaches	2 tablespoons flax meal
	1 teaspoon vanilla extract
½ cup plain or vanilla Greek yogurt	1 teaspoon orange extract
	1 tablespoon honey (optional)
½ ripe avocado	

1. Combine all of the ingredients in a blender and blend until smooth. 2. Pour the mixture into two bowls, and, if desired, sprinkle with additional toppings.

Per Serving:

calories: 213 | fat: 13g | protein: 6g | carbs: 23g | fiber: 7g | sodium: 41mg

Strawberry Basil Honey Ricotta Toast

Prep time: 10 minutes | Cook time: 0 minutes | Serves 2

4 slices of whole-grain bread	Sea salt
½ cup ricotta cheese (whole milk or low-fat)	1 cup fresh strawberries, sliced
1 tablespoon honey	4 large fresh basil leaves, sliced into thin shreds

1. Toast the bread. 2. In a small bowl, combine the ricotta, honey, and a pinch or two of sea salt. Taste and add additional honey or salt if desired. 3. Spread the mixture evenly over each slice of bread (about 2 tablespoons per slice). 4. Top each piece with sliced strawberries and a few pieces of shredded basil.

Per Serving:

calories: 275 | fat: 8g | protein: 15g | carbs: 41g | fiber: 5g | sodium: 323mg

Peach Sunrise Smoothie

Prep time: 10 minutes | Cook time: 0 minutes | Serves 1

1 large unpeeled peach, pitted and sliced (about ½ cup)	peach low-fat Greek yogurt
6 ounces (170 g) vanilla or	2 tablespoons low-fat milk
	6 to 8 ice cubes

1. Combine all ingredients in a blender and blend until thick and creamy. Serve immediately.

Per Serving:

calories: 228 | fat: 3g | protein: 11g | carbs: 42g | fiber: 3g | sodium: 127mg

Blueberry-Lemon Tea Cakes

Prep time: 10 minutes | Cook time: 25 minutes | Serves 12

4 eggs	2 teaspoons baking powder
½ cup granulated sugar	1 teaspoon kosher salt
Grated peel of 1 lemon	1 cup extra-virgin olive oil
1½ cups all-purpose flour	1½ cups fresh or frozen blueberries
¾ cup fine cornmeal	

1. Preheat the oven to 350°F(180°C). Grease a 12-cup muffin pan or line with paper liners. 2. With an electric mixer set to medium speed, beat the eggs and sugar together until they are pale and fluffy. Stir in the lemon peel. 3. In a medium bowl, stir together the flour, cornmeal, baking powder, and salt. With the mixer on low speed, alternate adding the flour mixture and oil to the egg mixture. Fold in the blueberries. 4. Dollop the batter into the muffin pan. Bake until the tops are golden and a toothpick inserted in the middle comes out clean, 20 to 25 minutes.

Per Serving:

calories: 317 | fat: 20g | protein: 4g | carbs: 31g | fiber: 2g | sodium: 217mg

Morning Buzz Iced Coffee

Prep time: 10 minutes | Cook time: 0 minutes | Serves 1

1 cup freshly brewed strong black coffee, cooled slightly	heavy cream (optional)
1 tablespoon extra-virgin olive oil	1 teaspoon MCT oil (optional)
	⅛ teaspoon almond extract
1 tablespoon half-and-half or	⅛ teaspoon ground cinnamon

1. Pour the slightly cooled coffee into a blender or large glass (if using an immersion blender). 2. Add the olive oil, half-and-half (if using), MCT oil (if using), almond extract, and cinnamon. 3. Blend well until smooth and creamy. Drink warm and enjoy.

Per Serving:

calories: 124 | fat: 14g | protein: 0g | carbs: 0g | fiber: 0g | sodium: 5mg

Amaranth Breakfast Bowl with Chocolate and Almonds

Prep time: 10 minutes | Cook time: 6 minutes | Serves 6

2 cups amaranth, rinsed and drained	1 teaspoon vanilla extract
2 cups almond milk	¼ teaspoon salt
2 cups water	½ cup toasted sliced almonds
¼ cup maple syrup	⅓ cup miniature semisweet chocolate chips
3 tablespoons cocoa powder	

1. Place amaranth, almond milk, water, maple syrup, cocoa powder, vanilla, and salt in the Instant Pot®. Stir to combine. Close lid, set steam release to Sealing, press the Rice button, and set time to 6 minutes. When the timer beeps, quick-release the pressure until the float valve drops, press the Cancel button, open lid, and stir well. 2. Serve hot, topped with almonds and chocolate chips.

Per Serving:

calories: 263 | fat: 12g | protein: 5g | carbs: 35g | fiber: 5g | sodium: 212mg

Almond Butter Banana Chocolate Smoothie

Prep time: 5 minutes | Cook time: 0 minutes | Serves 1

¾ cup almond milk	1 tablespoon almond butter
½ medium banana, preferably frozen	1 tablespoon unsweetened cocoa powder
¼ cup frozen blueberries	1 tablespoon chia seeds

1. In a blender or Vitamix, add all the ingredients. Blend to combine.

Per Serving:

calories: 300 | fat: 16g | protein: 8g | carbs: 37g | fiber: 10g | sodium: 125mg

Baked Ricotta with Pears

Prep time: 5 minutes |Cook time: 25 minutes| Serves: 4

Nonstick cooking spray	1 tablespoon sugar
1 (16-ounce / 454-g) container whole-milk ricotta cheese	1 teaspoon vanilla extract
2 large eggs	¼ teaspoon ground nutmeg
¼ cup white whole-wheat flour or whole-wheat pastry flour	1 pear, cored and diced
	2 tablespoons water
	1 tablespoon honey

1. Preheat the oven to 400°F(205ºC). Spray four 6-ounce ramekins with nonstick cooking spray. 2. In a large bowl, beat together the ricotta, eggs, flour, sugar, vanilla, and nutmeg. Spoon into the ramekins. Bake for 22 to 25 minutes, or until the ricotta is just about set. Remove from the oven and cool slightly on racks. 3. While the ricotta is baking, in a small saucepan over medium heat, simmer the pear in the water for 10 minutes, until slightly softened. Remove from the heat, and stir in the honey. 4. Serve the ricotta ramekins topped with the warmed pear.

Per Serving:

calories: 306 | fat: 17g | protein: 17g | carbs: 21g | fiber: 1g | sodium: 131mg

Greek Breakfast Power Bowl

Prep time: 15 minutes | Cook time: 20 minutes | Serves 2

3 tablespoons extra-virgin avocado oil or ghee, divided	1 tablespoon chopped fresh oregano
1 clove garlic, minced	Salt and black pepper, to taste
2 teaspoons chopped fresh rosemary	6 ounces (170 g) Halloumi cheese, cubed or sliced
1 small eggplant, roughly chopped	¼ cup pitted Kalamata olives
1 medium zucchini, roughly chopped	4 large eggs, soft-boiled (or hard-boiled or poached)
1 tablespoon fresh lemon juice	1 tablespoon extra-virgin olive oil, to drizzle
2 tablespoons chopped mint	

1. Heat a skillet (with a lid) greased with 2 tablespoons (30 ml) of the avocado oil over medium heat. Add the garlic and rosemary and cook for 1 minute. Add the eggplant, zucchini, and lemon juice. Stir and cover with a lid, then reduce the heat to medium-low. Cook for 10 to 15 minutes, stirring once or twice, until tender. 2. Stir in the mint and oregano. Optionally, reserve some herbs for topping. Season with salt and pepper to taste. Remove from the heat and transfer to a plate. Cover with the skillet lid to keep the veggies warm. 3. Grease the same pan with the remaining 1 tablespoon (15 ml) avocado oil and cook the Halloumi over medium-high heat for 2 to 3 minutes per side until lightly browned. Place the slices of cooked Halloumi on top of the cooked veggies. Top with the olives and cooked eggs and drizzle with the olive oil. 4. Always serve warm, as Halloumi hardens once it cools. Reheat before serving if necessary.

Per Serving:

calories: 748 | fat: 56g | protein: 40g | carbs: 25g | fiber: 10g | sodium: 275mg

Enjoy-Your-Veggies Breakfast

Prep time: 20 minutes | Cook time: 10 minutes | Serves 4

1 tablespoon olive oil	1 tablespoon low-sodium soy sauce
1 small sweet onion, peeled and diced	¼ cup water
2 large carrots, peeled and diced	1 cup diced peeled zucchini or summer squash
2 medium potatoes, peeled and diced	2 medium tomatoes, peeled and diced
1 stalk celery, diced	2 cups cooked brown rice
1 large red bell pepper, seeded and diced	½ teaspoon ground black pepper

1. Press the Sauté button on the Instant Pot® and heat oil. Add onion and cook until just tender, about 2 minutes. 2. Stir in carrots, potatoes, celery, and bell pepper and cook until just tender, about 2 minutes. Add soy sauce and water. Press the Cancel button. 3. Close lid, set steam release to Sealing, press the Manual button, and set time to 2 minutes. When the timer beeps, quick-release the pressure until the float valve drops. Press the Cancel button. 4. Open lid and add squash and tomatoes, and stir. Close lid, set steam release to Sealing, press the Manual button, and set time to 1 minute. When the timer beeps, quick-release the pressure until the float valve drops. Press the Cancel button and open lid. 5. Serve over rice and sprinkle with black pepper.

Per Serving:

calories: 224 | fat: 5g | protein: 6g | carbs: 41g | fiber: 5g | sodium: 159mg

Oat and Fruit Parfait

Prep time: 5 minutes | Cook time: 12 minutes | Serves 2

½ cup whole-grain rolled or quickcooking oats (not instant)	1 cup sliced fresh strawberries
½ cup walnut pieces	1½ cups vanilla low-fat Greek yogurt
1 teaspoon honey	Fresh mint leaves for garnish

1. Preheat the oven to 300°F(150ºC). 2. Spread the oats and walnuts in a single layer on a baking sheet. 3. Toast the oats and nuts just until you begin to smell the nuts, 10 to 12 minutes. Remove the pan from the oven and set aside. 4. In a small microwave-safe bowl, heat the honey just until warm, about 30 seconds. Add the strawberries and stir to coat. 5. Place 1 tablespoon of the strawberries in the bottom of each of 2 dessert dishes or 8-ounce glasses. Add a portion of yogurt and then a portion of oats and repeat the layers until the containers are full, ending with the berries. Serve immediately or chill until ready to eat.

Per Serving:

calories: 541 | fat: 25g | protein: 21g | carbs: 66g | fiber: 8g | sodium: 124mg

Breakfast Panini with Eggs, Olives, and Tomatoes

Prep time: 5 minutes | Cook time: 0 minutes | Serves 4

1 (12-ounce / 340-g) round whole-wheat pagnotta foggiana or other round, crusty bread	8 hard-boiled eggs, peeled and sliced into rounds
2 tablespoons olive oil	2 medium tomatoes, thinly sliced into rounds
½ cup sliced pitted cured olives, such as Kalamata	12 large leaves fresh basil

1. Split the bread horizontally and brush the cut sides with the olive oil. 2. Arrange the sliced olives on the bottom half of the bread in a single layer. Top with a layer of the egg slices, then the tomato slices, and finally the basil leaves. Cut the sandwich into quarters and serve immediately.

Per Serving:

calories: 427 | fat: 21g | protein: 23g | carbs: 39g | fiber: 7g | sodium: 674mg

Berry Baked Oatmeal

Prep time: 10 minutes | Cook time: 45 to 50 minutes | Serves 8

2 cups gluten-free rolled oats	2 tablespoons extra-virgin olive oil
2 cups (10-ounce / 283-g bag) frozen mixed berries (blueberries and raspberries work best)	2 teaspoons ground cinnamon
	1 teaspoon baking powder
2 cups plain, unsweetened almond milk	1 teaspoon vanilla extract
	½ teaspoon kosher salt
1 cup plain Greek yogurt	¼ teaspoon ground nutmeg
¼ cup maple syrup	⅛ teaspoon ground cloves

1. Preheat the oven to 375ºF (190ºC). 2. Mix all the ingredients together in a large bowl. Pour into a 9-by-13-inch baking dish. Bake for 45 to 50 minutes, or until golden brown.

Per Serving:

calories: 180 | fat: 6g | protein: 6g | carbs: 28g | fiber: 4g | sodium: 180mg

Nuts and Fruit Oatmeal

Prep time: 10 minutes | Cook time: 7 minutes | Serves 2

1 cup rolled oats	¼ cup chopped walnuts
1¼ cups water	1 tablespoon honey
¼ cup orange juice	¼ teaspoon ground ginger
1 medium pear, peeled, cored, and cubed	¼ teaspoon ground cinnamon
	⅛ teaspoon salt
¼ cup dried cherries	

1. Place oats, water, orange juice, pear, cherries, walnuts, honey, ginger, cinnamon, and salt in the Instant Pot®. Stir to combine. 2. Close lid, set steam release to Sealing, press the Manual button, and

set time to 7 minutes. When the timer beeps, let pressure release naturally, about 20 minutes. Press the Cancel button, open lid, and stir well. Serve warm.

Per Serving:

calories: 362 | fat: 8g | protein: 7g | carbs: 69g | fiber: 8g | sodium: 164mg

Berry Breakfast Smoothie

Prep time: 5 minutes | Cook time: 0 minutes | Serves 1

½ cup vanilla low-fat Greek yogurt	blueberries or strawberries (or a combination)
¼ cup low-fat milk	6 to 8 ice cubes
½ cup fresh or frozen	

1. Place the Greek yogurt, milk, and berries in a blender and blend until the berries are liquefied. Add the ice cubes and blend on high until thick and smooth. Serve immediately.

Per Serving:

calories: 158 | fat: 3g | protein: 9g | carbs: 25g | fiber: 1g | sodium: 110mg

Mexican Breakfast Pepper Rings

Prep time: 5 minutes | Cook time: 10 minutes | Serves 4

Olive oil	4 eggs
1 large red, yellow, or orange bell pepper, cut into four ¾-inch rings	Salt and freshly ground black pepper, to taste
	2 teaspoons salsa

1. Preheat the air fryer to 350ºF (177ºC). Lightly spray a baking pan with olive oil. 2. Place 2 bell pepper rings on the pan. Crack one egg into each bell pepper ring. Season with salt and black pepper. 3. Spoon ½ teaspoon of salsa on top of each egg. 4. Place the pan in the air fryer basket. Air fry until the yolk is slightly runny, 5 to 6 minutes or until the yolk is fully cooked, 8 to 10 minutes. 5. Repeat with the remaining 2 pepper rings. Serve hot.

Per Serving:

calories: 76 | fat: 4g | protein: 6g | carbs: 3g | fiber: 1g | sodium: 83mg

Berry Warming Smoothie

Prep time: 5 minutes | Cook time: 0 minutes | Serves 1

⅔ cup plain kefir or plain yogurt	¼ teaspoon grated ginger
½ cup frozen mixed berries	¼ teaspoon ground cinnamon
½ cup baby spinach	¼ teaspoon ground nutmeg
½ cup cucumber, chopped	⅛ teaspoon ground cardamom
2 tablespoons unsweetened shredded coconut	¼ teaspoon vanilla extract (optional)

1. In a blender or Vitamix, add all the ingredients. Blend to combine.

Per Serving:

calories: 165 | fat: 7g | protein: 7g | carbs: 20g | fiber: 4g | sodium: 100mg

Breakfast Hash

Prep time: 10 minutes | Cook time: 30 minutes | Serves 6

Oil, for spraying
3 medium russet potatoes, diced
½ yellow onion, diced
1 green bell pepper, seeded and diced

2 tablespoons olive oil
2 teaspoons granulated garlic
1 teaspoon salt
½ teaspoon freshly ground black pepper

1. Line the air fryer basket with parchment and spray lightly with oil. 2. In a large bowl, mix together the potatoes, onion, bell pepper, and olive oil. 3. Add the garlic, salt, and black pepper and stir until evenly coated. 4. Transfer the mixture to the prepared basket. 5. Air fry at 400°F (204°C) for 20 to 30 minutes, shaking or stirring every 10 minutes, until browned and crispy. If you spray the potatoes with a little oil each time you stir, they will get even crispier.

Per Serving:
calories: 133 | fat: 5g | protein: 3g | carbs: 21g | fiber: 2g | sodium: 395mg

Butternut Squash and Ricotta Frittata

Prep time: 10 minutes | Cook time: 33 minutes | Serves 2 to 3

1 cup cubed (½-inch) butternut squash (5½ ounces / 156 g)
2 tablespoons olive oil
Kosher salt and freshly ground black pepper, to taste
4 fresh sage leaves, thinly sliced

6 large eggs, lightly beaten
½ cup ricotta cheese
Cayenne pepper

1. In a bowl, toss the squash with the olive oil and season with salt and black pepper until evenly coated. Sprinkle the sage on the bottom of a cake pan and place the squash on top. Place the pan in the air fryer and bake at 400°F (204°C) for 10 minutes. Stir to incorporate the sage, then cook until the squash is tender and lightly caramelized at the edges, about 3 minutes more. 2. Pour the eggs over the squash, dollop the ricotta all over, and sprinkle with cayenne. Bake at 300°F (149°C) until the eggs are set and the frittata is golden brown on top, about 20 minutes. Remove the pan from the air fryer and cut the frittata into wedges to serve.

Per Serving:
calories: 289 | fat: 22g | protein: 18g | carbs: 5g | fiber: 1g | sodium: 184mg

Chapter 3
Beans and Grains

Garlic-Asparagus Israeli Couscous

**Prep time: 5 minutes |Cook time: 25 minutes|
Serves: 6**

1 cup garlic-and-herb goat cheese (about 4 ounces/ 113 g)	teaspoon)
1½ pounds (680 g) asparagus spears, ends trimmed and stalks chopped into 1-inch pieces (about 2¾ to 3 cups chopped)	¼ teaspoon freshly ground black pepper
	1¾ cups water
1 tablespoon extra-virgin olive oil	1 (8-ounce/ 227-g) box uncooked whole-wheat or regular Israeli couscous (about 1⅓ cups)
1 garlic clove, minced (about ½	¼ teaspoon kosher or sea salt

1. Preheat the oven to 425°F (220°C). Put the goat cheese on the counter to bring to room temperature. 2. In a large bowl, mix together the asparagus, oil, garlic, and pepper. Spread the asparagus on a large, rimmed baking sheet and roast for 10 minutes, stirring a few times. Remove the pan from the oven, and spoon the asparagus into a large serving bowl. 3. While the asparagus is roasting, in a medium saucepan, bring the water to a boil. Add the couscous and salt. Reduce the heat to medium-low, cover, and cook for 12 minutes, or until the water is absorbed. 4. Pour the hot couscous into the bowl with the asparagus. Add the goat cheese, mix thoroughly until completely melted, and serve.

Per Serving:
calories: 98 | fat: 1g | protein: 10g | carbs: 14g | fiber:4g | sodium: 262mg

Couscous with Apricots

Prep time: 10 minutes | Cook time: 15 minutes | Serves 4

2 tablespoons olive oil	water overnight
1 small onion, diced	½ cup slivered almonds or pistachios
1 cup whole-wheat couscous	
2 cups water or broth	½ teaspoon dried mint
½ cup dried apricots, soaked in	½ teaspoon dried thyme

1. Heat the olive oil in a large skillet over medium-high heat. Add the onion and cook until translucent and soft. 2. Stir in the couscous and cook for 2–3 minutes. 3. Add the water or broth, cover, and cook for 8–10 minutes until the water is mostly absorbed. 4. Remove from the heat and let stand for a few minutes. 5. Fluff with a fork and fold in the apricots, nuts, mint, and thyme.

Per Serving:
calories: 294 | fat: 15g | protein: 8g | carbs: 38g | fiber: 6g | sodium: 6mg

Chili-Spiced Beans

Prep time: 10 minutes | Cook time: 30 minutes | Serves 8

1 pound (454 g) dried pinto beans, soaked overnight and	drained
	1 medium onion, peeled and
chopped	1 teaspoon ground cumin
¼ cup chopped fresh cilantro	1 teaspoon ground coriander
1 (15-ounce / 425-g) can tomato sauce	½ teaspoon ground black pepper
	2 cups vegetable broth
¼ cup chili powder	1 cup water
2 tablespoons smoked paprika	

1. Place all ingredients in the Instant Pot® and stir to combine. 2. Close lid, set steam release to Sealing, press the Chili button, and cook for the default time of 30 minutes. When the timer beeps, quick-release the pressure until the float valve drops, open lid, and stir well. If beans are too thin, press the Cancel button, then press the Sauté button and let beans simmer, uncovered, until desired thickness is reached. Serve warm.

Per Serving:
calories: 86 | fat: 0g | protein: 5g | carbs: 17g | fiber: 4g | sodium: 323mg

Green Beans with Chickpeas, Herbs, and Mushrooms

Prep time: 20 minutes | Cook time: 40 minutes | Serves 8

2 cups dried chickpeas, soaked overnight and drained	¼ cup chopped fresh flat-leaf parsley
½ teaspoon salt	2 tablespoons chopped fresh chives
9 cups water, divided	
½ pound (227 g) fresh green beans, trimmed and cut into 1» pieces	2 tablespoons chopped fresh tarragon
4 ounces (113 g) sliced button mushrooms	¼ cup extra-virgin olive oil
	2 tablespoons red wine vinegar
½ red bell pepper, seeded, thinly sliced, and cut into 1» pieces	1 teaspoon Dijon mustard
	1 teaspoon honey
½ medium red onion, peeled and diced	½ teaspoon ground black pepper
	¼ teaspoon salt
	¼ cup grated Parmesan cheese

1. Add chickpeas, salt, and 8 cups water to the Instant Pot®. Close lid, set steam release to Sealing, press the Manual button, and set time to 40 minutes. 2. When the timer beeps, let pressure release naturally for 10 minutes, then quick-release the remaining pressure. Press the Cancel button. Open lid and drain chickpeas. Transfer to a large bowl and cool to room temperature. 3. Add remaining 1 cup water to the Instant Pot®. Add rack to pot, top with steamer basket, and add green beans. Close lid, set steam release to Sealing, press the Manual button, and set time to 0 minutes. When the timer beeps, open lid, remove steamer basket, and rinse green beans with cool water. Add to bowl with chickpeas. 4. Add to the bowl mushrooms, bell pepper, red onion, parsley, chives, and tarragon. Toss to mix. In a small bowl, combine olive oil, vinegar, mustard, honey, black pepper, and salt. Whisk to combine, then pour over chickpea and green bean mixture, and toss to coat. Top with cheese and serve immediately.

Per Serving:
calories: 291 | fat: 12g | protein: 13g | carbs: 33g | fiber: 10g | sodium: 312mg

Herbed Barley

Prep time: 10 minutes | Cook time: 30 minutes | Serves 4

2 tablespoons olive oil	1 bay leaf
½ cup diced onion	½ teaspoon thyme
½ cup diced celery	½ teaspoon rosemary
1 carrot, peeled and diced	¼ cup walnuts or pine nuts
3 cups water or chicken broth	Sea salt and freshly ground
1 cup barley	pepper, to taste

1. Heat the olive oil in a medium saucepan over medium-high heat. Sauté the onion, celery, and carrot over medium heat until they are tender. 2. Add the water or chicken broth, barley, and seasonings, and bring to a boil. Reduce the heat and simmer for 25 minutes, or until tender. 3. Stir in the nuts and season to taste.

Per Serving:

calories: 283 | fat: 11g | protein: 6g | carbs: 43g | fiber: 9g | sodium: 26mg

Moroccan White Beans with Lamb

Prep time: 25 minutes | Cook time: 22 minutes | Serves 6 to 8

1½ tablespoons table salt, for brining	1 red bell pepper, stemmed, seeded, and chopped
1 pound (454 g) dried great Northern beans, picked over and rinsed	2 tablespoons tomato paste
	3 garlic cloves, minced
	2 teaspoons paprika
1 (12-ounce/ 340-g) lamb shoulder chop (blade or round bone), ¾ to 1 inch thick, trimmed and halved	2 teaspoons ground cumin
	1½ teaspoons ground ginger
	¼ teaspoon cayenne pepper
½ teaspoon table salt	½ cup dry white wine
2 tablespoons extra-virgin olive oil, plus extra for serving	2 cups chicken broth
	2 tablespoons minced fresh parsley
1 onion, chopped	

1. Dissolve 1½ tablespoons salt in 2 quarts cold water in large container. Add beans and soak at room temperature for at least 8 hours or up to 24 hours. Drain and rinse well. 2. Pat lamb dry with paper towels and sprinkle with ½ teaspoon salt. Using highest sauté function, heat oil in Instant Pot for 5 minutes (or until just smoking). Brown lamb, about 5 minutes per side; transfer to plate. 3. Add onion and bell pepper to fat left in pot and cook, using highest sauté function, until softened, about 5 minutes. Stir in tomato paste, garlic, paprika, cumin, ginger, and cayenne and cook until fragrant, about 30 seconds. Stir in wine, scraping up any browned bits, then stir in broth and beans. 4. Nestle lamb into beans and add any accumulated juices. Lock lid in place and close pressure release valve. Select high pressure cook function and cook for 1 minute. Turn off Instant Pot and let pressure release naturally for 15 minutes. Quick-release any remaining pressure, then carefully remove lid, allowing steam to escape away from you. 5. Transfer lamb to cutting board, let cool slightly, then shred into bite-size pieces using 2 forks; discard excess fat and bones. Stir lamb and parsley into beans, and season with salt

and pepper to taste. Drizzle individual portions with extra oil before serving.

Per Serving:

calories: 350 | fat: 12g | protein: 20g | carbs: 40g | fiber: 15g | sodium: 410mg

Skillet Bulgur with Kale and Tomatoes

Prep time: 15 minutes | Cook time: 8 minutes | Serves 2

2 tablespoons olive oil	2 cups cooked bulgur wheat
2 cloves garlic, minced	1 pint cherry tomatoes, halved
1 bunch kale, trimmed and cut into bite-sized pieces	Sea salt and freshly ground pepper, to taste
Juice of 1 lemon	

1. Heat the olive oil in a large skillet over medium heat. Add the garlic and sauté for 1 minute. 2. Add the kale leaves and stir to coat. Cook for 5 minutes until leaves are cooked through and thoroughly wilted. 3. Add the lemon juice, then the bulgur and tomatoes. Season with sea salt and freshly ground pepper.

Per Serving:

calories: 311 | fat: 14g | protein: 8g | carbs: 43g | fiber: 10g | sodium: 21mg

Chickpea Fritters

Prep time: 15 minutes | Cook time: 15 minutes | Serves 4

3 tablespoons olive oil, plus extra for frying	1 teaspoon dried oregano
	1 teaspoon dried parsley
1 onion, chopped	Sea salt
2 garlic cloves, minced	Freshly ground black pepper
1 (15-ounce/ 425-g) can chickpeas, drained and rinsed	¾ cup all-purpose flour, plus more as needed
1 teaspoon dried thyme	

1. In a large skillet, heat 1 tablespoon of the olive oil over medium-high heat. Add the onion and garlic and sauté for 5 to 7 minutes, until the onion is soft. Transfer the onion-garlic mixture to a food processor and add the remaining 2 tablespoons olive oil, the chickpeas, thyme, oregano, and parsley. Season with salt and pepper and purée until a paste forms. (If the mixture is too wet, add 1 to 2 tablespoons of flour and pulse to incorporate.) 2. Place the flour in a bowl. Scoop about 2 tablespoons of the chickpea mixture and roll it into a ball. Dredge the ball in the flour to coat, then flatten the ball slightly and place it on a plate. Repeat with the remaining chickpea mixture. 3. Wipe out the skillet and pour in 2 inches of olive oil. Heat the oil over medium-high heat. Working in batches, fry the fritters in a single layer until golden, about 3 minutes per side. Transfer them to a paper towel–lined plate. Repeat to fry the remaining fritters. Serve immediately.

Per Serving:

calories: 290 | fat: 12g | protein: 8g | carbs: 38g | fiber: 6g | sodium: 45mg

Prassorizo (Leeks and Rice)

Prep time: 10 minutes | Cook time: 12 minutes | Serves 6

6 large leeks	½ teaspoon salt
5 cups water	¼ teaspoon ground black pepper
4 scallions, chopped	1 cup Arborio rice
⅓ cup minced fresh dill	⅓ cup extra-virgin olive oil
¼ cup minced fresh mint	3 tablespoons lemon juice
½ tablespoon dried thyme	

1. Cut white ends of leeks into thick slices. Discard green part of leeks. 2. Place leeks, water, scallions, dill, mint, thyme, salt, and pepper in the Instant Pot®. Stir well. Add rice and stir to combine. 3. Close lid, set steam release to Sealing, press the Rice button, and set time to 12 minutes. When the timer beeps, let pressure release naturally for 10 minutes, then quick-release the remaining pressure. 4. Open lid and stir well. Add olive oil and lemon juice. Serve hot.

Per Serving:

calories: 224 | fat: 12g | protein: 4g | carbs: 28g | fiber: 4g | sodium: 408mg

Earthy Whole Brown Lentil Dhal

Prep time: 10 minutes | Cook time: 6 to 8 hours | Serves 6

6⅓ cups hot water	4 garlic cloves, finely chopped
2 cups whole brown lentils	1 or 2 fresh green chiles, finely
1 tablespoon ghee	chopped
1 teaspoon freshly grated ginger	1 onion, chopped
1 teaspoon sea salt	1 teaspoon garam masala
1 teaspoon turmeric	Handful fresh coriander leaves,
7 to 8 ounces (198 to 227 g)	chopped
canned tomatoes	

1. Wash and clean the lentils, then set them aside to drain. 2. Heat the slow cooker to high and add all of the ingredients except the garam masala and coriander leaves. 3. Cover and cook on high for 6 hours, or on low for 8 hours. 4. Add the garam masala and fresh coriander leaves before serving, and enjoy.

Per Serving:

calories: 263 | fat: 3g | protein: 16g | carbs: 44g | fiber: 8g | sodium: 401mg

Lentils and Bulgur with Caramelized Onions

Prep time: 10 minutes | Cook time: 50 minutes | Serves 6

½ cup extra-virgin olive oil	over and rinsed
4 large onions, chopped	1 teaspoon freshly ground black
2 teaspoons salt, divided	pepper
6 cups water	1 cup bulgur wheat
2 cups brown lentils, picked	

1. In a medium pot over medium heat, cook the olive oil and onions for 7 to 10 minutes until the edges are browned. 2. Turn the heat to high, add the water, cumin, and salt, and bring this mixture to a boil, boiling for about 3 minutes. 3. Add the lentils and turn the heat to medium-low. Cover the pot and cook for 20 minutes, stirring occasionally. 4. Stir in the rice and cover; cook for an additional 20 minutes. 5. Fluff the rice with a fork and serve 1.In a large pot over medium heat, cook and stir the olive oil, onions, and 1 teaspoon of salt for 12 to 15 minutes, until the onions are a medium brown/golden color. 2. Put half of the cooked onions in a bowl. 3. Add the water, remaining 1 teaspoon of salt, and lentils to the remaining onions. Stir. Cover and cook for 30 minutes. 4. Stir in the black pepper and bulgur, cover, and cook for 5 minutes. Fluff with a fork, cover, and let stand for another 5 minutes. 5. Spoon the lentils and bulgur onto a serving plate and top with the reserved onions. Serve warm.

Per Serving:

calories: 479 | fat: 20g | protein: 20g | carbs: 60g | fiber: 24g | sodium: 789mg

Quinoa Salad with Tomatoes

Prep time: 10 minutes | Cook time: 22 minutes | Serves 4

2 tablespoons olive oil	leaf parsley
2 cloves garlic, peeled and	1 tablespoon lemon juice
minced	1 cup quinoa, rinsed and drained
1 cup diced fresh tomatoes	2 cups water
¼ cup chopped fresh Italian flat-	1 teaspoon salt

1. Press the Sauté button on the Instant Pot® and heat oil. Add garlic and cook 30 seconds, then add tomatoes, parsley, and lemon juice. Cook an additional 1 minute. Transfer mixture to a small bowl and set aside. Press the Cancel button. 2. Add quinoa and water to the Instant Pot®. Close lid, set steam release to Sealing, press the Multigrain button, and set time to 20 minutes. 3. When timer beeps, let pressure release naturally, about 20 minutes, then open lid. Fluff with a fork and stir in tomato mixture and salt. Serve immediately.

Per Serving:

calories: 223 | fat: 10g | protein: 6g | carbs: 29g | fiber: 3g | sodium: 586mg

Apple Couscous with Curry

Prep time: 10 minutes | Cook time: 10 minutes | Serves 4

2 teaspoons olive oil	couscous
2 leeks, white parts only, sliced	2 tablespoons curry powder
1 Granny Smith apple, diced	½ cup chopped pecans
2 cups cooked whole-wheat	

1. Heat the olive oil in a large skillet on medium heat and add leeks. Cook until soft and tender, about 5 minutes. 2. Add diced apple and cook until soft. 3. Add couscous and curry powder, then stir to combine. Remove from heat, mix in nuts, and serve.

Per Serving:

calories: 255 | fat: 12g | protein: 5g | carbs: 34g | fiber: 6g | sodium: 15mg

Fasolakia (Greek Green Beans)

Prep time: 5 minutes | Cook time: 45 minutes | Serves 2

⅓ cup olive oil (any variety)
1 medium onion (red or white), chopped
1 medium russet or white potato, sliced into ¼-inch (.5cm) thick slices
1 pound (454 g) green beans (fresh or frozen)

3 medium tomatoes, grated, or 1 (15-ounce / 425-g) can crushed tomatoes
¼ cup chopped fresh parsley
1 teaspoon granulated sugar
½ teaspoon salt
¼ teaspoon freshly ground black pepper

1. Add the olive oil a medium pot over medium-low heat. When the oil begins to shimmer, add the onions and sauté until soft, about 5 minutes. 2. Add the potatoes to the pot, and sauté for an additional 2–3 minutes. 3. Add the green beans and stir until the beans are thoroughly coated with the olive oil. Add the tomatoes, parsley, sugar, salt, and black pepper. Stir to combine. 4. Add just enough hot water to the pot to cover half the beans. Cover and simmer for 40 minutes or until there is no water left in the pot and the beans are soft. (Do not allow the beans to boil.) 5. Allow the beans to cool until they're warm or until they reach room temperature, but do not serve hot. Store in refrigerator for up to 3 days.

Per Serving:
calories: 536 | fat: 37g | protein: 9g | carbs: 50g | fiber: 11g | sodium: 617mg

No-Stir Polenta with Arugula, Figs, and Blue Cheese

Prep time: 15 minutes | Cook time: 40 minutes | Serves 4

1 cup coarse-ground cornmeal
½ cup oil-packed sun-dried tomatoes, chopped
1 teaspoon minced fresh thyme or ¼ teaspoon dried
½ teaspoon table salt
¼ teaspoon pepper
3 tablespoons extra-virgin olive

oil, divided
2 ounces (57 g) baby arugula
4 figs, cut into ½-inch-thick wedges
1 tablespoon balsamic vinegar
2 ounces (57 g) blue cheese, crumbled (½ cup)
2 tablespoons pine nuts, toasted

1. Arrange trivet included with Instant Pot in base of insert and add 1 cup water. Fold sheet of aluminum foil into 16 by 6-inch sling, then rest 1½-quart round soufflé dish in center of sling. Whisk 4 cups water, cornmeal, tomatoes, thyme, salt, and pepper together in bowl, then transfer mixture to soufflé dish. Using sling, lower soufflé dish into pot and onto trivet; allow narrow edges of sling to rest along sides of insert. 2. Lock lid in place and close pressure release valve. Select high pressure cook function and cook for 40 minutes. Turn off Instant Pot and quick-release pressure. Carefully remove lid, allowing steam to escape away from you. 3. Using sling, transfer soufflé dish to wire rack. Whisk 1 tablespoon oil into polenta, smoothing out any lumps. Let sit until thickened slightly, about 10 minutes. Season with salt and pepper to taste. 4. Toss arugula and figs with vinegar and remaining 2 tablespoons oil

in bowl, and season with salt and pepper to taste. Divide polenta among individual serving plates and top with arugula mixture, blue cheese, and pine nuts. Serve.

Per Serving:
calories: 360 | fat: 21g | protein: 7g | carbs: 38g | fiber: 8g | sodium: 510mg

White Beans with Garlic and Tomatoes

Prep time: 10 minutes | Cook time: 40 minutes | Serves 6

1 cup dried cannellini beans, soaked overnight and drained
4 cups water
4 cups vegetable stock
1 tablespoon olive oil
1 teaspoon salt

2 cloves garlic, peeled and minced
½ cup diced tomato
½ teaspoon dried sage
½ teaspoon ground black pepper

1. Add beans and water to the Instant Pot®. Close lid, set steam release to Sealing, press the Bean button, and cook for default time of 30 minutes. When timer beeps, quick-release the pressure until the float valve drops. 2. Press the Cancel button, open lid, drain and rinse beans, and return to pot along with stock. Soak for 1 hour. 3. Add olive oil, salt, garlic, tomato, sage, and pepper to beans. Close lid, set steam release to Sealing, press the Manual button, and set time to 10 minutes. When the timer beeps, quick-release the pressure until the float valve drops and open lid. Serve hot.

Per Serving:
calories: 128 | fat: 2g | protein: 7g | carbs: 20g | fiber: 4g | sodium: 809mg

Brown Rice and Chickpea Salad

Prep time: 5 minutes | Cook time: 22 minutes | Serves 8

2 cups brown rice
2¼ cups vegetable broth
2 tablespoons light olive oil
1 (15-ounce/ 425-g) can chickpeas, drained and rinsed
½ cup diced tomato
½ cup chopped red onion
½ cup diced cucumber

¼ cup chopped fresh basil
3 tablespoons extra-virgin olive oil
2 tablespoons balsamic vinegar
½ teaspoon ground black pepper
¼ teaspoon salt
¼ cup crumbled feta cheese

1. Place rice, broth, and light oil in the Instant Pot®. Close lid, set steam release to Sealing, press the Manual button, and set time to 22 minutes. 2. When the timer beeps, let pressure release naturally for 10 minutes, then quick-release the remaining pressure. Open lid, transfer rice to a large bowl, and set aside for 20 minutes. Fold in chickpeas, tomato, onion, cucumber, and basil. 3. In a small bowl, whisk together extra-virgin olive oil, balsamic vinegar, pepper, and salt. Pour over rice mixture and toss to coat. Top with feta. Serve at room temperature or refrigerate for at least 2 hours.

Per Serving:
calories: 417 | fat: 21g | protein: 13g | carbs: 45g | fiber: 7g | sodium: 366mg

Bulgur Salad with Cucumbers, Olives, and Dill

Prep time: 10 minutes | Cook time: 12 minutes | Serves 4

1 cup bulgur wheat	½ teaspoon salt
2 cups water	1 large English cucumber, chopped
¼ cup olive oil	½ medium red onion, peeled and diced
2 tablespoons balsamic vinegar	¼ cup chopped salt-cured olives
1 clove garlic, peeled and minced	¼ cup chopped fresh dill
½ teaspoon ground black pepper	

1. Add bulgur and water to the Instant Pot® and stir well. Close lid, set steam release to Sealing, press the Rice button, adjust pressure to Low, and set time to 12 minutes. When the timer beeps, quick-release the pressure until the float valve drops. Open lid and fluff bulgur with a fork. Transfer to a medium bowl and set aside to cool to room temperature, about 40 minutes. 2. Stir in oil, vinegar, garlic, pepper, salt, cucumber, onion, olives, and dill, and toss well. Refrigerate for 4 hours before serving.

Per Serving:

calories: 290 | fat: 27g | protein: 2g | carbs: 11g | fiber: 2g | sodium: 352mg

Black Beans with Corn and Tomato Relish

Prep time: 20 minutes | Cook time: 30 minutes | Serves 6

½ pound (227 g) dried black beans, soaked overnight and drained	½ medium red onion, peeled and chopped
1 medium white onion, peeled and sliced in half	¼ cup minced fresh cilantro
2 cloves garlic, peeled and lightly crushed	½ teaspoon ground cumin
8 cups water	¼ teaspoon smoked paprika
1 cup corn kernels	¼ teaspoon ground black pepper
1 large tomato, seeded and chopped	¼ teaspoon salt
	3 tablespoons extra-virgin olive oil
	3 tablespoons lime juice

1. Add beans, white onion, garlic, and water to the Instant Pot®. Close lid, set steam release to Sealing, press the Bean button, and cook for the default time of 30 minutes. When the timer beeps, let pressure release naturally, about 20 minutes. 2. Open lid and remove and discard onion and garlic. Drain beans well and transfer to a medium bowl. Cool to room temperature, about 30 minutes. 3. In a separate small bowl, combine corn, tomato, red onion, cilantro, cumin, paprika, pepper, and salt. Toss to combine. Add to black beans and gently fold to mix. Whisk together olive oil and lime juice in a small bowl and pour over black bean mixture. Gently toss to coat. Serve at room temperature or refrigerate for at least 2 hours.

Per Serving:

calories: 216 | fat: 7g | protein: 8g | carbs: 28g | fiber: 6g | sodium: 192mg

Lemon and Garlic Rice Pilaf

Prep time: 10 minutes | Cook time: 34 minutes | Serves 8

2 tablespoons olive oil	1 teaspoon dried thyme
1 medium yellow onion, peeled and chopped	1 teaspoon dried oregano
4 cloves garlic, peeled and minced	¼ teaspoon salt
1 tablespoon grated lemon zest	2 tablespoons white wine
½ teaspoon ground black pepper	2 tablespoons lemon juice
	2 cups brown rice
	2 cups vegetable broth

1. Press the Sauté button on the Instant Pot® and heat oil. Add onion and cook until soft, about 6 minutes. Add garlic and cook until fragrant, about 30 seconds. Add lemon zest, pepper, thyme, oregano, and salt. Cook until fragrant, about 1 minute. 2. Add wine and lemon juice and cook, stirring well, until liquid has almost evaporated, about 1 minute. Add rice and cook, stirring constantly, until coated and starting to toast, about 3 minutes. Press the Cancel button. 3. Stir in broth. Close lid, set steam release to Sealing, press the Manual button, and set time to 22 minutes. 4. When the timer beeps, let pressure release naturally for 10 minutes, then quick-release the remaining pressure until the float valve drops. Open lid and fluff rice with a fork. Serve warm.

Per Serving:

calories: 202 | fat: 5g | protein: 4g | carbs: 37g | fiber: 1g | sodium: 274mg

Simple Herbed Rice

Prep time: 10 minutes | Cook time: 32 minutes | Serves 8

2 tablespoons extra-virgin olive oil	2¼ cups brown rice
½ medium yellow onion, peeled and chopped	2 cups water
4 cloves garlic, peeled and minced	¼ cup chopped fresh flat-leaf parsley
¼ teaspoon salt	¼ cup chopped fresh basil
½ teaspoon ground black pepper	2 tablespoons chopped fresh oregano
	2 teaspoons fresh thyme leaves

1. Press the Sauté button on the Instant Pot® and heat oil. Add onion and cook until soft, about 6 minutes. Add garlic, salt, and pepper and cook until fragrant, about 30 seconds. Add rice and cook, stirring constantly, until well-coated and starting to toast, about 3 minutes. Press the Cancel button. 2. Stir in water. Close lid, set steam release to Sealing, press the Manual button, and set time to 22 minutes. When the timer beeps, let pressure release naturally for 10 minutes, then quick-release the remaining pressure. Open lid and fold in parsley, basil, oregano, and thyme. Serve warm.

Per Serving:

calories: 102 | fat: 4g | protein: 2g | carbs: 15g | fiber: 1g | sodium: 96mg

Spicy Black Beans with Root Veggies

Prep time: 20 minutes | Cook time: 8 hours | Serves 2

1 onion, chopped	2 cups vegetable broth
1 leek, white part only, sliced	2 teaspoons chili powder
3 garlic cloves, minced	½ teaspoon dried marjoram
1 jalapeño pepper, minced	leaves
2 Yukon Gold potatoes, peeled	½ teaspoon salt
and cubed	⅛ teaspoon freshly ground black
1 parsnip, peeled and cubed	pepper
1 carrot, sliced	⅛ teaspoon crushed red pepper
1 cup dried black beans, sorted	flakes
and rinsed	

1. In the slow cooker, combine all the ingredients. 2. Cover and cook on low for 7 to 8 hours, or until the beans and vegetables are tender, and serve.

Per Serving:

calories: 597 | fat: 2g | protein: 27g | carbs: 124g | fiber: 25g | sodium: 699mg

Brown Rice Pilaf with Golden Raisins

Prep time: 5 minutes |Cook time: 15 minutes| Serves: 6

1 tablespoon extra-virgin olive	½ teaspoon ground cinnamon
oil	2 cups instant brown rice
1 cup chopped onion (about ½	1¾ cups 100% orange juice
medium onion)	¼ cup water
½ cup shredded carrot (about 1	1 cup golden raisins
medium carrot)	½ cup shelled pistachios
1 teaspoon ground cumin	Chopped fresh chives (optional)

1. In a medium saucepan over medium-high heat, heat the oil. Add the onion and cook for 5 minutes, stirring frequently. Add the carrot, cumin, and cinnamon, and cook for 1 minute, stirring frequently. Stir in the rice, orange juice, and water. Bring to a boil, cover, then lower the heat to medium-low. Simmer for 7 minutes, or until the rice is cooked through and the liquid is absorbed. 2. Stir in the raisins, pistachios, and chives (if using) and serve.

Per Serving:

calories: 337 | fat: 9g | protein: 7g | carbs: 71g | fiber: 5g | sodium: 154mg

Sea Salt Soybeans

Prep time: 5 minutes | Cook time: 12 minutes | Serves 4

1 cup shelled edamame	1 teaspoon coarse sea salt
8 cups water, divided	2 tablespoons soy sauce
1 tablespoon vegetable oil	

1. Add edamame and 4 cups water to the Instant Pot®. Close lid, set steam release to Sealing, and set time to 1 minute. When the timer beeps, quick-release the pressure until the float valve drops. Press the Cancel button. 2. Open lid, drain and rinse edamame, and return to pot with the remaining 4 cups water. Soak for 1 hour. 3. Add oil. Close lid, set steam release to Sealing, press the Manual button, and set time to 11 minutes. When the timer beeps, let pressure release naturally, about 25 minutes, then open lid. 4. Drain edamame and transfer to a serving bowl. Sprinkle with salt and serve with soy sauce on the side for dipping.

Per Serving:

calories: 76 | fat: 5g | protein: 4g | carbs: 5g | fiber: 2g | sodium: 768mg

Chicken Artichoke Rice Bake

Prep time: 10 minutes | Cook time: 3 to 5 hours | Serves 4

Nonstick cooking spray	2 garlic cloves, minced
1 cup raw long-grain brown	10 ounces (283 g) fresh spinach,
rice, rinsed	chopped
2½ cups low-sodium chicken	1 teaspoon dried thyme
broth	½ teaspoon sea salt
1 (14-ounce/ 397-g) can	½ teaspoon freshly ground black
artichoke hearts, drained and	pepper
rinsed	1 pound (454 g) boneless,
½ small onion, diced	skinless chicken breast

1. Generously coat a slow-cooker insert with cooking spray. Put the rice, chicken broth, artichoke hearts, onion, garlic, spinach, thyme, salt, and pepper in a slow cooker. Gently stir to mix well. 2. Place the chicken on top of the rice mixture. 3. Cover the cooker and cook for 3 to 5 hours on Low heat. 4. Remove the chicken from the cooker, shred it, and stir it back into the rice in the cooker.

Per Serving:

calories: 323 | fat: 4g | protein: 32g | carbs: 44g | fiber: 6g | sodium: 741mg

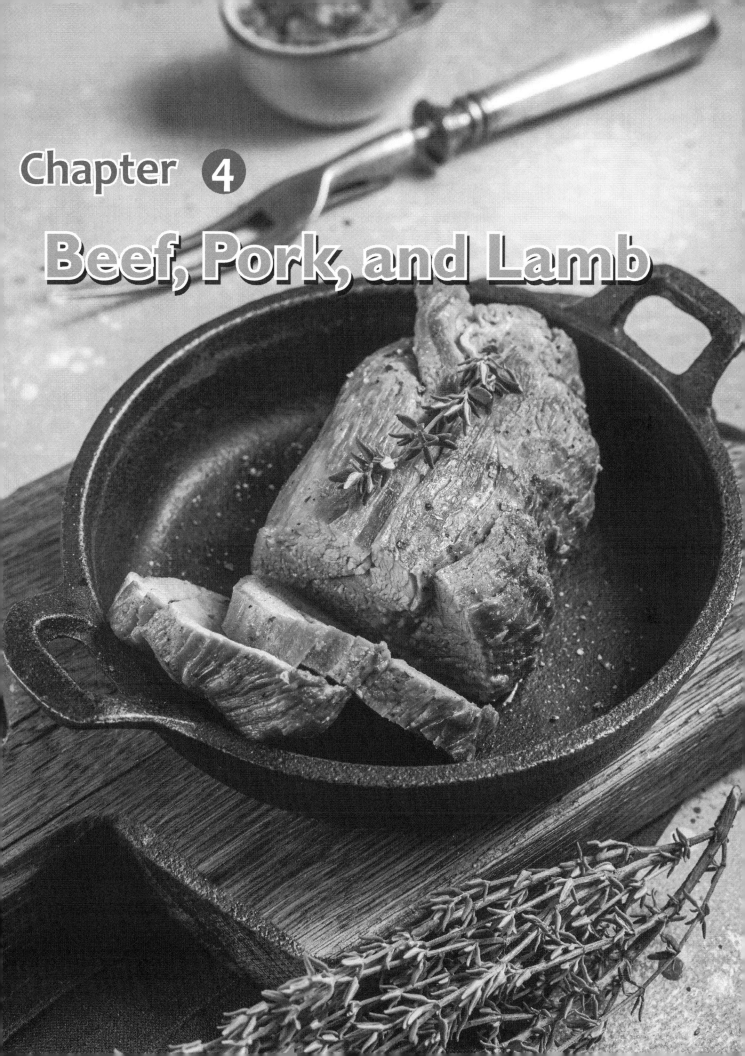

Chapter 4
Beef, Pork, and Lamb

Spicy Lamb Sirloin Chops

Prep time: 30 minutes | Cook time: 15 minutes | Serves 4

½ yellow onion, coarsely chopped	1 teaspoon ground cinnamon
4 coin-size slices peeled fresh ginger	1 teaspoon ground turmeric
	½ to 1 teaspoon cayenne pepper
5 garlic cloves	½ teaspoon ground cardamom
1 teaspoon garam masala	1 teaspoon kosher salt
1 teaspoon ground fennel	1 pound (454 g) lamb sirloin chops

1. In a blender, combine the onion, ginger, garlic, garam masala, fennel, cinnamon, turmeric, cayenne, cardamom, and salt. Pulse until the onion is finely minced and the mixture forms a thick paste, 3 to 4 minutes. 2. Place the lamb chops in a large bowl. Slash the meat and fat with a sharp knife several times to allow the marinade to penetrate better. Add the spice paste to the bowl and toss the lamb to coat. Marinate at room temperature for 30 minutes or cover and refrigerate for up to 24 hours. 3. Place the lamb chops in a single layer in the air fryer basket. Set the air fryer to 325ºF (163ºC) for 15 minutes, turning the chops halfway through the cooking time. Use a meat thermometer to ensure the lamb has reached an internal temperature of 145ºF (63ºC) (medium-rare).

Per Serving:

calories: 179 | fat: 7g | protein: 24g | carbs: 4g | fiber: 1g | sodium: 657mg

One-Pan Greek Pork and Vegetables

Prep time: 10 minutes | Cook time: 40 minutes | Serves 3

1 pound (454 g) pork shoulder, cut into 1-inch cubes	1 medium green bell pepper, seeded and sliced
¾ teaspoon fine sea salt, divided	1 medium carrot, peeled and julienned
½ teaspoon freshly ground black pepper, divided, plus more for serving	¼ cup dry red wine
	15 cherry tomatoes, halved
4 tablespoons extra virgin olive oil, divided	2 tablespoons hot water
1 medium red onion, sliced	½ teaspoon dried oregano

1. Scatter the cubed pork onto a cutting board and sprinkle with ¼ teaspoon of sea salt and ¼ teaspoon of black pepper. Flip the pieces over and sprinkle an additional ¼ teaspoon of sea salt and the remaining ¼ teaspoon of black pepper. 2. In a large pan wide enough to hold all the pork in a single layer, heat 3 tablespoons of olive oil over high heat. Once the oil is hot, add the pork pieces and brown for 2 minutes, then flip the pork pieces and brown for 2 more minutes. (Do not stir.) 3. Add the onions and sauté for 2 minutes and then add the bell peppers and carrots and sauté for 2 more minutes, ensuring all vegetables are coated with the oil. Reduce the heat to medium, cover the pan loosely, and cook for 5 minutes, stirring occasionally. 4. Add the wine and continue cooking for about 4 minutes, using a wooden spatula to scrape any browned bits from the bottom of the

pan. Add about 20 cherry tomato halves and stir gently, then drizzle with the remaining 1 tablespoon of olive oil and add the hot water. Reduce the heat to low and simmer for 15–20 minutes or until all the liquids are absorbed. Remove the pan from the heat. 5. Sprinkle the oregano over the top. Top with the remaining cherry tomato halves and season to taste with the remaining ¼ teaspoon of sea salt and additional black pepper before serving. Store covered in the refrigerator for up to 3 days.

Per Serving:

calories: 407 | fat: 27g | protein: 30g | carbs: 8g | fiber: 2g | sodium: 700mg

Parmesan-Crusted Pork Chops

Prep time: 5 minutes | Cook time: 12 minutes | Serves 4

1 large egg	pork chops
½ cup grated Parmesan cheese	½ teaspoon salt
4 (4-ounce / 113-g) boneless	¼ teaspoon ground black pepper

1. Whisk egg in a medium bowl and place Parmesan in a separate medium bowl. 2. Sprinkle pork chops on both sides with salt and pepper. Dip each pork chop into egg, then press both sides into Parmesan. 3. Place pork chops into ungreased air fryer basket. Adjust the temperature to 400ºF (204ºC) and air fry for 12 minutes, turning chops halfway through cooking. Pork chops will be golden and have an internal temperature of at least 145ºF (63ºC) when done. Serve warm.

Per Serving:

calories: 218 | fat: 9g | protein: 32g | carbs: 1g | fiber: 0g | sodium: 372mg

Garlic-Marinated Flank Steak

Prep time: 30 minutes | Cook time: 8 to 10 minutes | Serves 6

½ cup avocado oil	1½ teaspoons sea salt
¼ cup coconut aminos	1 teaspoon freshly ground black pepper
1 shallot, minced	
1 tablespoon minced garlic	¼ teaspoon red pepper flakes
2 tablespoons chopped fresh oregano, or 2 teaspoons dried	2 pounds (907 g) flank steak

1. In a blender, combine the avocado oil, coconut aminos, shallot, garlic, oregano, salt, black pepper, and red pepper flakes. Process until smooth. 2. Place the steak in a zip-top plastic bag or shallow dish with the marinade. Seal the bag or cover the dish and marinate in the refrigerator for at least 2 hours or overnight. 3. Remove the steak from the bag and discard the marinade. 4. Set the air fryer to 400ºF (204ºC). Place the steak in the air fryer basket (if needed, cut into sections and work in batches). Air fry for 4 to 6 minutes, flip the steak, and cook for another 4 minutes or until the internal temperature reaches 120ºF (49ºC) in the thickest part for medium-rare (or as desired).

Per Serving:

calories: 373 | fat: 26g | protein: 33g | carbs: 1g | fiber: 0g | sodium: 672mg

Pork Casserole with Fennel and Potatoes

Prep time: 20 minutes | Cook time: 6 to 8 hours | Serves 6

2 large fennel bulbs	4 garlic cloves, minced
3 pounds (1.4 kg) pork tenderloin, cut into 1½-inch pieces	1½ teaspoons dried thyme
	1 teaspoon dried parsley
	1 teaspoon sea salt
2 pounds (907 g) red potatoes, quartered	Freshly ground black pepper
	⅓ cup shredded Parmesan cheese
1 cup low-sodium chicken broth	

1. Cut the stalks off the fennel bulbs. Trim a little piece from the bottom of the bulbs to make them stable, then cut straight down through the bulbs to halve them. Cut the halves into quarters. Peel off and discard any wilted outer layers. Cut the fennel pieces crosswise into slices. 2. In a slow cooker, combine the fennel, pork, and potatoes. Stir to mix well. 3. In a small bowl, whisk together the chicken broth, garlic, thyme, parsley, and salt until combined. Season with pepper and whisk again. Pour the sauce over the pork. 4. Cover the cooker and cook for 6 to 8 hours on Low heat. 5. Top with Parmesan cheese for serving.

Per Serving:

calories: 412 | fat: 7g | protein: 55g | carbs: 31g | fiber: 5g | sodium: 592mg

Braised Short Ribs with Fennel and Pickled Grapes

Prep time: 20 minutes | Cook time: 55 minutes | Serves 4

1½ pounds (680 g) boneless beef short ribs, trimmed and cut into 2-inch pieces	1 onion, halved and sliced ½ inch thick
1 teaspoon table salt, divided	4 garlic cloves, minced
1 tablespoon extra-virgin olive oil	2 teaspoons fennel seeds
	½ cup chicken broth
1 fennel bulb, 2 tablespoons fronds chopped, stalks discarded, bulb halved, cored, and sliced into 1-inch-thick wedges	1 sprig fresh rosemary
	¼ cup red wine vinegar
	1 tablespoon sugar
	4 ounces (113 g) seedless red grapes, halved (½ cup)

1. Pat short ribs dry with paper towels and sprinkle with ½ teaspoon salt. Using highest sauté function, heat oil in Instant Pot for 5 minutes (or until just smoking). Brown short ribs on all sides, 6 to 8 minutes; transfer to plate. 2. Add fennel wedges, onion, and ¼ teaspoon salt to fat left in pot and cook, using highest sauté function, until vegetables are softened and lightly browned, about 5 minutes. Stir in garlic and fennel seeds and cook until fragrant, about 30 seconds. Stir in broth and rosemary sprig, scraping up any browned bits. Nestle short ribs into vegetable mixture and add any accumulated juices. Lock lid in place and close pressure release valve. Select high pressure cook function and cook for 35 minutes.

3. Meanwhile, microwave vinegar, sugar, and remaining ¼ teaspoon salt in bowl until simmering, about 1 minute. Add grapes and let sit, stirring occasionally, for 20 minutes. Drain grapes and return to now-empty bowl. (Drained grapes can be refrigerated for up to 1 week.) 4. Turn off Instant Pot and let pressure release naturally for 15 minutes. Quick-release any remaining pressure, then carefully remove lid, allowing steam to escape away from you. Transfer short ribs to serving dish, tent with aluminum foil, and let rest while finishing sauce. 5. Strain braising liquid through fine-mesh strainer into fat separator. Discard rosemary sprig and transfer vegetables to serving dish with beef. Let braising liquid settle for 5 minutes, then pour ¾ cup defatted liquid over short ribs and vegetables; discard remaining liquid. Sprinkle with grapes and fennel fronds. Serve.

Per Serving:

calories: 310 | fat: 17g | protein: 24g | carbs: 15g | fiber: 3g | sodium: 750mg

Hearty Stewed Beef in Tomato Sauce

Prep time: 20 minutes | Cook time: 1 hour 45 minutes | Serves 5

3 tablespoons extra virgin olive oil	4 cloves
	4 allspice berries
2 pounds (907 g) boneless beef chuck, cut into 2-inch (5cm) chunks	1 bay leaf
	¼ teaspoon freshly ground black pepper
1 medium onion (any variety), diced	15 ounces (425 g) canned crushed tomatoes or chopped fresh tomatoes
4 garlic cloves, minced	
⅓ cup white wine	1 cup hot water
2 tablespoons tomato paste	½ teaspoon fine sea salt
1 cinnamon stick	

1. Add the olive oil to a deep pan over medium heat. When the oil starts to shimmer, place half the beef in the pan. Brown the meat until a crust develops, about 3–4 minutes per side, then transfer the meat to a plate, and set aside. Repeat with the remaining pieces. 2. Add the onions to the pan and sauté for 3 minutes or until soft, using a wooden spatula to scrape the browned bits from the bottom of the pan. Add the garlic and sauté for 1 minute, then add the wine and deglaze the pan for 1 more minute, again using the wooden spatula to scrape any browned bits from the bottom of the pan. 3. Add the tomato paste to the pan while stirring rapidly, then add the cinnamon stick, cloves, allspice berries, bay leaf, black pepper, crushed tomatoes, and hot water. Mix well. 4. Add the beef back to the pan. Stir, then cover and reduce the heat to low. Simmer for 1 hour 30 minutes or until the beef is cooked through and tender, and the sauce has thickened. (If the sauce becomes too dry, add more hot water as needed.) 5. About 10 minutes before the cooking time is complete, add the sea salt and stir. When ready to serve, remove the cinnamon stick, bay leaf, allspice berries, and cloves. Store in the refrigerator for up to 3 days.

Per Serving:

calories: 357 | fat: 19g | protein: 39g | carbs: 8g | fiber: 2g | sodium: 403mg

The Best Spaghetti Sauce

Prep time: 10 minutes | Cook time: 1 hour | Serves 4

1 tablespoon extra-virgin olive oil	paste
1 pound (454 g) ground beef, about 90% lean	10 to 15 ounces (283 to 425 g) red wine
4 garlic cloves, minced or pressed	1 tablespoon sugar
1 medium to large onion, diced	1 tablespoon Worcestershire sauce
1 green bell pepper, diced	1 tablespoon Italian seasoning
1 (15-ounce / 425-g) can tomato sauce	Salt and freshly ground black pepper, to taste
1 (6-ounce / 170-g) can tomato	1 (15-ounce / 425-g) can diced tomatoes, drained

1. In a large skillet, heat the olive oil over medium heat. Add the ground beef and cook, breaking it up with a wooden spoon as it cooks, until nearly browned. Add the garlic, onion, and bell pepper and cook, stirring occasionally, until the onion is translucent. Drain any excess liquid from the skillet. 2. Add the tomato sauce and tomato paste and stir them into the beef mixture. Add the wine, sugar, Worcestershire, and Italian seasoning. Season with salt and pepper. Cook over low heat, stirring occasionally, for at least 1 hour, or as long as 4 hours, adding more water as needed to maintain the desired consistency. 3. Ten minutes before serving, stir in the diced tomatoes.

Per Serving:

1 cup: calories: 334 | fat: 14g | protein: 28g | carbs: 24g | fiber: 6g | sodium: 536mg

Beesteya (Moroccan-Style Lamb Pie)

Prep time: 15 minutes | Cook time: 1 hour | Serves 8

2 tablespoons olive oil	½ cup pistachios, toasted
1 medium onion, chopped (about 1¼ cups)	¼ cup chopped fresh cilantro
3 carrots, finely chopped (about 1 cup)	1 teaspoon ground cinnamon
1 teaspoon ground turmeric	6 eggs
2 garlic cloves, minced	1 (5-ounce / 142-g) container 2% Greek yogurt
1 pound (454 g) ground lamb, turkey, or lean beef	Olive oil cooking spray or other nonstick cooking spray
⅓ cup golden raisins	12 sheets frozen phyllo dough, thawed

1. Preheat the oven to 375°F (190°C). 2. In a large skillet, heat 1 tablespoon of the olive oil over medium heat. Add the onion and carrots and cook, stirring occasionally for 5 to 6 minutes, until the onion is translucent. Stir in the turmeric and garlic; cook for 1 minute. Add the remaining 1 tablespoon olive oil and the ground lamb to the skillet. Cook, breaking up the meat with a wooden spoon as it cooks, for 6 to 8 minutes, until the lamb is browned. 3. Stir in the raisins, pistachios, cilantro, and cinnamon until well combined; set aside. 4. In a medium bowl, whisk the eggs and yogurt together; set aside. 5.

Spray a 9-inch springform pan with olive oil cooking spray or other cooking spray. On a clean work surface, stack 4 phyllo sheets, spray both sides with cooking spray, and place in the stack in the prepared pan, extending the edges of the stack up the sides of the pan. Repeat with a second stack of 4 phyllo sheets; place them crosswise over the first stack, extending the edges over the top edge of the pan. 6. Fill the phyllo crust with the lamb mixture, then pour in the egg mixture. Spray the remaining 4 phyllo sheets with cooking spray and cut in half. Place them over the filling to cover it completely. Fold the phyllo toward the center over the filling. Spray with additional cooking spray. 7. Bake for 45 to 50 minutes, until golden brown. Let stand for 15 minutes before serving.

Per Serving:

1 cup: calories: 362 | fat: 19g | protein: 22g | carbs: 28g | fiber: 3g | sodium: 241mg

Lamb Chops with Shaved Zucchini Salad

Prep time: 20 minutes | Cook time: 40 minutes | Serves 4

4 (8- to 12-ounce/ 227- to 340-g) lamb shoulder chops (blade or round bone), about ¾ inch thick, trimmed	1 bay leaf
¾ teaspoon table salt, divided	4 zucchini (6 ounces / 170 g each), sliced lengthwise into ribbons
¾ teaspoon pepper, divided	1 teaspoon grated lemon zest plus 1 tablespoon juice
2 tablespoons extra-virgin olive oil, divided	2 ounces (57 g) goat cheese, crumbled (½ cup)
1 onion, chopped	¼ cup chopped fresh mint
5 garlic cloves, minced	2 tablespoons raisins
½ cup chicken broth	

1. Pat lamb chops dry with paper towels and sprinkle with ½ teaspoon salt and ½ teaspoon pepper. Using highest sauté function, heat 1½ teaspoons oil in Instant Pot for 5 minutes (or until just smoking). Brown half of chops on both sides, 6 to 8 minutes; transfer to plate. Repeat with 1½ teaspoons oil and remaining chops; transfer to plate. 2. Add onion to fat left in pot and cook, using highest sauté function, until softened, about 5 minutes. Stir in garlic and cook until fragrant, about 30 seconds. Stir in broth and bay leaf, scraping up any browned bits. Return chops to pot along with any accumulated juices (chops will overlap). Lock lid in place and close pressure release valve. Select high pressure cook function and cook for 20 minutes. 3. Turn off Instant Pot and let pressure release naturally for 15 minutes. Quick-release any remaining pressure, then carefully remove lid, allowing steam to escape away from you. Transfer chops to serving dish. Gently toss zucchini with lemon zest and juice, remaining 1 tablespoon oil, remaining ¼ teaspoon salt, and remaining ¼ teaspoon pepper in bowl. Arrange zucchini on serving dish with lamb, and sprinkle with goat cheese, mint, and raisins. Serve.

Per Serving:

calories: 390 | fat: 20g | protein: 38g | carbs: 14g | fiber: 2g | sodium: 720mg

Greek-Inspired Beef Kebabs

Prep timePrep Time: 15 minutes | Cook Time: 15 minutes | Serves 2	peppers
	½ cup olive oil
6 ounces (170 g) beef sirloin tip, trimmed of fat and cut into 2-inch pieces	¼ cup freshly squeezed lemon juice
	2 tablespoons balsamic vinegar
3 cups of any mixture of vegetables: mushrooms, zucchini, summer squash, onions, cherry tomatoes, red	2 teaspoons dried oregano
	1 teaspoon garlic powder
	1 teaspoon minced fresh rosemary
	1 teaspoon salt

1. Place the meat in a large shallow container or in a plastic freezer bag. 2. Cut the vegetables into similar-size pieces and place them in a second shallow container or freezer bag. 3. For the marinade, combine the olive oil, lemon juice, balsamic vinegar, oregano, garlic powder, rosemary, and salt in a measuring cup. Whisk well to combine. Pour half of the marinade over the meat, and the other half over the vegetables. 4. Place the meat and vegetables in the refrigerator to marinate for 4 hours. 5. When you are ready to cook, preheat the grill to medium-high (350–400°F) and grease the grill grate. 6. Thread the meat onto skewers and the vegetables onto separate skewers. 7. Grill the meat for 3 minutes on each side. They should only take 10 to 12 minutes to cook, but it will depend on how thick the meat is. 8. Grill the vegetables for about 3 minutes on each side or until they have grill marks and are softened.

Per Serving:

calories: 285 | fat: 18g | protein: 21g | carbs: 9g | fiber: 4g | sodium: 123mg

Pepper Steak

Prep time: 30 minutes | Cook time: 16 to 20 minutes | Serves 4

1 pound (454 g) cube steak, cut into 1-inch pieces	pepper
	¼ cup cornstarch
1 cup Italian dressing	1 cup thinly sliced bell pepper, any color
1½ cups beef broth	
1 tablespoon soy sauce	1 cup chopped celery
½ teaspoon salt	1 tablespoon minced garlic
¼ teaspoon freshly ground black	1 to 2 tablespoons oil

1. In a large resealable bag, combine the beef and Italian dressing. Seal the bag and refrigerate to marinate for 8 hours. 2. In a small bowl, whisk the beef broth, soy sauce, salt, and pepper until blended. 3. In another small bowl, whisk ¼ cup water and the cornstarch until dissolved. Stir the cornstarch mixture into the beef broth mixture until blended. 4. Preheat the air fryer to 375°F (191°C). 5. Pour the broth mixture into a baking pan. Cook for 4 minutes. Stir and cook for 4 to 5 minutes more. Remove and set aside. 6. Increase the air fryer temperature to 400°F (204°C). Line the air fryer basket with parchment paper. 7. Remove the steak from the marinade and place it in a medium bowl. Discard the marinade. Stir in the bell pepper, celery, and garlic. 8. Place the steak and pepper mixture on the parchment. Spritz with oil. 9. Cook for 4 minutes. Shake the basket and cook for 4 to 7 minutes more, until the vegetables are tender

and the meat reaches an internal temperature of 145°F (63°C). Serve with the gravy.

Per Serving:

calories: 302 | fat: 14g | protein: 27g | carbs: 15g | fiber: 1g | sodium: 635mg

Pork Souvlaki

Prep time: 1 hour 15 minutes | Cook time: 10 minutes | Serves 4

1 (1½-pound / 680-g) pork loin	1 tablespoon dried oregano
2 tablespoons garlic, minced	1 teaspoon salt
⅓ cup extra-virgin olive oil	Pita bread and tzatziki, for serving (optional)
⅓ cup lemon juice	

1. Cut the pork into 1-inch cubes and put them into a bowl or plastic zip-top bag. 2. In a large bowl, mix together the garlic, olive oil, lemon juice, oregano, and salt. 3. Pour the marinade over the pork and let it marinate for at least 1 hour. 4. Preheat a grill, grill pan, or lightly oiled skillet to high heat. Using wood or metal skewers, thread the pork onto the skewers. 5. Cook the skewers for 3 minutes on each side, for 12 minutes in total. 6. Serve with pita bread and tzatziki sauce, if desired.

Per Serving:

calories: 393 | fat: 25g | protein: 38g | carbs: 3g | fiber: 0g | sodium: 666mg

Moroccan Flank Steak with Harissa Couscous

Prep time: 5 minutes | Cook time: 15 minutes | Serves 4

1½ teaspoons coriander seeds	1 tablespoon harissa
1¼ teaspoons ground ginger	½ cup chopped pitted dried dates
½ teaspoon ground cumin	
¾ teaspoon ground cinnamon	1 cup uncooked couscous
¼ teaspoon ground cloves	Sea salt
1½ pounds (680 g) flank steak	Freshly ground black pepper
3 tablespoons olive oil	¼ cup chopped fresh Italian parsley
¾ cup chicken broth	

1. In a small bowl, combine the coriander, ginger, cumin, cinnamon, and cloves. Rub the steak all over with the seasoning mix. 2. In a large sauté pan, heat the olive oil over medium-high heat. Add the steak and cook for 2 to 3 minutes on each side for medium-rare. Transfer the steak to a plate and set aside to rest for 10 minutes. 3. In the same pan, mix together the meat juices with the broth, harissa, and dates. Bring to a boil over medium-high heat. Add the couscous, remove from the heat, cover, and let stand for 5 minutes. Season with salt and pepper. 4. Cut the steak across the grain into thin strips. 5. Serve the steak with the couscous, garnished with parsley.

Per Serving:

calories: 516 | fat: 16g | protein: 43g | carbs: 49g | fiber: 4g | sodium: 137mg

Greek Stuffed Tenderloin

Prep time: 10 minutes | Cook time: 10 minutes | Serves 4

1½ pounds (680 g) venison or beef tenderloin, pounded to ¼ inch thick	¼ cup finely chopped onions
3 teaspoons fine sea salt	2 cloves garlic, minced
1 teaspoon ground black pepper	For Garnish/Serving (Optional):
2 ounces (57 g) creamy goat cheese	Prepared yellow mustard
	Halved cherry tomatoes
	Extra-virgin olive oil
½ cup crumbled feta cheese (about 2 ounces / 57 g)	Sprigs of fresh rosemary
	Lavender flowers

1. Spray the air fryer basket with avocado oil. Preheat the air fryer to 400ºF (204ºC). 2. Season the tenderloin on all sides with the salt and pepper. 3. In a medium-sized mixing bowl, combine the goat cheese, feta, onions, and garlic. Place the mixture in the center of the tenderloin. Starting at the end closest to you, tightly roll the tenderloin like a jelly roll. Tie the rolled tenderloin tightly with kitchen twine. 4. Place the meat in the air fryer basket and air fry for 5 minutes. Flip the meat over and cook for another 5 minutes, or until the internal temperature reaches 135ºF (57ºC) for medium-rare. 5. To serve, smear a line of prepared yellow mustard on a platter, then place the meat next to it and add halved cherry tomatoes on the side, if desired. Drizzle with olive oil and garnish with rosemary sprigs and lavender flowers, if desired. 6. Best served fresh. Store leftovers in an airtight container in the fridge for 3 days. Reheat in a preheated 350ºF (177ºC) air fryer for 4 minutes, or until heated through.

Per Serving:

calories: 345 | fat: 17g | protein: 43g | carbs: 2g | fiber: 0g | sodium: 676mg

Lamb and Onion Tagine

Prep time: 10 minutes | Cook time: 2 hours 15 minutes | Serves 4

2 tablespoons finely chopped fresh flat-leaf parsley	3 tablespoons extra-virgin olive oil
2 tablespoons finely chopped fresh cilantro	4 bone-in leg of lamb steaks, ½' thick (about 2½ pounds / 1.1 kg)
2 cloves garlic, minced	1 can (28 ounces / 794 g) whole peeled plum tomatoes, drained
½ teaspoon ground turmeric	
½ teaspoon ground ginger	2 large red onions, 1 finely chopped, the other sliced in ⅛' rounds
1 teaspoon ground cinnamon, divided	
1 teaspoon plus a pinch kosher salt	2 teaspoons honey, divided
½ teaspoon ground black pepper	1 tablespoon toasted sesame seeds
2 tablespoons plus ⅓ cup water	

1. In a large bowl, combine the parsley, cilantro, garlic, turmeric, ginger, ¼ teaspoon of the cinnamon, 1 teaspoon of the salt, and the pepper. Add 2 tablespoons of the water and the oil and mix. Add the lamb steaks and turn to coat each one. Cover and refrigerate,

turning the steaks occasionally, for at least 1 hour. 2. Make a small cut into each tomato and squeeze out the seeds and excess juices. 3. In a 12' tagine or a deep heavy-bottom skillet, scatter the chopped onion. Arrange the lamb steaks snugly in a single layer. Drizzle the remaining marinade over the top. Add the tomatoes around the lamb. Drizzle 1 teaspoon of the honey and ¼ teaspoon of the cinnamon over the top. 4. Lay the onion rounds on top of the lamb. Drizzle the remaining 1 teaspoon honey. Sprinkle the remaining ½ teaspoon cinnamon and the pinch of salt. Turn the heat on to medium (medium-low if using a pot) and cook, uncovered, nudging the lamb occasionally, until the chopped onion below is translucent, about 15 minutes. 5. Pour in the ⅓ cup water around the outer edges of the food. Cover with a lid, slightly askew to keep air flowing in and out of the tagine or skillet. Reduce the heat to low and simmer gently, nudging the lamb occasionally to prevent sticking. Cook until the lamb is very tender, adding water as needed to keep the sauce moist, about 2 hours. 6. Sprinkle with the sesame seeds and serve.

Per Serving:

calories: 537 | fat: 25g | protein: 63g | carbs: 19g | fiber: 6g | sodium: 791mg

Nigerian Peanut-Crusted Flank Steak

Prep time: 30 minutes | Cook time: 8 minutes | Serves 4

Suya Spice Mix:	1 teaspoon kosher salt
¼ cup dry-roasted peanuts	½ teaspoon cayenne pepper
1 teaspoon cumin seeds	Steak:
1 teaspoon garlic powder	1 pound (454 g) flank steak
1 teaspoon smoked paprika	2 tablespoons vegetable oil
½ teaspoon ground ginger	

1. For the spice mix: In a clean coffee grinder or spice mill, combine the peanuts and cumin seeds. Process until you get a coarse powder. (Do not overprocess or you will wind up with peanut butter! Alternatively, you can grind the cumin with ⅓ cup ready-made peanut powder, such as PB2, instead of the peanuts.) 2. Pour the peanut mixture into a small bowl, add the garlic powder, paprika, ginger, salt, and cayenne, and stir to combine. This recipe makes about ½ cup suya spice mix. Store leftovers in an airtight container in a cool, dry place for up to 1 month. 3. For the steak: Cut the flank steak into ½-inch-thick slices, cutting against the grain and at a slight angle. Place the beef strips in a resealable plastic bag and add the oil and 2½ to 3 tablespoons of the spice mixture. Seal the bag and massage to coat all of the meat with the oil and spice mixture. Marinate at room temperature for 30 minutes or in the refrigerator for up to 24 hours. 4. Place the beef strips in the air fryer basket. Set the air fryer to 400ºF (204ºC) for 8 minutes, turning the strips halfway through the cooking time. 5. Transfer the meat to a serving platter. Sprinkle with additional spice mix, if desired.

Per Serving:

calories: 275 | fat: 17g | protein: 27g | carbs: 3g | fiber: 1g | sodium: 644mg

Beef and Mushroom Stroganoff

Prep time: 15 minutes | Cook time: 31 minutes | Serves 6

2 tablespoons olive oil	¼ teaspoon ground black pepper
1 medium onion, peeled and chopped	2 cups beef broth
2 cloves garlic, peeled and minced	1 pound (454 g) sliced button mushrooms
1 pound (454 g) beef stew meat, cut into 1" pieces	1 pound (454 g) wide egg noodles
3 tablespoons all-purpose flour	½ cup low-fat plain Greek yogurt
¼ teaspoon salt	

1. Press the Sauté button on the Instant Pot® and heat oil. Add onion and cook until soft, about 5 minutes. Add garlic and cook until fragrant, about 30 seconds. 2. Combine beef, flour, salt, and pepper in a medium bowl and toss to coat beef completely. Add beef to the pot and cook, stirring often, until browned, about 10 minutes. Stir in beef broth and scrape any brown bits from bottom of pot. Stir in mushrooms and press the Cancel button. 3. Close lid, set steam release to Sealing, press the Manual button, and set time to 10 minutes. When the timer beeps, quick-release the pressure until the float valve drops, open lid, and stir well. Press the Cancel button. 4. Add noodles and stir, making sure noodles are submerged in liquid. Close lid, set steam release to Sealing, press the Manual button, and set time to 5 minutes. 5. When the timer beeps, quick-release the pressure until the float valve drops. Open lid and stir well. Press the Cancel button and cool for 5 minutes, then stir in yogurt. Serve hot.

Per Serving:

calories: 446 | fat: 13g | protein: 19g | carbs: 63g | fiber: 4g | sodium: 721mg

Lamb Tagine

Prep time: 15 minutes | Cook time: 7 hours | Serves 6

1 navel orange	¼ teaspoon saffron threads, crushed in your palm
2 tablespoons all-purpose flour	¼ teaspoon ground red pepper
2 pounds (907 g) boneless leg of lamb, trimmed and cut into 1½-inch cubes	1 cup pitted dates
½ cup chicken stock	2 tablespoons honey
2 large white onions, chopped	3 cups hot cooked couscous, for serving
1 teaspoon pumpkin pie spice	
1 teaspoon ground cumin	2 tablespoons toasted slivered almonds, for serving
½ teaspoon sea salt	

1. Grate 2 teaspoons of zest from the orange into a small bowl.

Squeeze ¼ cup juice from the orange into another small bowl. 2. Add the flour to the orange juice, stirring with a whisk until smooth. Stir in the orange zest. 3. Heat a large nonstick skillet over medium-high heat. Add the lamb and sauté 7 minutes or until browned. Stir in the stock, scraping the bottom of the pan with a wooden spoon to loosen the flavorful brown bits. Stir in the orange juice mixture. 4. Stir the onions into the lamb mixture. Add the pumpkin pie spice, cumin, salt, saffron, and ground red pepper. 5. Pour the lamb mixture into the slow cooker. Cover and cook on low for 6 hours or until the lamb is tender. 6. Stir the dates and honey into the lamb mixture. Cover and cook on low for 1 hour or until thoroughly heated. 7. Serve the lamb tagine over the couscous and sprinkle with the almonds.

Per Serving:

calories: 451 | fat: 11g | protein: 37g | carbs: 53g | fiber: 5g | sodium: 329mg

Italian Braised Pork

Prep time: 10 minutes | Cook time: 4¹/□ hours | Serves 4

2½ pounds (1.1 kg) boneless pork shoulder	1 stalk celery, finely diced
Coarse sea salt	¾ teaspoon fennel seeds
Black pepper	½ cup dry red wine
2 tablespoons olive oil	1 (28-ounce / 794-g) can crushed tomatoes
1 large yellow onion, finely diced	4 cups prepared hot couscous, for serving
3 cloves garlic, minced	

1. Season the pork with salt and pepper. 2. In a large skillet, heat the olive oil over medium-high heat. Cook the pork, turning occasionally, until browned on all sides, about 8 minutes. Transfer the pork to the slow cooker. 3. Reduce the heat under the skillet to medium, and add the onion, garlic, celery, and fennel seeds. Cook, stirring often, until the onion is softened, about 4 minutes. 4. Add the wine and cook, stirring with a wooden spoon and scraping up the flavorful browned bits from the bottom of the pan, until the liquid is reduced by half, about 2 minutes. Add the wine mixture to the slow cooker, and stir in the tomatoes. 5. Cover and cook on high for 4 hours, or until the pork is very tender, or on low for 8 hours. 6. Transfer the pork to a cutting board. Shred the meat into bite-size pieces. Discard any pieces of fat. 7. Skim the fat off the sauce in the slow cooker and discard. Return the shredded pork to the slow cooker and stir to combine. Cook the pork and sauce for 5 minutes to reheat. 8. Serve hot over the couscous.

Per Serving:

calories: 669 | fat: 17g | protein: 72g | carbs: 49g | fiber: 7g | sodium: 187mg

Lamb and Vegetable Bake

Prep time: 20 minutes | Cook time: 1 hour 20 minutes | Serves 8

¼ cup olive oil

1 pound (454 g) boneless, lean lamb, cut into ½ -inch pieces

2 large red potatoes, scrubbed and diced

1 large onion, coarsely chopped

2 cloves garlic, minced

1 (28-ounce) can diced tomatoes with liquid (no salt added)

2 medium zucchini, cut into ½ -inch slices

1 red bell pepper, seeded and cut into 1-inch cubes

2 tablespoons flat-leaf parsley, chopped

1 teaspoon dried thyme

1 tablespoon paprika

½ teaspoon ground cinnamon

½ cup red wine

Sea salt and freshly ground pepper, to taste

1. Preheat the oven to 325ºF (165ºC) degrees. 2. Heat the olive oil in a large stew pot or cast-iron skillet over medium-high heat. 3. Add the lamb and brown the meat, stirring frequently. Transfer the lamb to an ovenproof baking dish. 4. Cook the potatoes, onion, and garlic in the skillet until tender, then transfer them to the baking dish. 5. Pour the tomatoes, zucchini, and pepper into the pan along with the herbs and spices, and simmer for 10 minutes. 6. Cover the lamb, onions, and potatoes with the tomato and pepper sauce and wine. 7. Cover with aluminum foil and bake for 1 hour. Uncover during the last 15 minutes of baking. 8. Season to taste, and serve with a green salad.

Per Serving:

calories: 264 | fat: 12g | protein: 15g | carbs: 24g | fiber: 5g | sodium: 75mg

Moroccan Meatballs

Prep time: 10 minutes |Cook time: 20 minutes| Serves: 4

¼ cup finely chopped onion (about ⅛ onion)

¼ cup raisins, coarsely chopped

1 teaspoon ground cumin

½ teaspoon ground cinnamon

¼ teaspoon smoked paprika

1 large egg

1 pound (454 g) ground beef (93% lean) or ground lamb

⅓ cup panko bread crumbs

1 teaspoon extra-virgin olive oil

1 (28-ounce/ 794-g) can low-sodium or no-salt-added crushed tomatoes

Chopped fresh mint, feta cheese, and/or fresh orange or lemon wedges, for serving (optional)

1. In a large bowl, combine the onion, raisins, cumin, cinnamon, smoked paprika, and egg. Add the ground beef and bread crumbs and mix gently with your hands. Divide the mixture into 20 even portions, then wet your hands and roll each portion into a ball. Wash your hands. 2. In a large skillet over medium-high heat, heat the oil. Add the meatballs and cook for 8 minutes, rolling around every minute or so with tongs or a fork to brown them on most sides. (They won't be cooked through.) Transfer the meatballs to a paper towel–lined plate. Drain the fat out of the pan, and carefully wipe out the hot pan with a paper towel. 3. Return the meatballs to the pan, and pour the tomatoes over the meatballs. Cover and cook on medium-high heat until the sauce begins to bubble. Lower the heat to medium, cover partially, and cook for 7 to 8 more minutes, until the meatballs are cooked through. Garnish with fresh mint, feta cheese, and/or a squeeze of citrus, if desired, and serve.

Per Serving:

calories: 351 | fat: 18g | protein: 28g | carbs: 23g | fiber: 5g | sodium: 170mg

Wedding Soup

Prep time: 15 minutes | Cook time: 17 minutes | Serves 6

3 (1-ounce/ 28-g) slices Italian bread, toasted

¾ pound (340 g) 90% lean ground beef

1 large egg, beaten

1 medium onion, peeled and chopped

3 cloves garlic, peeled and minced

¼ cup chopped fresh parsley

1 tablespoon minced fresh

oregano

1 tablespoon minced fresh basil

1 teaspoon salt

½ teaspoon ground black pepper

½ cup grated Parmesan cheese, divided

2 tablespoons olive oil

8 cups low-sodium chicken broth

5 ounces (142 g) baby spinach

1. Wet toasted bread with water and then squeeze out all the liquid. Place soaked bread in a large bowl. Add ground beef, egg, onion, garlic, parsley, oregano, basil, salt, pepper, and ¼ cup cheese. Mix well. Form the mixture into 1" balls. 2. Press the Sauté button on the Instant Pot® and heat oil. Brown meatballs in batches on all sides, about 3 minutes per side. Transfer meatballs to a plate. Press the Cancel button. 3. Add broth to pot, stirring well to release any browned bits. Add meatballs and stir well. Close lid, set steam release to Sealing, press the Manual button, and set time to 10 minutes. When the timer beeps, quick-release the pressure until the float valve drops. Open lid. 4. Add spinach and stir until wilted, about 1 minute. Ladle the soup into bowls and sprinkle with remaining ¼ cup cheese.

Per Serving:

calories: 270 | fat: 16g | protein: 24g | carbs: 10g | fiber: 1g | sodium: 590mg

Fajita Meatball Lettuce Wraps

Prep time: 10 minutes | Cook time: 10 minutes | Serves 4

1 pound (454 g) ground beef (85% lean)
½ cup salsa, plus more for serving if desired
¼ cup chopped onions
¼ cup diced green or red bell peppers
1 large egg, beaten
1 teaspoon fine sea salt
½ teaspoon chili powder

½ teaspoon ground cumin
1 clove garlic, minced
For Serving (Optional):
8 leaves Boston lettuce
Pico de gallo or salsa
Lime slices

1. Spray the air fryer basket with avocado oil. Preheat the air fryer to 350°F (177°C). 2. In a large bowl, mix together all the ingredients until well combined. 3. Shape the meat mixture into eight 1-inch balls. Place the meatballs in the air fryer basket, leaving a little space between them. Air fry for 10 minutes, or until cooked through and no longer pink inside and the internal temperature reaches 145°F (63°C). 4. Serve each meatball on a lettuce leaf, topped with pico de gallo or salsa, if desired. Serve with lime slices if desired. 5. Store leftovers in an airtight container in the fridge for 3 days or in the freezer for up to a month. Reheat in a preheated 350°F (177°C) air fryer for 4 minutes, or until heated through.

Per Serving:
calories: 289 | fat: 20g | protein: 24g | carbs: 4g | fiber: 1g | sodium: 815mg

Hamburger Steak with Mushroom Gravy

Prep time: 20 minutes | Cook time: 29 to 34 minutes | Serves 4

Mushroom Gravy:
1 (1 ounce / 28 g) envelope dry onion soup mix
⅓ cup cornstarch
1 cup diced mushrooms
Hamburger Steak:
1 pound (454 g) ground beef (85% lean)

¾ cup minced onion
½ cup Italian-style bread crumbs
2 teaspoons Worcestershire sauce
1 teaspoon salt
1 teaspoon freshly ground black pepper
1 to 2 tablespoons oil

Make the Mushroom Gravy 1. In a metal bowl, whisk the soup mix, cornstarch, mushrooms, and 2 cups water until blended. 2. Preheat the air fryer to 350°F (177°C). 3. Place the bowl in the air fryer basket. 4. Cook for 10 minutes. Stir and cook for 5 to 10 minutes more to your desired thickness. Make the Hamburger Steak 5. In a large bowl, mix the ground beef, onion, bread crumbs, Worcestershire sauce, salt, and pepper until blended. Shape the beef mixture into 4 patties. 6. Decrease the air fryer's temperature to 320°F (160°C). 7. Place the patties in the air fryer basket. 8. Cook for 7 minutes. Flip the patties, spritz them with oil, and cook for 7 minutes more, until the internal temperature reaches 145°F (63°C).

Per Serving:
calories: 383 | fat: 21g | protein: 24g | carbs: 23g | fiber: 1g | sodium: 810mg

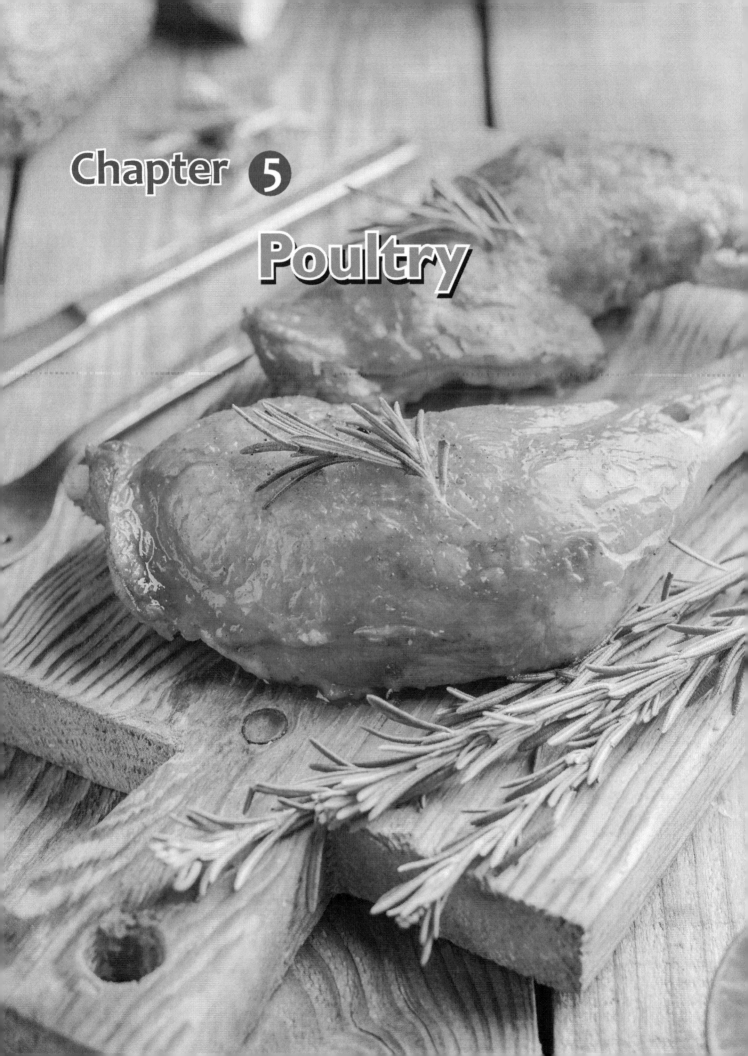

Chapter ⑤
Poultry

Turkey Meatloaf

Prep time: 10 minutes | Cook time: 50 minutes | Serves 4

8 ounces (227 g) sliced mushrooms	¼ cup almond meal
1 small onion, coarsely chopped	2 tablespoons almond milk
2 cloves garlic	1 tablespoon dried oregano
1½ pounds (680 g) 85% lean ground turkey	1 teaspoon salt
	½ teaspoon freshly ground black pepper
2 eggs, lightly beaten	1 Roma tomato, thinly sliced
1 tablespoon tomato paste	

1. Preheat the air fryer to 350ºF (177ºC). Lightly coat a round pan with olive oil and set aside. 2. In a food processor fitted with a metal blade, combine the mushrooms, onion, and garlic. Pulse until finely chopped. Transfer the vegetables to a large mixing bowl. 3. Add the turkey, eggs, tomato paste, almond meal, milk, oregano, salt, and black pepper. Mix gently until thoroughly combined. Transfer the mixture to the prepared pan and shape into a loaf. Arrange the tomato slices on top. 4. Air fry for 50 minutes or until the meatloaf is nicely browned and a thermometer inserted into the thickest part registers 165ºF (74ºC). Remove from the air fryer and let rest for about 10 minutes before slicing.

Per Serving:

calories: 353 | fat: 20g | protein: 38g | carbs: 7g | fiber: 2g | sodium: 625mg

Braised Chicken with Mushrooms and Tomatoes

Prep time: 20 minutes | Cook time: 25 minutes | Serves 4

1 tablespoon extra-virgin olive oil	2 teaspoons minced fresh sage
	½ cup dry red wine
1 pound (454 g) portobello mushroom caps, gills removed, caps halved and sliced ½ inch thick	1 (14½ ounces / 411 g) can diced tomatoes, drained
	4 (5 to 7 ounces / 142 to 198 g) bone-in chicken thighs, skin removed, trimmed
1 onion, chopped fine	
¾ teaspoon salt, divided	¼ teaspoon pepper
4 garlic cloves, minced	2 tablespoons chopped fresh parsley
1 tablespoon tomato paste	
1 tablespoon all-purpose flour	Shaved Parmesan cheese

1. Using highest sauté function, heat oil in Instant Pot until shimmering. Add mushrooms, onion, and ¼ teaspoon salt. Partially cover and cook until mushrooms are softened and have released their liquid, about 5 minutes. Stir in garlic, tomato paste, flour, and sage and cook until fragrant, about 1 minute. Stir in wine, scraping up any browned bits, then stir in tomatoes. 2. Sprinkle chicken with remaining ½ teaspoon salt and pepper. Nestle chicken skinned side up into pot and spoon some of sauce on top. Lock lid in place and close pressure release valve. Select high pressure cook function and cook for 15 minutes. 3. Turn off Instant Pot and quick-release pressure. Carefully remove lid, allowing steam to escape away from you. Transfer chicken to serving dish, tent with aluminum foil, and let rest while finishing sauce. 4. Using highest sauté function, bring sauce to simmer and cook until thickened slightly, about 5 minutes. Season sauce with salt and pepper to taste. Spoon sauce over chicken and sprinkle with parsley and Parmesan. Serve.

Per Serving:

calories: 230 | fat: 7g | protein: 21g | carbs: 15g | fiber:2g | sodium: 730mg

Chicken and Vegetable Fajitas

Prep time: 15 minutes | Cook time: 23 minutes | Serves 6

Chicken:	lengthwise
1 pound (454 g) boneless, skinless chicken thighs, cut crosswise into thirds	1 tablespoon vegetable oil
	½ teaspoon kosher salt
	½ teaspoon ground cumin
1 tablespoon vegetable oil	For Serving:
4½ teaspoons taco seasoning	Tortillas
Vegetables:	Sour cream
1 cup sliced onion	Shredded cheese
1 cup sliced bell pepper	Guacamole
1 or 2 jalapeños, quartered	Salsa

1. For the chicken: In a medium bowl, toss together the chicken, vegetable oil, and taco seasoning to coat. 2. For the vegetables: In a separate bowl, toss together the onion, bell pepper, jalapeño(s), vegetable oil, salt, and cumin to coat. 3. Place the chicken in the air fryer basket. Set the air fryer to 375ºF (191ºC) for 10 minutes. Add the vegetables to the basket, toss everything together to blend the seasonings, and set the air fryer for 13 minutes more. Use a meat thermometer to ensure the chicken has reached an internal temperature of 165ºF (74ºC). 4. Transfer the chicken and vegetables to a serving platter. Serve with tortillas and the desired fajita fixings.

Per Serving:

calories: 151 | fat: 8g | protein: 15g | carbs: 4g | fiber: 1g | sodium: 421mg

Italian Herb Grilled Chicken

Prep time: 20 minutes | Cook time: 10 minutes | Serves 4

½ cup lemon juice	1 teaspoon red pepper flakes
½ cup extra-virgin olive oil	1 teaspoon salt
3 tablespoons garlic, minced	2 pounds (907 g) boneless and skinless chicken breasts
2 teaspoons dried oregano	

1. In a large bowl, mix together the lemon juice, olive oil, garlic, oregano, red pepper flakes, and salt. 2. Fillet the chicken breast in half horizontally to get 2 thin pieces, repeating with all of the breasts. 3. Put the chicken in the bowl with the marinade and let sit for at least 10 minutes before cooking. 4. Preheat a grill, grill pan, or lightly oiled skillet to high heat. Once hot, cook the chicken for 4 minutes on each side. Serve warm.

Per Serving:

calories: 529 | fat: 33g | protein: 52g | carbs: 5g | fiber: 1g | sodium: 583mg

Roast Chicken

Prep time: 20 minutes | Cook time: 55 minutes | Serves 4

¼ cup white wine	1 large roasting chicken, giblets
2 tablespoons olive oil, divided	removed
1 tablespoon Dijon mustard	3 large carrots, peeled and cut
1 garlic clove, minced	into chunks
1 teaspoon dried rosemary	1 fennel bulb, peeled and cut
Juice and zest of 1 lemon	into ½-inch cubes
Sea salt and freshly ground	2 celery stalks, cut into chunks
pepper, to taste	

1. Preheat the oven to 400ºF (205ºC). 2. Combine the white wine, 1 tablespoon of olive oil, mustard, garlic, rosemary, lemon juice and zest, sea salt, and freshly ground pepper in a small bowl. 3. Place the chicken in a shallow roasting pan on a roasting rack. 4. Rub the entire chicken, including the cavity, with the wine and mustard mixture. 5. Place the chicken in the oven and roast for 15 minutes. 6. Toss the vegetables with the remaining tablespoon of olive oil, and place around the chicken. 7. Turn the heat down to 375ºF (190ºC). 8. Roast an additional 40–60 minutes, basting the chicken every 15 minutes with the drippings in the bottom of the pan. 9. Cook chicken until internal temperature reaches 180ºF (82ºC) in between the thigh and the body of the chicken. When you remove the instant-read thermometer, the juices should run clear. 10. Let the chicken rest for at least 10–15 minutes before serving.

Per Serving:

calories: 387 | fat: 14g | protein: 50g | carbs: 12g | fiber: 4g | sodium: 306mg

Fiesta Chicken Plate

Prep time: 15 minutes | Cook time: 12 to 15 minutes | Serves 4

1 pound (454 g) boneless,	beans
skinless chicken breasts (2 large	½ cup salsa
breasts)	2 cups shredded lettuce
2 tablespoons lime juice	1 medium tomato, chopped
1 teaspoon cumin	2 avocados, peeled and sliced
½ teaspoon salt	1 small onion, sliced into thin
½ cup grated Pepper Jack	rings
cheese	Sour cream
1 (16-ounce / 454-g) can refried	Tortilla chips (optional)

1. Split each chicken breast in half lengthwise. 2. Mix lime juice, cumin, and salt together and brush on all surfaces of chicken breasts. 3. Place in air fryer basket and air fry at 390ºF (199ºC) for 12 to 15 minutes, until well done. 4. Divide the cheese evenly over chicken breasts and cook for an additional minute to melt cheese. 5. While chicken is cooking, heat refried beans on stovetop or in microwave. 6. When ready to serve, divide beans among 4 plates. Place chicken breasts on top of beans and spoon salsa over. Arrange the lettuce, tomatoes, and avocados artfully on each plate and scatter with the onion rings. 7. Pass sour cream at the table and serve with tortilla chips if desired.

Per Serving:

calories: 497 | fat: 27g | protein: 38g | carbs: 26g | fiber: 12g | sodium: 722mg

Grilled Rosemary-Lemon Turkey Cutlets

Prep time: 10 minutes | Cook time: 30 minutes | Serves 4

2 tablespoons olive oil	Kosher salt and ground black
2 tablespoons fresh lemon juice	pepper, to taste
1 teaspoon finely chopped fresh	2 ripe tomatoes, diced
rosemary	½ red onion, diced
1 clove garlic, minced	1 tablespoon balsamic vinegar
4 turkey cutlets (6 ounces /	2 cups (2 ounces / 57 g) baby
170 g each), pounded to ¼'	arugula
thickness	

1. In a large bowl, combine the oil, lemon juice, rosemary, and garlic. Add the turkey cutlets and let marinate at room temperature while you prepare the grill, about 20 minutes. 2. Coat a grill rack or grill pan with olive oil and prepare the grill to medium-high heat. 3. Season the turkey with the salt and pepper. Grill the cutlets until grill marks form and the turkey is cooked through, about 4 minutes per side. 4. Meanwhile, in a medium bowl, combine the tomatoes, onion, and vinegar and season to taste with the salt and pepper. 5. Top each cutlet with ½ cup baby arugula and a quarter of the tomato mixture.

Per Serving:

calories: 269 | fat: 8g | protein: 43g | carbs: 6g | fiber: 1g | sodium: 398mg

Chicken in Cream Sauce

Prep time: 10 minutes | Cook time: 35 minutes | Serves 6

3 tablespoons olive oil	3 garlic cloves, minced
6 (4-ounce / 113-g) boneless,	½ teaspoon dried thyme
skinless chicken breasts	½ teaspoon dried marjoram
½ zucchini, chopped into 2-inch	½ teaspoon dried basil
pieces	½ cup baby spinach
1 celery stalk, chopped	1 cup heavy (whipping) cream
1 red bell pepper, thinly sliced	¼ cup chopped fresh Italian
2 tomatoes on the vine, chopped	parsley (optional)

1. In a large skillet, heat the olive oil over medium-high heat. Add the chicken and cook for 8 to 10 minutes on each side, until cooked through. Transfer the chicken to a plate and set aside. 2. Add the zucchini, celery, bell pepper, tomatoes, and garlic and sauté for 8 to 10 minutes, until the vegetables are softened. Add the thyme, marjoram, and basil and cook for 1 minute. Add the spinach and cook until wilted, about 3 minutes. 3. Add the cream and mix well. Return the chicken to the skillet and cook until warmed through, about 4 minutes. 4. Garnish with the parsley, if desired, and serve.

Per Serving:

calories: 341 | fat: 24g | protein: 27g | carbs: 4g | fiber: 1g | sodium: 83mg

Braised Chicken and Mushrooms

Prep time: 20 minutes | Cook time: 1 hour 30 minutes | Serves 4

3 tablespoons extra-virgin olive oil	mushrooms, cleaned and cut in half
8 pieces chicken, thighs and drumsticks	1 teaspoon salt
1½ cups garlic cloves, peeled	4 cups chicken broth
1 large onion, chopped	Rice or noodles, for serving (optional)
1 pound (454 g) cremini	

1. In a large pot or Dutch oven over medium heat, heat the olive oil and add chicken, browning on all sides, for about 8 minutes. Remove the chicken and place onto a dish; set aside. 2. Add the garlic, onion, mushrooms, and salt to the pot. Stir and cook for 8 minutes. 3. Add the broth to the pot and stir everything together. Add the chicken back into the pot, cover, and turn the heat to medium-low. Let simmer for 1 hour. 4. Uncover the pot and let simmer for another 10 minutes. 5. Serve with rice or noodles, if desired.

Per Serving:

calories: 521 | fat: 31g | protein: 38g | carbs: 24g | fiber: 3g | sodium: 742mg

Chettinad Chicken

Prep time: 15 minutes | Cook time: 4 to 6 hours | Serves 6

1 tablespoon white poppy seeds	20 curry leaves
1 teaspoon coriander seeds	3 onions, finely sliced
2 teaspoons cumin seeds	2 star anise
1 teaspoon fennel seeds	4 tomatoes
4 to 5 dried red chiles	1 teaspoon turmeric
2-inch piece cinnamon stick	Sea salt
6 green cardamom pods	1 teaspoon chili powder
4 cloves	12 chicken thighs on the bone, skinned and trimmed
1½ cups grated coconut	
4 garlic cloves	Juice of 2 or 3 limes
1 tablespoon freshly grated ginger	Handful fresh coriander leaves, chopped
2 tablespoons coconut oil	

1. In a frying pan, toast the poppy seeds, coriander seeds, cumin seeds, fennel seeds, dried red chiles, cinnamon, green cardamom pods, and cloves until fragrant, about 1 minute. Remove from the pan and set aside to cool. Once cooled, grind to a fine powder in a spice grinder. 2. In the same pan, toast the grated coconut for 3 to 4 minutes until it just starts to turn golden. Remove from the pan and spread on a plate to cool. Once cooled, grind and mix with the ground spices. 3. Crush the garlic and ginger in a mortar and pestle and set aside. 4. Either heat the slow cooker to sauté or use a pan on the stove. Heat the coconut oil and add the curry leaves, when they stop spluttering, add the sliced onions and fry them until they are light brown. Stir in the crushed garlic and ginger, and stir for a minute or two. 5. Add to the slow cooker along with the ground spices and anise. Chop and add the tomatoes, the turmeric, and the

salt, and stir in the chili powder. 6. Place the chicken pieces in the cooker, cover and cook on low for 6 hours, or on high for 4 hours, until tender and cooked through. 7. Check the seasoning and adjust if needed, squeeze in the lime juice, and serve topped with fresh coriander leaves.

Per Serving:

calories: 628 | fat: 28g | protein: 79g | carbs: 13g | net carbs: 9g | fiber: 4g

calories: 628 | fat: 28g | protein: 79g | carbs: 13g | sugars: 6g | fiber: 4g | sodium: 393mg

Fajita-Stuffed Chicken Breast

Prep time: 15 minutes | Cook time: 25 minutes | Serves 4

2 (6-ounce / 170-g) boneless, skinless chicken breasts	seeded and sliced
¼ medium white onion, peeled and sliced	1 tablespoon coconut oil
	2 teaspoons chili powder
	1 teaspoon ground cumin
1 medium green bell pepper,	½ teaspoon garlic powder

1. Slice each chicken breast completely in half lengthwise into two even pieces. Using a meat tenderizer, pound out the chicken until it's about ¼-inch thickness. 2. Lay each slice of chicken out and place three slices of onion and four slices of green pepper on the end closest to you. Begin rolling the peppers and onions tightly into the chicken. Secure the roll with either toothpicks or a couple pieces of butcher's twine. 3. Drizzle coconut oil over chicken. Sprinkle each side with chili powder, cumin, and garlic powder. Place each roll into the air fryer basket. 4. Adjust the temperature to 350ºF (177ºC) and air fry for 25 minutes. 5. Serve warm.

Per Serving:

calories: 168 | fat: 7g | protein: 25g | carbs: 3g | fiber: 1g | sodium: 320mg

Blackened Chicken

Prep time: 10 minutes | Cook time: 20 minutes | Serves 4

1 large egg, beaten	chicken breasts (about 1 pound / 454 g each), halved
¾ cup Blackened seasoning	
2 whole boneless, skinless	1 to 2 tablespoons oil

1. Place the beaten egg in one shallow bowl and the Blackened seasoning in another shallow bowl. 2. One at a time, dip the chicken pieces in the beaten egg and the Blackened seasoning, coating thoroughly. 3. Preheat the air fryer to 360ºF (182ºC). Line the air fryer basket with parchment paper. 4. Place the chicken pieces on the parchment and spritz with oil. 5. Cook for 10 minutes. Flip the chicken, spritz it with oil, and cook for 10 minutes more until the internal temperature reaches 165ºF (74ºC) and the chicken is no longer pink inside. Let sit for 5 minutes before serving.

Per Serving:

calories: 225 | fat: 10g | protein: 28g | carbs: 8g | fiber: 6g | sodium: 512mg

Chicken Jalfrezi

Prep time: 15 minutes | Cook time: 15 minutes | Serves 4

Chicken:
1 pound (454 g) boneless, skinless chicken thighs, cut into 2 or 3 pieces each
1 medium onion, chopped
1 large green bell pepper, stemmed, seeded, and chopped
2 tablespoons olive oil
1 teaspoon ground turmeric
1 teaspoon garam masala
1 teaspoon kosher salt
½ to 1 teaspoon cayenne pepper
Sauce:
¼ cup tomato sauce
1 tablespoon water
1 teaspoon garam masala
½ teaspoon kosher salt
½ teaspoon cayenne pepper
Side salad, rice, or naan bread, for serving

1. For the chicken: In a large bowl, combine the chicken, onion, bell pepper, oil, turmeric, garam masala, salt, and cayenne. Stir and toss until well combined. 2. Place the chicken and vegetables in the air fryer basket. Set the air fryer to 350ºF (177ºC) for 15 minutes, stirring and tossing halfway through the cooking time. Use a meat thermometer to ensure the chicken has reached an internal temperature of 165ºF (74ºC). 3. Meanwhile, for the sauce: In a small microwave-safe bowl, combine the tomato sauce, water, garam masala, salt, and cayenne. Microwave on high for 1 minute. Remove and stir. Microwave for another minute; set aside. 4. When the chicken is cooked, remove and place chicken and vegetables in a large bowl. Pour the sauce over all. Stir and toss to coat the chicken and vegetables evenly. 5. Serve with rice, naan, or a side salad.

Per Serving:
calories: 224 | fat: 12g | protein: 23g | carbs: 6g | fiber: 2g | sodium: 827mg

Chicken and Potato Tagine

Prep time: 20 minutes | Cook time: 55 minutes | Serves 6

1 chicken, cut up into 8 pieces
1 medium onion, thinly sliced
3 cloves garlic, minced
¼ cup olive oil
½ teaspoon ground cumin
½ teaspoon freshly ground pepper
¼ teaspoon ginger
Pinch saffron threads
1 teaspoon paprika
Sea salt, to taste
2 cups water
3 cups potatoes, peeled and diced
½ cup flat-leaf parsley, chopped
½ cup fresh cilantro, chopped
1 cup fresh or frozen green peas

1. Place the chicken, onion, garlic, olive oil, and seasonings into a Dutch oven. Add about 2 cups water and bring to a boil over medium-high heat. Reduce heat and cover. Simmer for 30 minutes. 2. Add the potatoes, parsley, and cilantro, and simmer an additional 20 minutes, or until the potatoes are almost tender. 3. Add the peas at the last moment, simmering for an additional 5 minutes. Serve hot.

Per Serving:
calories: 345 | fat: 14g | protein: 36g | carbs: 19g | fiber: 3g | sodium: 155mg

Smoky Chicken Leg Quarters

Prep time: 30 minutes | Cook time: 23 to 27 minutes | Serves 6

½ cup avocado oil
2 teaspoons smoked paprika
1 teaspoon sea salt
1 teaspoon garlic powder
½ teaspoon dried rosemary
½ teaspoon dried thyme
½ teaspoon freshly ground black pepper
2 pounds (907 g) bone-in, skin-on chicken leg quarters

1. In a blender or small bowl, combine the avocado oil, smoked paprika, salt, garlic powder, rosemary, thyme, and black pepper. 2. Place the chicken in a shallow dish or large zip-top bag. Pour the marinade over the chicken, making sure all the legs are coated. Cover and marinate for at least 2 hours or overnight. 3. Place the chicken in a single layer in the air fryer basket, working in batches if necessary. Set the air fryer to 400ºF (204ºC) and air fry for 15 minutes. Flip the chicken legs, then reduce the temperature to 350ºF (177ºC). Cook for 8 to 12 minutes more, until an instant-read thermometer reads 160ºF (71ºC) when inserted into the thickest piece of chicken. 4. Allow to rest for 5 to 10 minutes before serving.

Per Serving:
calories: 347 | fat: 25g | protein: 29g | carbs: 1g | fiber: 0g | sodium: 534mg

Moroccan Chicken with Apricots, Almonds, and Olives

Prep time: 10 minutes | Cook time: 2 hours | Serves 4

3 pounds (1.4 kg) skinless chicken thighs
1 yellow onion, cut into ½-inch wedges
1 teaspoon ground cumin
½ teaspoon ground ginger
½ teaspoon ground coriander
¼ teaspoon ground cinnamon
¼ teaspoon cayenne pepper
Sea salt
Black pepper
1 bay leaf
⅓ cup chicken stock
1 (15-ounce / 425-g) can chickpeas, drained and rinsed
½ cup green olives
½ cup dried turkish apricots
⅓ cup sliced almonds, toasted

1. In a large bowl, mix the chicken thighs and the onion. Add the cumin, coriander, ginger, cinnamon, and cayenne and toss to coat. Season the spiced chicken and onion with salt and pepper. 2. Transfer the chicken and onion to the slow cooker. Add the bay leaf and chicken stock to the slow cooker. 3. Cover and cook on high for 2 hours. 4. Stir in the chickpeas, olives, and apricots. Cover and cook until the chicken is tender and cooked through and the apricots are plump, about 1 hour more. 5. Remove the bay leaf and season the juices with salt and pepper. 6. Meanwhile, preheat the oven to 350°F(180°C). Spread the almonds in a pie plate and toast for about 7 minutes, until fragrant and lightly golden. Watch them so they don't burn. 7. Spoon the hot chicken, vegetables, and juices into shallow bowls, sprinkle with the toasted almonds, and serve.

Per Serving:
calories: 625 | fat: 22g | protein: 75g | carbs: 31g | fiber: 8g | sodium: 597mg

Baked Chicken Caprese

**Prep time: 5minutes |Cook time: 25 minutes|
Serves: 4**

Nonstick cooking spray	1 cup shredded mozzarella or 4
1 pound (454 g) boneless,	ounces (113 g) fresh mozzarella
skinless chicken breasts	cheese, diced
2 tablespoons extra-virgin olive	1 (14½-ounce / 411-g) can low-
oil	sodium or no-salt-added crushed
¼ teaspoon freshly ground black	tomatoes
pepper	2 tablespoons fresh torn basil
¼ teaspoon kosher or sea salt	leaves
1 large tomato, sliced thinly	4 teaspoons balsamic vinegar

1. Set one oven rack about 4 inches below the broiler element. Preheat the oven to 450°F(235°C). Line a large, rimmed baking sheet with aluminum foil. Place a wire cooling rack on the aluminum foil, and spray the rack with nonstick cooking spray. Set aside. 2. Cut the chicken into 4 pieces (if they aren't already). Put the chicken breasts in a large zip-top plastic bag. With a rolling pin or meat mallet, pound the chicken so it is evenly flattened, about ¼-inch thick. Add the oil, pepper, and salt to the bag. Reseal the bag, and massage the ingredients into the chicken. Take the chicken out of the bag and place it on the prepared wire rack. 3. Cook the chicken for 15 to 18 minutes, or until the internal temperature of the chicken is 165°F(74°C) on a meat thermometer and the juices run clear. Turn the oven to the high broiler setting. Layer the tomato slices on each chicken breast, and top with the mozzarella. Broil the chicken for another 2 to 3 minutes, or until the cheese is melted (don't let the chicken burn on the edges). Remove the chicken from the oven. 4. While the chicken is cooking, pour the crushed tomatoes into a small, microwave-safe bowl. Cover the bowl with a paper towel, and microwave for about 1 minute on high, until hot. When you're ready to serve, divide the tomatoes among four dinner plates. Place each chicken breast on top of the tomatoes. Top with the basil and a drizzle of balsamic vinegar.

Per Serving:
calories: 304 | fat: 15g | protein: 34g | carbs: 7g | fiber: 3g | sodium: 215mg

Sautéed Chicken with Tomatoes over Haricots Verts

**Prep time: 5 minutes | Cook time: 25 minutes |
Serves 4**

2 tablespoons olive oil	1 medium onion, diced, or 1 cup
8 thin-cut boneless, skinless	frozen diced onions
chicken breasts	1 small handful of mixed fresh
3 cups haricots verts (very thin	parsley, oregano, and basil,
whole green beans)	minced, or 2 teaspoons Italian
2 cups cherry or grape tomatoes,	seasoning
halved	½ cup low-sodium chicken
1 or 2 garlic cloves, minced or	broth or white wine
pressed (½ teaspoon; optional)	

1. Preheat the oven (or a toaster oven) to 250°F (121°C). 2. In a large nonstick skillet, heat the olive oil over medium-high heat in a nonstick skillet. Working in batches as needed (you may only be able to do 2 to 4 breasts at a time, depending on the size of your skillet), add the chicken and cook for 1 minute, then reduce the heat to medium and cook for 2 to 3 minutes more. Turn the breast and cook for 2 minutes more, until browned on both sides but not cooked through (the chicken will finish cooking in the sauce). Remove and place on baking sheet in oven or transfer the chicken to a platter and cover to keep warm. Repeat until you have cooked all the chicken. 3. Immediately start cooking the green beans in a microwave or in a steamer basket over a pot of boiling water for about 5 minutes, or until crisp-tender. 4. In the same skillet, sauté the tomatoes, garlic (if using), and frozen diced onions (no need to thaw them first) over medium-low heat. Add the herbs and the broth and cook until the liquid has reduced and thickened slightly. Return all the chicken to the skillet and spoon the sauce over the chicken. 5. Divide the haricots verts among four plates. Place two chicken breasts on top of the beans on each plate, top with the sauce, and serve.

Per Serving:
1 cup: calories: 232 | fat: 10g | protein: 25g | carbs: 11g | fiber: 4g | sodium: 168mg

Lemon Chicken with Artichokes and Crispy Kale

**Prep time: 15 minutes | Cook time: 35 minutes
| Serves 4**

3 tablespoons extra-virgin olive	pepper
oil, divided	1½ pounds (680 g) boneless,
2 tablespoons lemon juice	skinless chicken breast
Zest of 1 lemon	2 (14-ounce / 397-g) cans
2 garlic cloves, minced	artichoke hearts, drained
2 teaspoons dried rosemary	1 bunch (about 6 ounces / 170
½ teaspoon kosher salt	g) lacinato kale, stemmed and
¼ teaspoon freshly ground black	torn or chopped into pieces

1. In a large bowl or zip-top bag, combine 2 tablespoons of the olive oil, the lemon juice, lemon zest, garlic, rosemary, salt, and black pepper. Mix well and then add the chicken and artichokes. Marinate for at least 30 minutes, and up to 4 hours in the refrigerator. 2. Preheat the oven to 350°F (180°C). Line a baking sheet with parchment paper or foil. Remove the chicken and artichokes from the marinade and spread them in a single layer on the baking sheet. Roast for 15 minutes, turn the chicken over, and roast another 15 minutes. Remove the baking sheet and put the chicken, artichokes, and juices on a platter or large plate. Tent with foil to keep warm. 3. Change the oven temperature to broil. In a large bowl, combine the kale with the remaining 1 tablespoon of the olive oil. Arrange the kale on the baking sheet and broil until golden brown in spots and as crispy as you like, about 3 to 5 minutes. Place the kale on top of the chicken and artichokes.

Per Serving:
calories: 430 | fat: 16g | protein: 46g | carbs: 29g | fiber: 19g | sodium: 350mg

Chicken Cutlets with Greek Salsa

Prep time: 15 minutes | Cook time: 15 minutes | Serves 2

2 tablespoons olive oil, divided
¼ teaspoon salt, plus additional to taste
Zest of ½ lemon
Juice of ½ lemon
8 ounces (227 g) chicken cutlets, or chicken breast sliced through the middle to make 2 thin pieces
1 cup cherry or grape tomatoes, halved or quartered (about 4 ounces / 113 g)
½ cup minced red onion (about ⅓ medium onion)
1 medium cucumber, peeled, seeded and diced (about 1 cup)
5 to 10 pitted Greek olives, minced (more or less depending on size and your taste)
1 tablespoon minced fresh parsley
1 tablespoon minced fresh oregano
1 tablespoon minced fresh mint
1 ounce (28 g) crumbled feta cheese
1 tablespoon red wine vinegar

1. In a medium bowl, combine 1 tablespoon of olive oil, the salt, lemon zest, and lemon juice. Add the chicken and let it marinate while you make the salsa. 2. In a small bowl, combine the tomatoes, onion, cucumber, olives, parsley, oregano, mint, feta cheese, and red wine vinegar, and toss lightly. Cover and let rest in the refrigerator for at least 30 minutes. Taste the salsa before serving and add a pinch of salt or extra herbs if desired. 3. To cook the chicken, heat the remaining 1 tablespoon of olive oil in a large nonstick skillet over medium-high heat. Add the chicken pieces and cook for 3 to 6 minutes on each side, depending on the thickness. If the chicken sticks to the pan, it's not quite ready to flip. 4. When chicken is cooked through, top with the salsa and serve.

Per Serving:

calories: 357 | fat: 23g | protein: 31g | carbs: 8g | fiber: 2g | sodium: 202mg

Coconut Chicken Meatballs

Prep time: 10 minutes | Cook time: 14 minutes | Serves 4

1 pound (454 g) ground chicken
2 scallions, finely chopped
1 cup chopped fresh cilantro leaves
¼ cup unsweetened shredded coconut
1 tablespoon hoisin sauce
1 tablespoon soy sauce
2 teaspoons Sriracha or other hot sauce
1 teaspoon toasted sesame oil
½ teaspoon kosher salt
1 teaspoon black pepper

1. In a large bowl, gently mix the chicken, scallions, cilantro, coconut, hoisin, soy sauce, Sriracha, sesame oil, salt, and pepper until thoroughly combined (the mixture will be wet and sticky). 2. Place a sheet of parchment paper in the air fryer basket. Using a small scoop or teaspoon, drop rounds of the mixture in a single layer onto the parchment paper. 3. Set the air fryer to 350°F (177°C) for 10 minutes, turning the meatballs halfway through the cooking time. Raise the air fryer temperature to 400°F (204°C) and cook for 4 minutes more to brown the outsides of the meatballs. Use a meat thermometer to ensure the meatballs have reached an internal temperature of 165°F (74°C). 4. Transfer the meatballs to a serving platter. Repeat with any remaining chicken mixture.

Per Serving:

calories: 213 | fat: 13g | protein: 21g | carbs: 4g | fiber: 1g | sodium: 501mg

Garlic Chicken (Shish Tawook)

Prep time: 15 minutes | Cook time: 15 minutes | Serves 4 to 6

2 tablespoons garlic, minced
2 tablespoons tomato paste
1 teaspoon smoked paprika
½ cup lemon juice
½ cup extra-virgin olive oil
1½ teaspoons salt
½ teaspoon freshly ground black
pepper
2 pounds (907 g) boneless and skinless chicken (breasts or thighs)
Rice, tzatziki, or hummus, for serving (optional)

1. In a large bowl, add the garlic, tomato paste, paprika, lemon juice, olive oil, salt, and pepper and whisk to combine. 2. Cut the chicken into ½-inch cubes and put them into the bowl; toss to coat with the marinade. Set aside for at least 10 minutes. 3. To grill, preheat the grill on high. Thread the chicken onto skewers and cook for 3 minutes per side, for a total of 9 minutes. 4. To cook in a pan, preheat the pan on high heat, add the chicken, and cook for 9 minutes, turning over the chicken using tongs. 5. Serve the chicken with rice, tzatziki, or hummus, if desired.

Per Serving:

calories: 350 | fat: 22g | protein: 34g | carbs: 3g | fiber: 0g | sodium: 586mg

Grilled Chicken and Vegetables with Lemon-Walnut Sauce

Prep time: 20 minutes | Cook time: 16 minutes | Serves 4

1 cup chopped walnuts, toasted
1 small shallot, very finely chopped
½ cup olive oil, plus more for brushing
Juice and zest of 1 lemon
4 boneless, skinless chicken breasts
Sea salt and freshly ground pepper, to taste
2 zucchini, sliced diagonally ¼-inch thick
½ pound (227 g) asparagus
1 red onion, sliced ⅓-inch thick
1 teaspoon Italian seasoning

1. Preheat a grill to medium-high. 2. Put the walnuts, shallots, olive oil, lemon juice, and zest in a food processor and process until smooth and creamy. 3. Season the chicken with sea salt and freshly ground pepper, and grill on an oiled grate until cooked through, about 7–8 minutes a side or until an instant-read thermometer reaches 180°F (82°C) in the thickest part. 4. When the chicken is halfway done, put the vegetables on the grill. Sprinkle Italian seasoning over the chicken and vegetables to taste. 5. To serve, lay the grilled veggies on a plate, place the chicken breast on the grilled vegetables, and spoon the lemon-walnut sauce over the chicken and vegetables.

Per Serving:

calories: 800 | fat: 54g | protein: 68g | carbs: 13g | fiber: 5g | sodium: 134mg

Chicken Cacciatore with Wild Mushrooms and Fresh Fennel

Prep time: 10 minutes | Cook time: 1 hour and 10 minutes | Serves 6 to 8

½ ounce (14 g) dried porcini mushrooms	3 cloves garlic, minced
1 cup boiling water	1 tablespoon minced fresh rosemary
2 tablespoons olive oil	2 teaspoons freshly grated orange zest
12 boneless, skinless chicken thighs (about 3 pounds / 1.4 kg), trimmed of fat	1 teaspoon fresh thyme leaves
	3 tablespoons red wine vinegar
1 large green bell pepper, seeded and cut into rings	¾ cup dry white wine
1 large onion, halved and thinly sliced	2 tablespoons tomato paste
1 large fennel bulb, trimmed, halved, cored and thinly sliced	1 teaspoon salt

1. Preheat the oven to 350°F (180°C) . 2. Soak the porcinis in the boiling water for about 20 minutes. 3. While the mushrooms are soaking, heat the olive oil in a large skillet over medium-high heat. Brown the chicken pieces on all sides, working in batches if needed. Transfer the chicken to a 9-by-13-inch baking dish as the pieces are browned. 4. Reduce the heat under the skillet to medium. Add the pepper, onion, and fennel and cook, stirring frequently, until softened, about 5 minutes. Stir in the garlic, rosemary, orange zest, and thyme and cook, stirring, for another 30 seconds. Add the vinegar and cook, stirring, 1 minute longer. Remove from the heat. 5. Remove the mushrooms from the water, reserving the soaking water, and chop them coarsely. Add the chopped mushrooms and the soaking water to the pan along with the wine, tomato paste, and salt. 6. Bring to a simmer over medium heat, then add the hot mixture to the baking dish, pouring it over the chicken legs. Cover with aluminum foil and bake in the preheated oven for 45 minutes. Remove from the oven and let it rest for 5 to 10 minutes before serving. Serve hot.

Per Serving:

calories: 468 | fat: 19g | protein: 58g | carbs: 9g | fiber: 3g | sodium: 527mg

Chicken Piccata with Mushrooms

Prep time: 25 minutes | Cook time: 25 minutes | Serves 4

1 pound (454 g) thinly sliced chicken breasts	2 cups sliced mushrooms
1½ teaspoons salt, divided	½ cup dry white wine or chicken stock
½ teaspoon freshly ground black pepper	¼ cup freshly squeezed lemon juice
¼ cup ground flaxseed	¼ cup roughly chopped capers
2 tablespoons almond flour	Zucchini noodles, for serving
8 tablespoons extra-virgin olive oil, divided	¼ cup chopped fresh flat-leaf Italian parsley, for garnish
4 tablespoons butter, divided	

1. Season the chicken with 1 teaspoon salt and the pepper. On a plate, combine the ground flaxseed and almond flour and dredge each chicken breast in the mixture. Set aside. 2. In a large skillet, heat 4 tablespoons olive oil and 1 tablespoon butter over medium-high heat. Working in batches if necessary, brown the chicken, 3 to 4 minutes per side. Remove from the skillet and keep warm. 3. Add the remaining 4 tablespoons olive oil and 1 tablespoon butter to the skillet along with mushrooms and sauté over medium heat until just tender, 6 to 8 minutes. 4. Add the white wine, lemon juice, capers, and remaining ½ teaspoon salt to the skillet and bring to a boil, whisking to incorporate any little browned bits that have stuck to the bottom of the skillet. Reduce the heat to low and whisk in the final 2 tablespoons butter. 5. Return the browned chicken to skillet, cover, and simmer over low heat until the chicken is cooked through and the sauce has thickened, 5 to 6 more minutes. 6. Serve chicken and mushrooms warm over zucchini noodles, spooning the mushroom sauce over top and garnishing with chopped parsley.

Per Serving:

calories: 596 | fat: 48g | protein: 30g | carbs: 8g | fiber: 4g | sodium: 862mg

Chapter 6
Fish and Seafood

Saffron Rice with Whitefish

Prep time: 10 minutes | Cook time: 35 minutes | Serves 4

4 tablespoons extra-virgin olive oil, divided	4½ cups water
1 large onion, chopped	1 teaspoon saffron threads
3 cod fillets, rinsed and patted dry	1½ teaspoons salt
	1 teaspoon turmeric
	2 cups long-grain rice, rinsed

1. In a large pot over medium heat, cook 2 tablespoons of olive oil and the onions for 5 minutes. 2. While the onions are cooking, preheat another large pan over high heat. Add the remaining 2 tablespoons of olive oil and the cod fillets. Cook the cod for 2 minutes on each side, then remove from the pan and set aside. 3. Once the onions are done cooking, add the water, saffron, salt, turmeric, and rice, stirring to combine. Cover and cook for 12 minutes. 4. Cut the cod up into 1-inch pieces. Place the cod pieces in the rice, lightly toss, cover, and cook for another 10 minutes. 5. Once the rice is done cooking, fluff with a fork, cover, and let stand for 5 minutes. Serve warm.

Per Serving:

calories: 564 | fat: 15g | protein: 26g | carbs: 78g | fiber: 2g | sodium: 945mg

Monkfish with Sautéed Leeks, Fennel, and Tomatoes

Prep time: 20 minutes | Cook time: 35 minutes | Serves 4

1 to 1½ pounds (454 to 680 g) monkfish	½ onion, julienned
3 tablespoons lemon juice, divided	3 garlic cloves, minced
1 teaspoon kosher salt, divided	2 bulbs fennel, cored and thinly sliced, plus ¼ cup fronds for garnish
⅛ teaspoon freshly ground black pepper	1 (14½-ounce / 411-g) can no-salt-added diced tomatoes
2 tablespoons extra-virgin olive oil	2 tablespoons fresh parsley, chopped
1 leek, white and light green parts only, sliced in half lengthwise and thinly sliced	2 tablespoons fresh oregano, chopped
	¼ teaspoon red pepper flakes

1. Place the fish in a medium baking dish and add 2 tablespoons of the lemon juice, ¼ teaspoon of the salt, and the black pepper. Place in the refrigerator. 2. Heat the olive oil in a large skillet or sauté pan over medium heat. Add the leek and onion and sauté until translucent, about 3 minutes. Add the garlic and sauté for 30 seconds. Add the fennel and sauté 4 to 5 minutes. Add the tomatoes and simmer for 2 to 3 minutes. 3. Stir in the parsley, oregano, red pepper flakes, the remaining ¾ teaspoon salt, and the remaining 1 tablespoon lemon juice. Place the fish on top of the leek mixture, cover, and simmer for 20 to 25 minutes, turning over halfway through, until the fish is opaque and pulls apart easily. Garnish with the fennel fronds.

Per Serving:

calories: 220 | fat: 9g | protein: 22g | carbs: 11g | fiber: 3g | sodium: 345mg

Weeknight Sheet Pan Fish Dinner

Prep time: 10 minutes |Cook time: 10 minutes| Serves: 4

Nonstick cooking spray	thick)
2 tablespoons extra-virgin olive oil	2½ cups green beans (about 12 ounces)
1 tablespoon balsamic vinegar	1 pint cherry or grape tomatoes (about 2 cups)
4 (4-ounce / 113-g) fish fillets, such as cod or tilapia (½ inch	

1. Preheat the oven to 400°F (205°C). Coat two large, rimmed baking sheets with nonstick cooking spray. 2. In a small bowl, whisk together the oil and vinegar. Set aside. 3. Place two pieces of fish on each baking sheet. 4. In a large bowl, combine the beans and tomatoes. Pour in the oil and vinegar, and toss gently to coat. Pour half of the green bean mixture over the fish on one baking sheet, and the remaining half over the fish on the other. Turn the fish over, and rub it in the oil mixture to coat. Spread the vegetables evenly on the baking sheets so hot air can circulate around them. 5. Bake for 5 to 8 minutes, until the fish is just opaque and not translucent. The fish is done and ready to serve when it just begins to separate into flakes (chunks) when pressed gently with a fork.

Per Serving:

calories: 190 | fat: 8g | protein: 22g | carbs: 8g | fiber: 3g | sodium: 70mg

Bouillabaisse

Prep time: 30 minutes | Cook time: 50 minutes | Serves 8

½ cup olive oil	1 teaspoon dried thyme
2 onions, diced	½ teaspoon saffron
4 tomatoes, peeled and chopped	10 clams, scrubbed
5 cloves garlic, minced	10 mussels, scrubbed
3 pints low-salt fish stock	1 pound (454 g) shrimp, peeled, deveined, and tails removed
8 small red potatoes, cubed and cooked	1 pound (454 g) fresh monkfish fillets, cut into chunks
1 cup white wine	1 pound (454 g) fresh cod, cut into chunks
1 bunch basil leaves, finely chopped	½ cup flat-leaf parsley, chopped
1 tablespoon Tabasco or other hot sauce	

1. Heat the olive oil in a large stockpot over medium-high heat. 2. Add the onions and cook for 5 minutes, or until the onions are soft and translucent. 3. Add the tomatoes and garlic, and simmer 5 minutes more. 4. Add the fish stock, potatoes, wine, basil, hot sauce, thyme, and saffron, and simmer for 20 minutes. 5. Purée half of this mixture in the blender, then return to stockpot. 6. Add the shellfish, shrimp, fish, and parsley, and simmer 20 minutes. Serve with brown rice.

Per Serving:

calories: 458 | fat: 16g | protein: 39g | carbs: 35g | fiber: 4g | sodium: 344mg

Salmon with Garlicky Broccoli Rabe and White Beans

Prep time: 20 minutes | Cook time: 10 minutes | Serves 4

2 tablespoons extra-virgin olive oil, plus extra for drizzling	salmon fillets, 1½ inches thick
4 garlic cloves, sliced thin	½ teaspoon table salt
½ cup chicken or vegetable broth	¼ teaspoon pepper
¼ teaspoon red pepper flakes	1 pound (454 g) broccoli rabe, trimmed and cut into 1-inch pieces
1 lemon, sliced ¼ inch thick, plus lemon wedges for serving	1 (15-ounce / 425-g) can cannellini beans, rinsed
4 (6-ounce / 170-g) skinless	

1. Using highest sauté function, cook oil and garlic in Instant Pot until garlic is fragrant and light golden brown, about 3 minutes. Using slotted spoon, transfer garlic to paper towel–lined plate and season with salt to taste; set aside for serving. Turn off Instant Pot, then stir in broth and pepper flakes. 2. Fold sheet of aluminum foil into 16 by 6-inch sling. Arrange lemon slices widthwise in 2 rows across center of sling. Sprinkle flesh side of salmon with salt and pepper, then arrange skinned side down on top of lemon slices. Using sling, lower salmon into Instant Pot; allow narrow edges of sling to rest along sides of insert. Lock lid in place and close pressure release valve. Select high pressure cook function and cook for 3 minutes. 3. Turn off Instant Pot and quick-release pressure. Carefully remove lid, allowing steam to escape away from you. Using sling, transfer salmon to large plate. Tent with foil and let rest while preparing broccoli rabe mixture. 4. Stir broccoli rabe and beans into cooking liquid, partially cover, and cook, using highest sauté function, until broccoli rabe is tender, about 5 minutes. Season with salt and pepper to taste. Gently lift and tilt salmon fillets with spatula to remove lemon slices. Serve salmon with broccoli rabe mixture and lemon wedges, sprinkling individual portions with garlic chips and drizzling with extra oil.

Per Serving:

calories: 510 | fat: 30g | protein: 43g | carbs: 15g | fiber: 6g | sodium: 650mg

Greek Stuffed Squid

Prep time: 15 minutes | Cook time: 30 minutes | Serves 4

8 ounces (227 g) frozen spinach, thawed and drained (about 1½ cup)	¼ cup chopped sun-dried tomatoes
4 ounces (113 g) crumbled goat cheese	¼ cup chopped fresh flat-leaf Italian parsley
½ cup chopped pitted olives (I like Kalamata in this recipe)	2 garlic cloves, finely minced
½ cup extra-virgin olive oil, divided	¼ teaspoon freshly ground black pepper
	2 pounds (907 g) baby squid, cleaned and tentacles removed

1. Preheat the oven to 350°F(180°C). 2. In a medium bowl, combine the spinach, goat cheese, olives, ¼ cup olive oil, sun-dried tomatoes, parsley, garlic, and pepper. 3. Pour 2 tablespoons olive oil in the bottom of an 8-inch square baking dish and spread to coat the bottom. 4. Stuff each cleaned squid with 2 to 3 tablespoons of the cheese mixture, depending on the size of squid, and place in the prepared baking dish. 5. Drizzle the tops with the remaining 2 tablespoons olive oil and bake until the squid are cooked through, 25 to 30 minutes. Remove from the oven and allow to cool 5 to 10 minutes before serving.

Per Serving:

calories: 595 | fat: 41g | protein: 44g | carbs: 13g | fiber: 2g | sodium: 397mg

Honey-Balsamic Salmon

Prep time: 5 minutes | Cook time: 8 minutes | Serves 2

Oil, for spraying	2 teaspoons red pepper flakes
2 (6-ounce / 170-g) salmon fillets	2 teaspoons olive oil
¼ cup balsamic vinegar	½ teaspoon salt
2 tablespoons honey	¼ teaspoon freshly ground black pepper

1. Line the air fryer basket with parchment and spray lightly with oil. 2. Place the salmon in the prepared basket. 3. In a small bowl, whisk together the balsamic vinegar, honey, red pepper flakes, olive oil, salt, and black pepper. Brush the mixture over the salmon. 4. Roast at 390°F (199°C) for 7 to 8 minutes, or until the internal temperature reaches 145°F (63°C). Serve immediately.

Per Serving:

calories: 353 | fat: 12g | protein: 35g | carbs: 24g | fiber: 1g | sodium: 590mg

Italian Tuna Roast

Prep time: 15 minutes | Cook time: 21 to 24 minutes | Serves 8

Cooking spray	1 teaspoon lemon juice
1 tablespoon Italian seasoning	1 tuna loin (approximately 2 pounds / 907 g, 3 to 4 inches thick)
⅛ teaspoon ground black pepper	
1 tablespoon extra-light olive oil	

1. Spray baking dish with cooking spray and place in air fryer basket. Preheat the air fryer to 390°F (199°C). 2. Mix together the Italian seasoning, pepper, oil, and lemon juice. 3. Using a dull table knife or butter knife, pierce top of tuna about every half inch: Insert knife into top of tuna roast and pierce almost all the way to the bottom. 4. Spoon oil mixture into each of the holes and use the knife to push seasonings into the tuna as deeply as possible. 5. Spread any remaining oil mixture on all outer surfaces of tuna. 6. Place tuna roast in baking dish and roast at 390°F (199°C) for 20 minutes. Check temperature with a meat thermometer. Cook for an additional 1 to 4 minutes or until temperature reaches 145°F (63°C). 7. Remove basket from the air fryer and let tuna sit in the basket for 10 minutes.

Per Serving:

calories: 178 | fat: 7g | protein: 26g | carbs: 0g | fiber: 0g | sodium: 44mg

Ouzo Mussels

Prep time: 10 minutes | Cook time: 15 minutes | Serves 4

1 tablespoon olive oil	or water
2 shallots, chopped	½ cup ouzo
4 cloves garlic, sliced	Grated peel of 1 lemon
1 pound (454 g) mussels, scrubbed and debearded	2 tablespoons chopped fresh flat-leaf parsley
1 cup low-sodium chicken broth	

1. In a large pot over medium heat, warm the oil. Cook the shallots and garlic until softened, 5 minutes. Increase the heat and add the mussels, broth or water, and ouzo. Cover, bring to a boil, and cook until the mussels have opened, about 8 minutes. 2. Discard any unopened mussels. Sprinkle the lemon peel and parsley over the top. Serve the mussels with their broth.

Per Serving:

calories: 238 | fat: 6g | protein: 16g | carbs: 22g | fiber: 0g | sodium: 344mg

Shrimp and Feta Saganaki

Prep time: 10 minutes | Cook time: 35 minutes | Serves 2

1¼ pounds (567 g) raw medium shrimp (about 20), peeled and deveined	1 small hot chili, sliced
	1 teaspoon red pepper flakes
	14 ounces (397 g) canned crushed tomatoes or whole tomatoes chopped in a food processor
¼ teaspoon fine sea salt	
¼ teaspoon freshly ground black pepper	
4 tablespoons extra virgin olive oil, divided	1 teaspoon dried oregano, divided
5 garlic cloves, minced	3 ounces (85 g) crumbled feta, divided
¼ cup ouzo (anise-flavored liquor)	1 tablespoon chopped fresh basil
½ large onion (any variety), chopped	

1. Preheat the oven to 400°F (205°C). Pat the shrimp dry with paper towels, then season with the sea salt and black pepper. 2. Add 2 tablespoons of the olive oil to a large skillet over medium-high heat. When the oil begins to shimmer, add the shrimp and sauté for about 2 minutes and then add the garlic and sauté for 1 more minute or until the shrimp turn pink. 3. Add the ouzo and sauté for 2 minutes or until the alcohol has evaporated. Remove the pan from the heat and set aside. 4. Add the remaining 2 tablespoons of olive oil to a medium pot or saucepan placed over medium heat. When the olive oil begins to shimmer, add the onions and sauté for 5 minutes or until translucent. Add the sliced chili and red pepper flakes and sauté for 2 more minutes. Add the tomatoes, cover, and simmer for 7 minutes or until the sauce thickens. 5. Pour the tomato sauce into an oven-proof casserole dish or cast-iron skillet large enough to hold the shrimp in a single layer. Sprinkle ½ teaspoon of the oregano and half of the feta over the sauce, then place the shrimp on top of the sauce, lightly pressing each shrimp into the sauce. Sprinkle the remaining feta and oregano over the shrimp. 6. Transfer to the oven and bake for 15 minutes, then top with the chopped basil. Store covered in the refrigerator for up to 2 days.

Per Serving:

calories: 652 | fat: 38g | protein: 66g | carbs: 15g | fiber: 5g | sodium: 704mg

Pistachio-Crusted Halibut

Prep time: 5 minutes | Cook time: 7 minutes | Serves 2

1 tablespoon Dijon mustard	pistachios
1 teaspoon lemon juice	¼ teaspoon salt
2 tablespoons panko bread crumbs	2 (5-ounce / 142-g) halibut fillets
¼ cup chopped unsalted	1 cup water

1. Preheat broiler. Line a baking sheet with parchment paper. 2. In a small bowl, combine mustard, lemon juice, bread crumbs, pistachios, and salt to form a thick paste. 3. Pat fillets dry with a paper towel. Rub paste on the top of each fillet and place in the steamer basket. 4. Pour water in the Instant Pot® and insert rack. Place steamer basket on rack. Close lid, set steam release to Sealing, press the Manual button, and set time to 5 minutes. When the timer beeps, quick-release the pressure until the float valve drops and then open lid. Transfer fillets to prepared baking sheet. 5. Broil for approximately 1–2 minutes until tops are browned. Remove from oven and serve hot.

Per Serving:

calories: 235 | fat: 9g | protein: 35g | carbs: 4g | fiber: 2g | sodium: 411mg

Lemon-Oregano Grilled Shrimp

Prep time: 10 minutes | Cook time: 6 minutes | Serves 6

½ cup oregano leaves	½ teaspoon freshly ground black pepper, plus more for seasoning shrimp
1 clove garlic, minced	
1 teaspoon finely grated lemon zest	
3 tablespoons lemon juice	½ cup olive oil, plus 2 tablespoons, divided
¾ teaspoon salt, plus more for seasoning shrimp	2½ pounds (1.1 kg) large shrimp, peeled and deveined

1. In a small bowl, stir together the oregano, garlic, lemon zest, lemon juice, salt, and pepper. Whisk in ½ cup of olive oil until well combined. 2. Preheat the grill to high heat. 3. Place the shrimp in a large bowl and toss with the remaining 2 tablespoons of olive oil and a pinch or two of salt and pepper. Thread the shrimp onto skewers, 3 to 5 at a time depending on the size of the shrimp. Place the skewers on the grill and cook for 2 to 3 minutes per side, just until the shrimp are cooked through and just beginning to char. As the shrimp are cooked, transfer the skewers to a serving platter. Spoon the sauce over the skewers and serve immediately.

Per Serving:

calories: 389 | fat: 26g | protein: 36g | carbs: 8g | fiber: 3g | sodium: 530mg

Spicy Trout over Sautéed Mediterranean Salad

Prep time: 10 minutes | Cook time: 30 minutes | Serves 4

2 pounds (907 g) rainbow trout fillets (about 6 fillets)	1 garlic clove, finely minced
Salt	1 large carrot, thinly sliced
Ground white pepper	2 Roma tomatoes, chopped
1 tablespoon extra-virgin olive oil	8 pitted kalamata olives, chopped
1 pound (454 g) asparagus	¼ cup ground cumin
4 medium golden potatoes, thinly sliced	2 tablespoons dried parsley
	2 tablespoons paprika
1 scallion, thinly sliced, green and white parts separated	1 tablespoon vegetable bouillon seasoning
	½ cup dry white wine

1. Lightly season the fish with salt and white pepper and set aside. 2. In a large sauté pan or skillet, heat the oil over medium heat. Add and stir in the asparagus, potatoes, the white part of the scallions, and garlic to the hot oil. Cook and stir for 5 minutes, until fragrant. Add the carrot, tomatoes, and olives; continue to cook for 5 to 7 minutes, until the carrots are slightly tender. 3. Sprinkle the cumin, parsley, paprika, and vegetable bouillon seasoning over the pan. Season with salt. Stir to incorporate. Put the trout on top of the vegetables and add the wine to cover the vegetables. 4. Reduce the heat to low, cover, and cook for 5 to 7 minutes, until the fish flakes easily with a fork and juices run clear. Top with scallion greens and serve.

Per Serving:

calories: 493 | fat: 19g | protein: 40g | carbs: 41g | fiber: 7g | sodium: 736mg

Nut-Crusted Baked Fish

Prep time: 10 minutes | Cook time: 20 minutes | Serves 4

½ cup extra-virgin olive oil, divided	Zest and juice of 1 lemon, divided
1 pound (454 g) flaky white fish (such as cod, haddock, or halibut), skin removed	1 teaspoon ground cumin
	1 teaspoon ground allspice
½ cup shelled finely chopped pistachios	½ teaspoon salt (use 1 teaspoon if pistachios are unsalted)
½ cup ground flaxseed	¼ teaspoon freshly ground black pepper

1. Preheat the oven to 400°F(205ºC). 2. Line a baking sheet with parchment paper or aluminum foil and drizzle 2 tablespoons olive oil over the sheet, spreading to evenly coat the bottom. 3. Cut the fish into 4 equal pieces and place on the prepared baking sheet. 4. In a small bowl, combine the pistachios, flaxseed, lemon zest, cumin, allspice, salt, and pepper. Drizzle in ¼ cup olive oil and stir well. 5. Divide the nut mixture evenly atop the fish pieces. Drizzle the lemon juice and remaining 2 tablespoons oil over the fish and bake until cooked through, 15 to 20 minutes, depending on the thickness of the fish.

Per Serving:

calories: 499 | fat: 41g | protein: 26g | carbs: 41g | fiber: 6g | sodium: 358mg

Lemon Pesto Salmon

Prep time: 5 minutes | Cook time: 10 minutes | Serves 2

10 ounces (283 g) salmon fillet (1 large piece or 2 smaller ones)	2 tablespoons prepared pesto sauce
Salt	1 large fresh lemon, sliced
Freshly ground black pepper	

1. Oil the grill grate and heat the grill to medium-high heat. Alternatively, you can roast the salmon in a 350°F (180ºC) oven. 2. Prepare the salmon by seasoning with salt and freshly ground black pepper, and then spread the pesto sauce on top. 3. Make a bed of fresh lemon slices about the same size as your fillet on the hot grill (or on a baking sheet if roasting), and rest the salmon on top of the lemon slices. Place any additional lemon slices on top of the salmon. 4. Grill the salmon for 6 to 10 minutes, or until it's opaque and flakes apart easily. If roasting, it will take about 20 minutes. There is no need to flip the fish over.

Per Serving:

calories: 315 | fat: 21g | protein: 29g | carbs: 1g | fiber: 0g | sodium: 176mg

Trout in Parsley Sauce

Prep time: 10 minutes | Cook time: 3 minutes | Serves 4

4 (½-pound / 227-g) river trout, rinsed and patted dry	1 small shallot, peeled and minced
¾ teaspoon salt, divided	2 tablespoons olive oil mayonnaise
4 cups torn lettuce leaves, divided	½ teaspoon lemon juice
1 teaspoon white wine vinegar	¼ teaspoon sugar
½ cup water	2 tablespoons toasted sliced almonds
½ cup minced fresh flat-leaf parsley	

1. Season trout with ½ teaspoon salt inside and out. Put 3 cups lettuce leaves in the bottom of the Instant Pot®. Arrange trout over lettuce and top trout with remaining 1 cup lettuce. Stir vinegar into water and pour into pot. 2. Close lid, set steam release to Sealing, press the Manual button, and set time to 3 minutes. When the timer beeps, quick-release the pressure until the float valve drops and open lid. 3. Use a spatula to move fish to a serving plate. Peel and discard skin from fish. Remove and discard fish heads if desired. 4. In a small bowl, mix together parsley, shallot, mayonnaise, lemon juice, sugar, and remaining ¼ teaspoon salt. Evenly divide among the fish, spreading it over them. Sprinkle toasted almonds over the sauce. Serve immediately.

Per Serving:

calories: 159 | fat: 9g | protein: 15g | carbs: 4g | fiber: 1g | sodium: 860mg

Blackened Red Snapper

Prep time: 13 minutes | Cook time: 8 to 10 minutes | Serves 4

1½ teaspoons black pepper	4 (4 ounces / 113 g) red snapper
¼ teaspoon thyme	fillet portions, skin on
¼ teaspoon garlic powder	4 thin slices lemon
⅛ teaspoon cayenne pepper	Cooking spray
1 teaspoon olive oil	

1. Mix the spices and oil together to make a paste. Rub into both sides of the fish. 2. Spray the air fryer basket with nonstick cooking spray and lay snapper steaks in basket, skin-side down. 3. Place a lemon slice on each piece of fish. 4. Roast at 390°F (199°C) for 8 to 10 minutes. The fish will not flake when done, but it should be white through the center.

Per Serving:

calories: 128 | fat: 3g | protein: 23g | carbs: 1g | fiber: 1g | sodium: 73mg

Cod with Warm Tabbouleh Salad

Prep time: 10 minutes | Cook time: 6 minutes | Serves 4

1 cup medium-grind bulgur, rinsed	olive oil, divided, plus extra for drizzling
1 teaspoon table salt, divided	¼ teaspoon pepper
1 lemon, sliced ¼ inch thick, plus 2 tablespoons juice	1 small shallot, minced
4 (6-ounce / 170-g) skinless cod fillets, 1½ inches thick	10 ounces (283 g) cherry tomatoes, halved
3 tablespoons extra-virgin	1 cup chopped fresh parsley
	½ cup chopped fresh mint

1. Arrange trivet included with Instant Pot in base of insert and add ½ cup water. Fold sheet of aluminum foil into 16 by 6-inch sling, then rest 1½-quart round soufflé dish in center of sling. Combine 1 cup water, bulgur, and ½ teaspoon salt in dish. Using sling, lower soufflé dish into pot and onto trivet; allow narrow edges of sling to rest along sides of insert. 2. Lock lid in place and close pressure release valve. Select high pressure cook function and cook for 3 minutes. Turn off Instant Pot and quick-release pressure. Carefully remove lid, allowing steam to escape away from you. Using sling, transfer soufflé dish to wire rack; set aside to cool. Remove trivet; do not discard sling or water in pot. 3. Arrange lemon slices widthwise in 2 rows across center of sling. Brush cod with 1 tablespoon oil and sprinkle with remaining ½ teaspoon salt and pepper. Arrange cod skinned side down in even layer on top of lemon slices. Using sling, lower cod into Instant Pot; allow narrow edges of sling to rest along sides of insert. Lock lid in place and close pressure release valve. Select high pressure cook function and cook for 3 minutes. 4. Meanwhile, whisk remaining 2 tablespoons oil, lemon juice, and shallot together in large bowl. Add bulgur, tomatoes, parsley, and mint, and gently toss to combine. Season with salt and pepper to taste. 5. Turn off Instant Pot and quick-release pressure. Carefully remove lid, allowing steam to escape away from you. Using sling, transfer cod to large plate. Gently lift and tilt fillets with spatula

to remove lemon slices. Serve cod with salad, drizzling individual portions with extra oil.

Per Serving:

calories: 380 | fat: 12g | protein: 36g | carbs: 32g | fiber: 6g | sodium: 690mg

Shrimp Fra Diavolo

Prep time: 10 minutes | Cook time: 10 minutes | Serves 4

2 tablespoons extra-virgin olive oil	¼ teaspoon red pepper flakes
1 onion, diced small	1 (14½-ounce / 411-g) can no-salt-added diced tomatoes
1 fennel bulb, cored and diced small, plus ¼ cup fronds for garnish	1 pound (454 g) shrimp, peeled and deveined
1 bell pepper, diced small	Juice of 1 lemon
½ teaspoon dried oregano	Zest of 1 lemon
½ teaspoon dried thyme	2 tablespoons fresh parsley, chopped, for garnish
½ teaspoon kosher salt	

1. Heat the olive oil in a large skillet or sauté pan over medium heat. Add the onion, fennel, bell pepper, oregano, thyme, salt, and red pepper flakes and sauté until translucent, about 5 minutes. 2. Deglaze the pan with the juice from the canned tomatoes, scraping up any brown bits, and bring to a boil. Add the diced tomatoes and the shrimp. Lower heat to a simmer, cover, and cook until the shrimp are cooked through, about 3 minutes. 3. Turn off the heat. Add the lemon juice and lemon zest, and toss well to combine. Garnish with the parsley and the fennel fronds.

Per Serving:

calories: 240 | fat: 9g | protein: 25g | carbs: 13g | fiber: 3g | sodium:335 mg

Poached Salmon

Prep time: 10 minutes | Cook time: 5 minutes | Serves 4

1 lemon, sliced ¼ inch thick	½ teaspoon table salt
4 (6-ounce / 170-g) skinless salmon fillets, 1½ inches thick	¼ teaspoon pepper

1. Add ½ cup water to Instant Pot. Fold sheet of aluminum foil into 16 by 6-inch sling. Arrange lemon slices widthwise in 2 rows across center of sling. Sprinkle flesh side of salmon with salt and pepper, then arrange skinned side down on top of lemon slices. 2. Using sling, lower salmon into Instant Pot; allow narrow edges of sling to rest along sides of insert. Lock lid in place and close pressure release valve. Select high pressure cook function and cook for 3 minutes. 3. Turn off Instant Pot and quick-release pressure. Carefully remove lid, allowing steam to escape away from you. Using sling, transfer salmon to large plate. Gently lift and tilt fillets with spatula to remove lemon slices. Serve.

Per Serving:

calories: 350 | fat: 23g | protein: 35g | carbs: 0g | fiber: 0g | sodium: 390mg

Sage-Stuffed Whole Trout with Roasted Vegetables

Prep time: 10 minutes | Cook time: 35 minutes | Serves 4

2 red bell peppers, seeded and cut into 1-inch-wide strips	3 tablespoons olive oil, divided
1 (15-ounce / 425-g) can artichoke hearts, drained and cut into quarters	1½ teaspoons salt, divided
	¾ teaspoon freshly ground black pepper, divided
1 large red onion, halved through the stem and cut into 1-inch-wide wedges	2 whole rainbow trout, cleaned with head on
	3 cups sage leaves
4 cloves garlic, halved	Juice of ½ lemon

1. Preheat the oven to 475ºF (245ºC). 2. In a large baking dish, toss the bell peppers, artichoke hearts, onion, and garlic with 2 tablespoons of the olive oil. Sprinkle with 1 teaspoon of salt and ½ teaspoon of pepper. Roast the vegetables in the preheated oven for 20 minutes. Reduce the heat to 375ºF(190ºC). 3. While the vegetables are roasting, prepare the fish. Brush the fish inside and out with the remaining 1 tablespoon of olive oil and season with the remaining ½ teaspoon of salt and ¼ teaspoon of pepper. Stuff each fish with half of the sage leaves. 4. Remove the vegetables from the oven and place the fish on top. Put back in the oven and bake at 375ºF (190ºC) for about 15 minutes more, until the fish is cooked through. Remove from the oven, squeeze the lemon juice over the fish, and let rest for 5 minutes. 5. To serve, halve the fish. Spoon roasted vegetables onto 4 serving plates and serve half a fish alongside each, topped with some of the sage leaves.

Per Serving:

calories: 349 | fat: 16g | protein: 24g | carbs: 34g | fiber: 17g | sodium: 879mg

Trout Cooked in Parchment

Prep time: 10 minutes | Cook time: 10 minutes | Serves 4

4 (4 ounces / 113 g each) trout fillets	Zest and juice of 1 lemon
3 cloves garlic, finely chopped	⅓ cup extra-virgin olive oil
8 fresh sage leaves, finely chopped	1 teaspoon unrefined sea salt or salt
½ cup finely chopped fresh parsley	Freshly ground pepper
	Lemon wedges

1. Preheat the oven to 425ºF (220ºC). Combine the garlic, sage, parsley, lemon zest and juice, olive oil, salt, and pepper in a small bowl. Cut four pieces of parchment paper—each more than double the size of the trout. 2. Place 1 trout on top of each piece of parchment and equally distribute ¼ of garlic herb mixture on each fish. Brush any remaining garlic herb mixture over the fish and fold the parchment over the fish. Fold and crimp the edges to seal tightly and place in a baking dish. 3. Bake about 10 minutes, until fish is cooked through. Remove from the oven, and serve with lemon wedges, allowing guests to open their own individual packages at the table.

Per Serving:

calories: 339 | fat: 26g | protein: 24g | carbs: 3g | fiber: 1g | sodium: 646mg

Citrus-Marinated Scallops

Prep time: 10 minutes | Cook time: 10 minutes | Serves 4

Juice and zest of 2 lemons	to taste
¼ cup extra-virgin olive oil	1 clove garlic, minced
Unrefined sea salt or salt, to taste	1½ pounds (680 g) dry scallops, side muscle removed
Freshly ground black pepper,	

1. In a large shallow bowl or baking dish, combine the lemon juice and zest, olive oil, salt, pepper, and garlic. Mix well to combine. Add the scallops to the marinade; cover and refrigerate 1 hour. 2. Heat a large skillet over medium-high heat. Drain the scallops and place them in skillet. Cook 4 to 5 minutes per side, until cooked through.

Per Serving:

calories: 243 | fat: 14g | protein: 21g | carbs: 7g | fiber: 0g | sodium: 567mg

Seared Scallops with Braised Dandelion Greens

Prep time: 5 minutes | Cook time: 15 minutes | Serves 4

3 tablespoons olive oil, divided	pepper, divided
2 cloves garlic, thinly sliced	1 cup chopped fresh mint
1 pound (454 g) dandelion greens	1 cup chopped fresh flat-leaf parsley
1 cup low-sodium chicken broth or water	1 pound (454 g) scallops, muscle tabs removed
½ teaspoon kosher salt, divided	Lemon wedges, for serving
¼ teaspoon ground black	

1. In a large skillet over medium-high heat, warm 1 tablespoon of the oil. Cook the garlic until softened, about 2 minutes. Add the dandelion greens and broth or water and bring to a boil. Cover and cook until the greens are wilted, 2 minutes. Season with ¼ teaspoon of the salt and ⅛ teaspoon of the pepper. Cover and cook until the greens are tender, 5 to 10 minutes. Stir in the mint and parsley. 2. Meanwhile, pat the scallops dry and season with the remaining ¼ teaspoon salt and the remaining ⅛ teaspoon pepper. In a large nonstick skillet over medium heat, warm 1 tablespoon of the oil. Add the scallops in a single layer and cook without disturbing until browned, 1 to 2 minutes. Add the remaining 1 tablespoon oil to the skillet, flip the scallops, and cook until browned on the other side, 1 to 2 minutes. Serve the scallops over the braised greens and with the lemon wedges.

Per Serving:

calories: 235 | fat: 12g | protein: 18g | carbs: 17g | fiber: 5g | sodium: 850mg

Shrimp and Asparagus Risotto

Prep time: 15 minutes | Cook time: 20 minutes | Serves 4

¼ cup extra-virgin olive oil, divided	3 cups chicken or vegetable broth, plus extra as needed
8 ounces (227 g) asparagus, trimmed and cut on bias into 1-inch lengths	1 pound (454 g) large shrimp (26 to 30 per pound), peeled and deveined
½ onion, chopped fine	2 ounces (57 g) Parmesan cheese, grated (1 cup)
¼ teaspoon table salt	1 tablespoon lemon juice
1½ cups Arborio rice	1 tablespoon minced fresh chives
3 garlic cloves, minced	
½ cup dry white wine	

1. Using highest sauté function, heat 1 tablespoon oil in Instant Pot until shimmering. Add asparagus, partially cover, and cook until just crisp-tender, about 4 minutes. Using slotted spoon, transfer asparagus to bowl; set aside. 2. Add onion, 2 tablespoons oil, and salt to now-empty pot and cook, using highest sauté function, until onion is softened, about 5 minutes. Stir in rice and garlic and cook until grains are translucent around edges, about 3 minutes. Stir in wine and cook until nearly evaporated, about 1 minute. 3. Stir in broth, scraping up any rice that sticks to bottom of pot. Lock lid in place and close pressure release valve. Select high pressure cook function and cook for 7 minutes. 4. Turn off Instant Pot and quick-release pressure. Carefully remove lid, allowing steam to escape away from you. Stir shrimp and asparagus into risotto, cover, and let sit until shrimp are opaque throughout, 5 to 7 minutes. Add Parmesan and remaining 1 tablespoon oil, and stir vigorously until risotto becomes creamy. Adjust consistency with extra hot broth as needed. Stir in lemon juice and season with salt and pepper to taste. Sprinkle individual portions with chives before serving.

Per Serving:

calories: 707 | fat: 24g | protein: 45g | carbs: 76g | fiber: 5g | sodium: 360mg

Shrimp over Black Bean Linguine

Prep time: 10 minutes | Cook time: 15 minutes | Serves 4

1 pound (454 g) black bean linguine or spaghetti	oil
1 pound (454 g) fresh shrimp, peeled and deveined	1 onion, finely chopped
4 tablespoons extra-virgin olive	3 garlic cloves, minced
	¼ cup basil, cut into strips

1. Bring a large pot of water to a boil and cook the pasta according to the package instructions. 2. In the last 5 minutes of cooking the pasta, add the shrimp to the hot water and allow them to cook for 3 to 5 minutes. Once they turn pink, take them out of the hot water, and, if you think you may have overcooked them, run them under cool water. Set aside. 3. Reserve 1 cup of the pasta cooking water and drain the noodles. In the same pan, heat the oil over medium-high heat and cook the onion and garlic for 7 to 10 minutes. Once the onion is translucent, add the pasta back in and toss well. 4. Plate the pasta, then top with shrimp and garnish with basil.

Per Serving:

calories: 668 | fat: 19g | protein: 57g | carbs: 73g | fiber: 31g | sodium: 615mg

Cod with Parsley Pistou

Prep time: 15 minutes | Cook time: 10 minutes | Serves 4

1 cup packed roughly chopped fresh flat-leaf Italian parsley	½ teaspoon freshly ground black pepper
1 to 2 small garlic cloves, minced	1 cup extra-virgin olive oil, divided
Zest and juice of 1 lemon	1 pound (454 g) cod fillets, cut into 4 equal-sized pieces
1 teaspoon salt	

1. In a food processer, combine the parsley, garlic, lemon zest and juice, salt, and pepper. Pulse to chop well. 2. While the food processor is running, slowly stream in ¾ cup olive oil until well combined. Set aside. 3. In a large skillet, heat the remaining ¼ cup olive oil over medium-high heat. Add the cod fillets, cover, and cook 4 to 5 minutes on each side, or until cooked through. Thicker fillets may require a bit more cooking time. Remove from the heat and keep warm. 4. Add the pistou to the skillet and heat over medium-low heat. Return the cooked fish to the skillet, flipping to coat in the sauce. Serve warm, covered with pistou.

Per Serving:

calories: 580 | fat: 55g | protein: 21g | carbs: 2g | fiber: 1g | sodium: 591mg

Flounder Fillets

Prep time: 10 minutes | Cook time: 5 to 8 minutes | Serves 4

1 egg white	4 (4-ounce / 113-g) flounder fillets
1 tablespoon water	
1 cup panko bread crumbs	Salt and pepper, to taste
2 tablespoons extra-light virgin olive oil	Oil for misting or cooking spray

1. Preheat the air fryer to 390ºF (199ºC). 2. Beat together egg white and water in shallow dish. 3. In another shallow dish, mix panko crumbs and oil until well combined and crumbly (best done by hand). 4. Season flounder fillets with salt and pepper to taste. Dip each fillet into egg mixture and then roll in panko crumbs, pressing in crumbs so that fish is nicely coated. 5. Spray the air fryer basket with nonstick cooking spray and add fillets. Air fry at 390ºF (199ºC) for 3 minutes. 6. Spray fish fillets but do not turn. Cook 2 to 5 minutes longer or until golden brown and crispy. Using a spatula, carefully remove fish from basket and serve.

Per Serving:

calories: 252 | fat: 10g | protein: 19g | carbs: 19g | fiber: 1g | sodium: 212mg

Cod with Jalapeño

Prep time: 5 minutes | Cook time: 14 minutes | Serves 4

4 cod fillets, boneless

1 jalapeño, minced

1 tablespoon avocado oil

½ teaspoon minced garlic

1. In the shallow bowl, mix minced jalapeño, avocado oil, and minced garlic. 2. Put the cod fillets in the air fryer basket in one layer and top with minced jalapeño mixture. 3. Cook the fish at 365ºF (185ºC) for 7 minutes per side.

Per Serving:

calorie: 141 | fat: 5g | protein: 21g | carbs: 1g | fiber: 0g | sodium: | 78mg

Salmon Fritters with Zucchini

Prep time: 15 minutes | Cook time: 12 minutes | Serves 4

2 tablespoons almond flour

1 zucchini, grated

1 egg, beaten

6 ounces (170 g) salmon fillet, diced

1 teaspoon avocado oil

½ teaspoon ground black pepper

1. Mix almond flour with zucchini, egg, salmon, and ground black pepper. 2. Then make the fritters from the salmon mixture. 3. Sprinkle the air fryer basket with avocado oil and put the fritters inside. 4. Cook the fritters at 375ºF (191ºC) for 6 minutes per side.

Per Serving:

calories: 102 | fat: 4g | protein: 11g | carbs: 4g | fiber: 1g | sodium: 52mg

Chapter 7
Vegetables and Sides

Braised Radishes with Sugar Snap Peas and Dukkah

Prep time: 20 minutes | Cook time: 5 minutes | Serves 4

¼ cup extra-virgin olive oil, divided
1 shallot, sliced thin
3 garlic cloves, sliced thin
1½ pounds (680 g) radishes, 2 cups greens reserved, radishes trimmed and halved if small or quartered if large
½ cup water
½ teaspoon table salt
8 ounces (227 g) sugar snap

peas, strings removed, sliced thin on bias
8 ounces (227 g) cremini mushrooms, trimmed and sliced thin
2 teaspoons grated lemon zest plus 1 teaspoon juice
1 cup plain Greek yogurt
½ cup fresh cilantro leaves
3 tablespoons dukkah

1. Using highest sauté function, heat 2 tablespoons oil in Instant Pot until shimmering. Add shallot and cook until softened, about 2 minutes. Stir in garlic and cook until fragrant, about 30 seconds. Stir in radishes, water, and salt. Lock lid in place and close pressure release valve. Select high pressure cook function and cook for 1 minute. 2. Turn off Instant Pot and quick-release pressure. Carefully remove lid, allowing steam to escape away from you. Stir in snap peas, cover, and let sit until heated through, about 3 minutes. Add radish greens, mushrooms, lemon zest and juice, and remaining 2 tablespoons oil and gently toss to combine. Season with salt and pepper to taste. 3. Spread ¼ cup yogurt over bottom of 4 individual serving plates. Using slotted spoon, arrange vegetable mixture on top and sprinkle with cilantro and dukkah. Serve.

Per Serving:
calories: 310 | fat: 23g | protein: 10g | carbs: 17g | fiber: 5g | sodium: 320mg

Stuffed Artichokes

Prep time: 20 minutes | Cook time: 5 to 7 hours | Serves 4 to 6

4 to 6 fresh large artichokes
½ cup bread crumbs
½ cup grated Parmesan cheese or Romano cheese
4 garlic cloves, minced
½ teaspoon sea salt
½ teaspoon freshly ground black

pepper
¼ cup water
2 tablespoons extra-virgin olive oil
2 tablespoons chopped fresh parsley for garnish (optional)

1. To trim and prepare the artichokes, cut off the bottom along with 1 inch from the top of each artichoke. Pull off and discard the lowest leaves nearest the stem end. Trim off any pointy tips of artichoke leaves that are poking out. Set aside. 2. In a small bowl, stir together the bread crumbs, Parmesan cheese, garlic, salt, and pepper. 3. Spread apart the artichoke leaves and stuff the bread-crumb mixture into the spaces, down to the base. 4. Pour the water into a slow cooker. 5. Place the artichokes in the slow cooker in a single layer. Drizzle the olive oil over the artichokes. 6. Cover the cooker and cook for 5 to 7 hours on Low heat, or until the artichokes are tender.

7. Garnish with fresh parsley if desired.

Per Serving:
calories: 224 | fat: 12g | protein: 12g | carbs: 23g | fiber: 8g | sodium: 883mg

Herbed Shiitake Mushrooms

Prep time: 10 minutes | Cook time: 5 minutes | Serves 4

8 ounces (227 g) shiitake mushrooms, stems removed and caps roughly chopped
1 tablespoon olive oil
½ teaspoon salt
Freshly ground black pepper, to taste

1 teaspoon chopped fresh thyme leaves
1 teaspoon chopped fresh oregano
1 tablespoon chopped fresh parsley

1. Preheat the air fryer to 400°F (204°C). 2. Toss the mushrooms with the olive oil, salt, pepper, thyme and oregano. Air fry for 5 minutes, shaking the basket once or twice during the cooking process. The mushrooms will still be somewhat chewy with a meaty texture. If you'd like them a little more tender, add a couple of minutes to this cooking time. 3. Once cooked, add the parsley to the mushrooms and toss. Season again to taste and serve.

Per Serving:
calories: 50 | fat: 4g | protein: 1g | carbs: 4g | fiber: 2g | sodium: 296mg

Wild Mushroom Soup

Prep time: 30 minutes | Cook time: 16 minutes | Serves 8

3 tablespoons olive oil
1 stalk celery, diced
1 medium carrot, peeled and diced
½ medium yellow onion, peeled and diced
1 clove garlic, peeled and minced
1 (8-ounce / 227-g) container hen of the woods mushrooms, sliced
1 (8-ounce / 227-g) container

porcini or chanterelle mushrooms, sliced
2 cups sliced shiitake mushrooms
2 tablespoons dry sherry
4 cups vegetable broth
2 cups water
1 tablespoon chopped fresh tarragon
½ teaspoon salt
½ teaspoon ground black pepper

1. Press the Sauté button on the Instant Pot® and heat oil. Add celery, carrot, and onion. Cook, stirring often, until softened, about 5 minutes. Add garlic and cook 30 seconds until fragrant, then add mushrooms and cook until beginning to soften, about 5 minutes. 2. Add sherry, broth, water, tarragon, salt, and pepper to pot, and stir well. Press the Cancel button. Close lid, set steam release to Sealing, press the Manual button, and set time to 5 minutes. 3. When the timer beeps, let pressure release naturally, about 15 minutes. Press the Cancel button, open lid, and stir well. Serve hot.

Per Serving:
calories: 98 | fat: 6g | protein: 1g | carbs: 11g | fiber: 2g | sodium: 759mg

Saffron Couscous with Almonds, Currants, and Scallions

Prep time: 5 minutes | Cook time: 35 minutes | Serves 8

2 cups whole wheat couscous	3 cups low-sodium chicken
1 tablespoon olive oil	broth or vegetable broth
5 scallions, thinly sliced, whites	½ cup slivered almonds
and greens kept separate	¼ cup dried currants
1 large pinch saffron threads,	Kosher salt and ground black
crumbled	pepper, to taste

1. In a medium saucepan over medium heat, toast the couscous, stirring occasionally, until lightly browned, about 5 minutes. Transfer to a bowl. 2. In the same saucepan, add the oil and scallion whites. Cook, stirring, until lightly browned, about 5 minutes. Sprinkle in the saffron and stir to combine. Pour in the broth and bring to a boil. 3. Remove the saucepan from the heat, stir in the couscous, cover, and let sit until all the liquid is absorbed and the couscous is tender, about 15 minutes. 4. Fluff the couscous with a fork. Fluff in the scallion greens, almonds, and currants. Season to taste with the salt and pepper.

Per Serving:
calories: 212 | fat: 6g | protein: 8g | carbs: 34g | fiber: 4g | sodium: 148mg

Spicy Creamer Potatoes

Prep time: 10 minutes | Cook time: 8 hours | Makes 7 (1-cup) servings

2 pounds (907 g) creamer	lemon juice
potatoes	2 tablespoons water
1 onion, chopped	1 tablespoon chili powder
3 garlic cloves, minced	½ teaspoon ground cumin
1 chipotle chile in adobo sauce,	½ teaspoon salt
minced	⅛ teaspoon freshly ground black
2 tablespoons freshly squeezed	pepper

1. In the slow cooker, combine all the ingredients and stir. 2. Cover and cook on low for 7 to 8 hours, or until the potatoes are tender, and serve.

Per Serving:
calories: 113 | fat: 0g | protein: 3g | carbs: 25g | fiber: 4g | sodium: 208mg

Sautéed Crunchy Greens

Prep time: 10 minutes | Cook time: 5 minutes | Serves 4

3 tablespoons olive oil	Juice of ½ lemon
2 cloves garlic, minced	Sea salt and freshly ground
2 large bunches Swiss chard or	pepper, to taste
kale, sliced, stems removed	3 tablespoons sunflower seeds

1. In a large skillet, heat the olive oil, and add the garlic on medium heat. Sauté for about a minute, and add the Swiss chard. 2. Cook

until wilted, about 2 more minutes. 3. Add the lemon juice, sea salt and freshly ground pepper to taste, and sunflower seeds. 4. Serve and enjoy!

Per Serving:
calories: 142 | fat: 14g | protein: 2g | carbs: 4g | fiber: 2g | sodium: 116mg

One-Pan Herb-Roasted Tomatoes, Green Beans, and Baby Potatoes

Prep time: 10 minutes | Cook time: 30 minutes | Serves 6

¼ cup chopped mixed fresh	1 pound (454 g) baby potatoes,
herbs, such as flat-leaf parsley,	halved
oregano, mint, and dill	1 pound (454 g) green beans,
3 tablespoons olive oil	trimmed and halved
½ teaspoon kosher salt	2 large shallots, cut into wedges
½ teaspoon ground black pepper	2 pints cherry tomatoes

1. Preheat the oven to 400°F (205°C). 2. In a small bowl, whisk together the herbs, oil, salt, and pepper. Place the potatoes, string beans, and shallots on a large rimmed baking sheet. Drizzle the herb mixture over the vegetables and toss thoroughly to coat. 3. Roast the vegetables until the potatoes are just tender, about 15 minutes. Remove from the oven and toss in the tomatoes. Roast until the tomatoes blister and the potatoes are completely tender, about 15 minutes.

Per Serving:
calories: 173 | fat: 8g | protein: 5g | carbs: 26g | fiber: 5g | sodium: 185mg

Mushroom-Stuffed Zucchini

Prep time: 15 minutes | Cook time: 46 minutes | Serves 2

2 tablespoons olive oil	finely chopped
2 cups button mushrooms,	1 tablespoon Italian seasoning
finely chopped	Sea salt and freshly ground
2 cloves garlic, finely chopped	pepper, to taste
2 tablespoons chicken broth	2 medium zucchini, cut in half
1 tablespoon flat-leaf parsley,	lengthwise

1. Preheat oven to 350°F (180°C). 2. Heat a large skillet over medium heat, and add the olive oil. Add the mushrooms and cook until tender, about 4 minutes. Add the garlic and cook for 2 more minutes. 3. Add the chicken broth and cook another 3–4 minutes. 4. Add the parsley and Italian seasoning, and season with sea salt and freshly ground pepper. 5. Stir and remove from heat. 6. Scoop out the insides of the halved zucchini and stuff with mushroom mixture. 7. Place zucchini in a casserole dish, and drizzle a tablespoon of water or broth in the bottom. 8. Cover with foil and bake for 30–40 minutes until zucchini are tender. Serve immediately.

Per Serving:
calories: 189 | fat: 14g | protein: 5g | carbs: 12g | fiber: 3g | sodium: 335mg

Puréed Cauliflower Soup

Prep time: 15 minutes | Cook time: 11 minutes | Serves 6

2 tablespoons olive oil	4 cups cauliflower florets
1 medium onion, peeled and chopped	2 cups vegetable stock
1 stalk celery, chopped	½ cup half-and-half
1 medium carrot, peeled and chopped	¼ cup low-fat plain Greek yogurt
3 sprigs fresh thyme	2 tablespoons chopped fresh chives

1. Press the Sauté button on the Instant Pot® and heat oil. Add onion, celery, and carrot. Cook until just tender, about 6 minutes. Add thyme, cauliflower, and stock. Stir well, then press the Cancel button. 2. Close lid, set steam release to Sealing, press the Manual button, and set time to 5 minutes. When the timer beeps, let pressure release naturally, about 15 minutes. 3. Open lid, remove and discard thyme stems, and with an immersion blender, purée soup until smooth. Stir in half-and-half and yogurt. Garnish with chives and serve immediately.

Per Serving:
calories: 113 | fat: 7g | protein: 3g | carbs: 9g | fiber: 2g | sodium: 236mg

Caponata (Sicilian Eggplant)

Prep time: 1 hour 5 minutes | Cook time: 40 minutes | Serves 2

3 medium eggplant, cut into ½-inch cubes (about 1½ pounds / 680 g)	3 medium tomatoes (about 15 ounces / 425 g), chopped
½ teaspoon fine sea salt	3 tablespoons red wine vinegar
¼ cup extra virgin olive oil	2 tablespoons granulated sugar
1 medium onion (red or white), chopped	Salt to taste
1 tablespoon dried oregano	Freshly ground black pepper to taste
½ cup green olives, pitted and halved	2 tablespoons chopped fresh basil
2 tablespoons capers, rinsed	1 tablespoon toasted pine nuts (optional)

1. Place the eggplant in a large colander. Sprinkle ½ teaspoon sea salt over the top and set the eggplant aside to rest for about an hour. 2. Add the olive oil to a large pan over medium heat. When the oil starts to shimmer, add the eggplant and sauté until it starts to turn golden brown, about 5 minutes. Add the onions and continue sautéing until the onions become soft. 3. Add the oregano, olives, capers, and tomatoes (with juices) to the pan. Reduce the heat to medium-low and simmer for about 20–25 minutes. 4. While the onions and tomatoes are cooking, combine the vinegar and sugar in a small bowl. Stir until the sugar is completely dissolved, then add the mixture to the pan. Continue cooking for 2–3 more minutes or until you can no longer smell the vinegar and then remove the pan from the heat. 5. Season the mixture to taste with salt and black pepper. Just prior to serving, top each serving with a sprinkle of chopped basil and toasted pine nuts, if using. Store in the refrigerator for up to 3 days.

Per Serving:
calories: 473 | fat: 32g | protein: 6g | carbs: 47g | fiber: 15g | sodium: 702mg

Roasted Broccolini with Garlic and Romano

Prep time: 5 minutes | Cook time: 10 minutes | Serves 2

1 bunch broccolini (about 5 ounces / 142 g)	¼ teaspoon salt
1 tablespoon olive oil	2 tablespoons grated Romano cheese
½ teaspoon garlic powder	

1. Preheat the oven to 400°F(205°C) and set the oven rack to the middle position. Line a sheet pan with parchment paper or foil. 2. Slice the tough ends off the broccolini and place in a medium bowl. Add the olive oil, garlic powder, and salt and toss to combine. Arrange broccolini on the lined sheet pan. 3. Roast for 7 minutes, flipping pieces over halfway through the roasting time. 4. Remove the pan from the oven and sprinkle the cheese over the broccolini. With a pair of tongs, carefully flip the pieces over to coat all sides. Return to the oven for another 2 to 3 minutes, or until the cheese melts and starts to turn golden.

Per Serving:
calories: 114 | fat: 9g | protein: 4g | carbs: 5g | fiber: 2g | sodium: 400mg

Steamed Cauliflower with Olive Oil and Herbs

Prep time: 10 minutes | Cook time: 0 minutes | Serves 6

1 head cauliflower, cut into florets (about 6 cups)	oregano
1 cup water	1 teaspoon chopped fresh thyme leaves
4 tablespoons olive oil	1 teaspoon chopped fresh sage
1 clove garlic, peeled and minced	¼ teaspoon salt
2 tablespoons chopped fresh	¼ teaspoon ground black pepper

1. Place cauliflower florets in a steamer basket. Place the rack in the Instant Pot®, add water, then top with the steamer basket. Close lid, set steam release to Sealing, press the Manual button, and set time to 0 minutes. 2. While cauliflower cooks, prepare the dressing. Whisk together olive oil, garlic, oregano, thyme, sage, salt, and pepper. 3. When the timer beeps, quick-release the pressure until the float valve drops. Press the Cancel button and open lid. Carefully transfer cauliflower to a serving bowl and immediately pour dressing over cauliflower. Carefully toss to coat. Let stand for 5 minutes. Serve hot.

Per Serving:
calories: 105 | fat: 9g | protein: 0g | carbs: 0g | fiber: 2g | sodium: 128mg

Sicilian-Style Roasted Cauliflower with Capers, Currants, and Crispy Breadcrumbs

Prep time: 10 minutes | Cook time: 55 minutes | Serves 4

1 large head of cauliflower (2 pounds / 907 g), cut into 2-inch florets	patted dry
	¾ cup fresh whole-wheat breadcrumbs
6 tablespoons olive oil, divided	½ cup chicken broth
1 teaspoon salt	1 teaspoon anchovy paste
½ teaspoon freshly ground black pepper	⅓ cup golden raisins
	1 tablespoon white wine vinegar
3 garlic cloves, thinly sliced	2 tablespoons chopped flat-leaf parsley
2 tablespoons salt-packed capers, soaked, rinsed, and	

1. Preheat the oven to 425°F(220°C). 2. In a medium bowl, toss the cauliflower florets with 3 tablespoons olive oil, and the salt and pepper. Spread the cauliflower out in a single layer on a large, rimmed baking sheet and roast in the preheated oven, stirring occasionally, for about 45 minutes, until the cauliflower is golden brown and crispy at the edges. 3. While the cauliflower is roasting, put the remaining 3 tablespoons of olive oil in a small saucepan and heat over medium-low heat. Add the garlic and cook, stirring, for about 5 minutes, until the garlic begins to turn golden. Stir in the capers and cook for 3 minutes more. Add the breadcrumbs, stir to mix well, and cook until the breadcrumbs turn golden brown and are crisp. Use a slotted spoon to transfer the breadcrumbs to a bowl or plate. 4. In the same saucepan, stir together the broth and anchovy paste and bring to a boil over medium-high heat. Stir in the raisins and vinegar and cook, stirring occasionally, for 5 minutes, until the liquid has mostly been absorbed. 5. When the cauliflower is done, transfer it to a large serving bowl. Add the raisin mixture and toss to mix. Top with the breadcrumbs and serve immediately, garnished with parsley.

Per Serving:

calories: 364 | fat: 22g | protein: 8g | carbs: 37g | fiber: 6g | sodium: 657mg

Baked Tomatoes with Spiced Amaranth Stuffing

Prep time: 10 minutes | Cook time: 50 minutes | Serves 6

1 tablespoon olive oil	½ teaspoon ground cinnamon
1 small onion, diced	½ cup golden raisins
1 clove garlic, minced	½ cup toasted pine nuts
1 cup amaranth	¾ teaspoon salt
1 cup vegetable broth or water	½ teaspoon freshly ground black pepper
1 cup diced tomatoes, drained	
¼ cup chopped fresh parsley	6 large ripe tomatoes

1. Preheat the oven to 375°F (190°C). 2. Heat the olive oil over medium heat in a medium saucepan. Add the onion and garlic and cook, stirring frequently, until the onion is softened, about 5 minutes. Stir in the amaranth and then the broth or water and bring to a boil over high heat. Lower the heat to low, cover, and cook, stirring occasionally, for about 20 minutes, until the amaranth is tender and the liquid has been absorbed. 3. Remove the pan from the heat and stir in the diced tomatoes, parsley, cinnamon, raisins, pine nuts, salt, and pepper. 4. Cut a slice off the bottom of each tomato to make a flat bottom for it to sit on. Scoop out the seeds and core of the tomato to make a shell for filling. Arrange the hollowed-out tomatoes in a baking dish. 5. Fill the tomatoes with the amaranth mixture and bake in the preheated oven for about 25 minutes, until the tomatoes have softened, but still hold their shape. Serve hot.

Per Serving:

calories: 306 | fat: 13g | protein: 10g | carbs: 43g | fiber: 7g | sodium: 439mg

Honey and Spice Glazed Carrots

Prep time: 5 minutes | Cook time: 5 minutes | Serves 4

4 large carrots, peeled and sliced on the diagonal into ½-inch-thick rounds	½ cup honey
	1 tablespoon red wine vinegar
	1 tablespoon chopped flat-leaf parsley
1 teaspoon ground cinnamon	
1 teaspoon ground ginger	1 tablespoon chopped cilantro
3 tablespoons olive oil	2 tablespoons toasted pine nuts

1. Bring a large saucepan of lightly salted water to a boil and add the carrots. Cover and cook for about 5 minutes, until the carrots are just tender. Drain in a colander, then transfer to a medium bowl. 2. Add the cinnamon, ginger, olive oil, honey, and vinegar and toss to combine well. Add the parsley and cilantro and toss again to incorporate. Garnish with the pine nuts. Serve immediately or let cool to room temperature.

Per Serving:

calories: 281 | fat: 14g | protein: 1g | carbs: 43g | fiber: 2g | sodium: 48mg

Roasted Harissa Carrots

Prep time: 10 minutes | Cook time: 15 minutes | Serves 4

1 pound (454 g) carrots, peeled and sliced into 1-inch-thick rounds	2 tablespoons harissa
	1 teaspoon honey
	1 teaspoon ground cumin
2 tablespoons extra-virgin olive oil	½ teaspoon kosher salt
	½ cup fresh parsley, chopped

1. Preheat the oven to 450°F (235°C). Line a baking sheet with parchment paper or foil. 2. In a large bowl, combine the carrots, olive oil, harissa, honey, cumin, and salt. Arrange in a single layer on the baking sheet. Roast for 15 minutes. Remove from the oven, add the parsley, and toss together.

Per Serving:

calories: 120 | fat: 8g | protein: 1g | carbs: 13g | fiber: 4g | sodium: 255mg

Braised Fennel

Prep time: 10 minutes | Cook time: 50 minutes | Serves 4

2 large fennel bulbs	leaves and stalks separated
¼ cup extra-virgin avocado oil or ghee, divided	1 cup water
	3 tablespoons fresh lemon juice
1 small shallot or red onion	Salt and black pepper, to taste
1 clove garlic, sliced	¼ cup extra-virgin olive oil, to drizzle
4 to 6 thyme sprigs	
1 small bunch fresh parsley,	

1. Cut off the fennel stalks where they attach to the bulb. Reserve the stalks. Cut the fennel bulb in half, trim the hard bottom part, and cut into wedges. 2. Heat a saucepan greased with 2 tablespoons of the avocado oil over medium-high heat. Sauté the shallot, garlic, thyme sprigs, parsley stalks, and hard fennel stalks for about 5 minutes. Add the water, bring to a boil, and simmer over medium heat for 10 minutes. Remove from the heat, set aside for 10 minutes, and then strain the stock, discarding the aromatics. 3. Preheat the oven to 350°F (180°C) fan assisted or 400°F (205°C) conventional. 4. Heat an ovenproof skillet greased with the remaining 2 tablespoons of avocado oil over medium-high heat and add the fennel wedges. Sear until caramelized, about 5 minutes, turning once. Pour the stock and the lemon juice over the fennel wedges, and season with salt and pepper. Loosely cover with a piece of aluminum foil. Bake for about 30 minutes. When done, the fennel should be easy to pierce with the tip of a knife. 5. Remove from the oven and scatter with the chopped parsley leaves and drizzle with the olive oil. To store, let cool and refrigerate for up to 5 days.

Per Serving:

calories: 225 | fat: 20g | protein: 2g | carbs: 12g | fiber: 5g | sodium: 187mg

Mediterranean Cauliflower Tabbouleh

Prep time: 15 minutes | Cook time: 5 minutes | Serves 6

6 tablespoons extra-virgin olive oil, divided	½ cup chopped pitted Kalamata olives
4 cups riced cauliflower	2 tablespoons minced red onion
3 garlic cloves, finely minced	Juice of 1 lemon (about 2 tablespoons)
1½ teaspoons salt	
½ teaspoon freshly ground black pepper	2 cups baby arugula or spinach leaves
½ large cucumber, peeled, seeded, and chopped	2 medium avocados, peeled, pitted, and diced
½ cup chopped mint leaves	1 cup quartered cherry tomatoes
½ cup chopped Italian parsley	

1. In a large skillet, heat 2 tablespoons of olive oil over medium-high heat. Add the riced cauliflower, garlic, salt, and pepper and sauté until just tender but not mushy, 3 to 4 minutes. Remove from the heat and place in a large bowl. 2. Add the cucumber, mint, parsley, olives, red onion, lemon juice, and remaining 4 tablespoons olive oil and toss well. Place in the refrigerator, uncovered, and refrigerate for at least 30 minutes, or up to 2 hours. 3. Before serving, add the arugula, avocado, and tomatoes and toss to combine well. Season to taste with salt and pepper and serve cold or at room temperature.

Per Serving:

calories: 273 | fat: 25g | protein: 4g | carbs: 13g | fiber: 7g | sodium: 697mg

White Beans with Rosemary, Sage, and Garlic

Prep time: 10 minutes | Cook time: 10 minutes | Serves 2

1 tablespoon olive oil	1 teaspoon minced fresh rosemary (from 1 sprig) plus 1 whole fresh rosemary sprig
2 garlic cloves, minced	
1 (15-ounce / 425-g) can white cannellini beans, drained and rinsed	½ cup low-sodium chicken stock
	Salt
¼ teaspoon dried sage	

1. Heat the olive oil in a sauté pan over medium-high heat. Add the garlic and sauté for 30 seconds. 2. Add the beans, sage, minced and whole rosemary, and chicken stock and bring the mixture to a boil. 3. Reduce the heat to medium and simmer the beans for 10 minutes, or until most of the liquid is evaporated. If desired, mash some of the beans with a fork to thicken them. 4. Season with salt. Remove the rosemary sprig before serving

Per Serving:

calories: 155 | fat: 7g | protein: 6g | carbs: 17g | fiber: 8g | sodium: 153mg

Balsamic Beets

Prep time: 15 minutes | Cook time: 3 to 4 hours | Serves 8

Cooking spray or 1 tablespoon extra-virgin olive oil	1 tablespoon honey
	2 fresh thyme sprigs
3 pounds (1.4 kg) beets, scrubbed, peeled, and cut into wedges	1 teaspoon kosher salt, plus more for seasoning
	½ teaspoon freshly ground black pepper, plus more for seasoning
2 garlic cloves, minced	
1 cup white grape or apple juice	1 tablespoon cold water
½ cup balsamic vinegar	1 tablespoon cornstarch

1. Use the cooking spray or olive oil to coat the inside (bottom and sides) of the slow cooker. Add the beets, garlic, juice, vinegar, honey, thyme, salt, and pepper. Stir to combine. Cover and cook on high for 3 to 4 hours. 2. About 10 minutes before serving, combine the water and cornstarch in a small bowl, stirring until no lumps remain. Add to the slow cooker and continue to cook for 10 minutes, or until the sauce thickens. 3. Discard the thyme. Season with additional salt and pepper, as needed. Serve.

Per Serving:

calories: 129 | fat: 2g | protein: 3g | carbs: 26g | fiber: 5g | sodium: 429mg

Sautéed Mustard Greens and Red Peppers

Prep time: 10 minutes | Cook time: 5 minutes | Serves 4

1 tablespoon olive oil	Sea salt and freshly ground
½ red pepper, diced	pepper, to taste
2 cloves garlic, minced	1 teaspoon white wine vinegar
1 bunch mustard greens	

1. Heat olive oil in a large saucepan over medium heat. Add bell pepper and garlic, and sauté for 1 minute, stirring often. 2. Add greens to pan and immediately cover to begin steaming. Set a timer for 2 minutes. 3. After 1 minute, lift lid and stir greens well, then immediately put lid back on for remaining minute. Remove the lid, season with sea salt and freshly ground pepper, sprinkle with vinegar, and serve.

Per Serving:

calories: 42 | fat: 4g | protein: 1g | carbs: 2g | fiber: 1g | sodium: 7mg

Vegetable Terrine

Prep time: 30 minutes | Cook time: 5 to 7 hours | Serves 6

1 small eggplant, thinly sliced lengthwise	4 large tomatoes, sliced
2 green bell peppers, halved, seeded, and sliced	1 teaspoon sea salt
	¼ teaspoon freshly ground black pepper
2 red bell peppers, halved, seeded, and sliced	Nonstick cooking spray
1 portobello mushroom, cut into ¼-inch-thick slices	1 cup grated Parmesan cheese
	2 tablespoons extra-virgin olive oil
1 zucchini, thinly sliced lengthwise	1 tablespoon red wine vinegar
1 large red onion, cut into ¼-inch-thick rounds	2 teaspoons freshly squeezed lemon juice
2 yellow squash, thinly sliced lengthwise	1 teaspoon dried basil
	1 garlic clove, minced

1. Season the eggplant, green and red bell peppers, mushroom, zucchini, onion, squash, and tomatoes with salt and black pepper, but keep all the vegetables separate. 2. Generously coat a slow-cooker insert with cooking spray, or line the bottom and sides with parchment paper or aluminum foil. 3. Starting with half of the eggplant, line the bottom of the prepared slow cooker with overlapping slices. Sprinkle with 2 tablespoons of Parmesan cheese. 4. Add a second layer using half of the green and red bell peppers. Sprinkle with 2 more tablespoons of Parmesan cheese. 5. Add a third layer using half of the mushroom slices. Sprinkle with 2 more tablespoons of Parmesan cheese. 6. Add a fourth layer using half of the zucchini slices. Sprinkle with 2 more tablespoons of Parmesan cheese. 7. Add a fifth layer using half of the red onion slices. Sprinkle with another 2 tablespoons of Parmesan cheese. 8. Add a sixth layer using half of the yellow squash slices. Sprinkle with 2 more tablespoons of Parmesan cheese. 9. Add a final seventh layer with half of the tomato slices. Sprinkle with 2 more tablespoons of Parmesan cheese. 10. Repeat the layering with the remaining vegetables and Parmesan cheese in the same order until all of the vegetables have been used. 11. In a small bowl, whisk together the olive oil, vinegar, lemon juice, basil, and garlic until combined. Pour the mixture over the vegetables. Top with any remaining Parmesan cheese. 12. Cover the cooker and cook for 5 to 7 hours on Low heat. 13. Let cool to room temperature before slicing and serving.

Per Serving:

calories: 217 | fat: 11g | protein: 12g | carbs: 24g | fiber: 7g | sodium: 725mg

Fried Zucchini Salad

Prep time: 10 minutes | Cook time: 5 to 7 minutes | Serves 4

2 medium zucchini, thinly sliced	Zest and juice of ½ lemon
5 tablespoons olive oil, divided	1 clove garlic, minced
¼ cup chopped fresh parsley	¼ cup crumbled feta cheese
2 tablespoons chopped fresh mint	Freshly ground black pepper, to taste

1. Preheat the air fryer to 400°F (204°C). 2. In a large bowl, toss the zucchini slices with 1 tablespoon of the olive oil. 3. Working in batches if necessary, arrange the zucchini slices in an even layer in the air fryer basket. Pausing halfway through the cooking time to shake the basket, air fry for 5 to 7 minutes until soft and lightly browned on each side. 4. Meanwhile, in a small bowl, combine the remaining 4 tablespoons olive oil, parsley, mint, lemon zest, lemon juice, and garlic. 5. Arrange the zucchini on a plate and drizzle with the dressing. Sprinkle the feta and black pepper on top. Serve warm or at room temperature.

Per Serving:

calories: 194 | fat: 19g | protein: 3g | carbs: 4g | fiber: 1g | sodium: 96mg

Rustic Cauliflower and Carrot Hash

Prep time: 10 minutes | Cook time: 10 minutes | Serves 4

3 tablespoons extra-virgin olive oil	4 cups cauliflower pieces, washed
1 large onion, chopped	1 teaspoon salt
1 tablespoon garlic, minced	½ teaspoon ground cumin
2 cups carrots, diced	

1. In a large skillet over medium heat, cook the olive oil, onion, garlic, and carrots for 3 minutes. 2. Cut the cauliflower into 1-inch or bite-size pieces. Add the cauliflower, salt, and cumin to the skillet and toss to combine with the carrots and onions. 3. Cover and cook for 3 minutes. 4. Toss the vegetables and continue to cook uncovered for an additional 3 to 4 minutes. 5. Serve warm.

Per Serving:

calories: 159 | fat: 11g | protein: 3g | carbs: 15g | fiber: 5g | sodium: 657mg

Ratatouille

Prep time: 15 minutes | Cook time: 20 minutes | Serves 2 to 3

2 cups ¾-inch cubed peeled eggplant	halved lengthwise
1 small red, yellow, or orange bell pepper, stemmed, seeded, and diced	3 tablespoons olive oil
	1 teaspoon dried oregano
	½ teaspoon dried thyme
1 cup cherry tomatoes	1 teaspoon kosher salt
6 to 8 cloves garlic, peeled and	½ teaspoon black pepper

1. In a medium bowl, combine the eggplant, bell pepper, tomatoes, garlic, oil, oregano, thyme, salt, and pepper. Toss to combine. 2. Place the vegetables in the air fryer basket. Set the air fryer to 400ºF (204ºC) for 20 minutes, or until the vegetables are crisp-tender.

Per Serving:

calories: 161 | fat: 14g | protein: 2g | carbs: 9g | fiber: 3g | sodium: 781mg

Lemon-Rosemary Beets

Prep time: 10 minutes | Cook time: 8 hours | Serves 7

2 pounds (907 g) beets, peeled and cut into wedges	1 tablespoon apple cider vinegar
2 tablespoons fresh lemon juice	¾ teaspoon sea salt
2 tablespoons extra-virgin olive oil	½ teaspoon black pepper
	2 sprigs fresh rosemary
2 tablespoons honey	½ teaspoon lemon zest

1. Place the beets in the slow cooker. 2. Whisk the lemon juice, extra-virgin olive oil, honey, apple cider vinegar, salt, and pepper together in a small bowl. Pour over the beets. 3. Add the sprigs of rosemary to the slow cooker. 4. Cover and cook on low for 8 hours, or until the beets are tender. 5. Remove and discard the rosemary sprigs. Stir in the lemon zest. Serve hot.

Per Serving:

calories: 111 | fat: 4g | protein: 2g | carbs: 18g | fiber: 4g | sodium: 351mg

Sesame-Ginger Broccoli

Prep time: 10 minutes | Cook time: 15 minutes | Serves 4

3 tablespoons toasted sesame oil	½ teaspoon black pepper
2 teaspoons sesame seeds	1 (16-ounce / 454-g) package
1 tablespoon chili-garlic sauce	frozen broccoli florets (do not
2 teaspoons minced fresh ginger	thaw)
½ teaspoon kosher salt	

1. In a large bowl, combine the sesame oil, sesame seeds, chili-garlic sauce, ginger, salt, and pepper. Stir until well combined. Add the broccoli and toss until well coated. 2. Arrange the broccoli in the air fryer basket. Set the air fryer to 325ºF (163ºC) for 15 minutes, or until the broccoli is crisp, tender, and the edges are lightly browned,

gently tossing halfway through the cooking time.

Per Serving:

calories: 143 | fat: 11g | protein: 4g | carbs: 9g | fiber: 4g | sodium: 385mg

Zesty Fried Asparagus

Prep time: 3 minutes | Cook time: 10 minutes | Serves 4

Oil, for spraying	1 tablespoon granulated garlic
10 to 12 spears asparagus, trimmed	1 teaspoon chili powder
	½ teaspoon ground cumin
2 tablespoons olive oil	¼ teaspoon salt

1. Line the air fryer basket with parchment and spray lightly with oil. 2. If the asparagus are too long to fit easily in the air fryer, cut them in half. 3. Place the asparagus, olive oil, garlic, chili powder, cumin, and salt in a zip-top plastic bag, seal, and toss until evenly coated. 4. Place the asparagus in the prepared basket. 5. Roast at 390ºF (199ºC) for 5 minutes, flip, and cook for another 5 minutes, or until bright green and firm but tender.

Per Serving:

calories: 74 | fat: 7g | protein: 1g | carbs: 3g | fiber: 1g | sodium: 166mg

Roasted Eggplant

Prep time: 15 minutes | Cook time: 15 minutes | Serves 4

1 large eggplant	¼ teaspoon salt
2 tablespoons olive oil	½ teaspoon garlic powder

1. Remove top and bottom from eggplant. Slice eggplant into ¼-inch-thick round slices. 2. Brush slices with olive oil. Sprinkle with salt and garlic powder. Place eggplant slices into the air fryer basket. 3. Adjust the temperature to 390ºF (199ºC) and set the timer for 15 minutes. 4. Serve immediately.

Per Serving:

calories: 98 | fat: 7g | protein: 2g | carbs: 8g | fiber: 3g | sodium: 200mg

Steamed Vegetables

Prep time: 10 minutes | Cook time: 5 to 7 hours | Serves 6

2 pounds (907 g) fresh vegetables of your choice, sliced	¼ teaspoon freshly ground black pepper
1 teaspoon dried thyme	2 tablespoons extra-virgin olive
1 teaspoon dried rosemary	oil
1 teaspoon sea salt	

1. Put the vegetables in a slow cooker and season them with thyme, rosemary, salt, and pepper. 2. Drizzle the olive oil on top. 3. Cover the cooker and cook for 5 to 7 hours on Low heat, or until the vegetables are tender.

Per Serving:

calories: 85 | fat: 5g | protein: 1g | carbs: 11g | fiber: 3g | sodium: 442mg

Baba Ghanoush

Prep time: 15 minutes | Cook time: 2 to 4 hours | Serves 6

1 large eggplant (2 to 4 pounds / 907 g to 1.8 kg), peeled and diced
¼ cup freshly squeezed lemon juice
2 garlic cloves, minced
2 tablespoons tahini
1 teaspoon extra-virgin olive oil,
plus more as needed
¼ teaspoon sea salt, plus more as needed
⅛ teaspoon freshly ground black pepper, plus more as needed
2 tablespoons chopped fresh parsley

1. In a slow cooker, combine the eggplant, lemon juice, garlic, tahini, olive oil, salt, and pepper. Stir to mix well. 2. Cover the cooker and cook for 2 to 4 hours on Low heat. 3. Using a spoon or potato masher, mash the mixture. If you prefer a smoother texture, transfer it to a food processor and blend to your desired consistency. Taste and season with olive oil, salt, and pepper as needed. 4. Garnish with fresh parsley for serving.

Per Serving:

calories: 81 | fat: 4g | protein: 3g | carbs: 12g | fiber: 4g | sodium: 108mg

Garlicky Sautéed Zucchini with Mint

Prep time: 5 minutes | Cook time: 10 minutes | Serves 4

3 large green zucchini
3 tablespoons extra-virgin olive oil
1 large onion, chopped
3 cloves garlic, minced
1 teaspoon salt
1 teaspoon dried mint

1. Cut the zucchini into ½-inch cubes. 2. In a large skillet over medium heat, cook the olive oil, onions, and garlic for 3 minutes, stirring constantly. 3. Add the zucchini and salt to the skillet and toss to combine with the onions and garlic, cooking for 5 minutes. 4. Add the mint to the skillet, tossing to combine. Cook for another 2 minutes. Serve warm.

Per Serving:

calories: 147 | fat: 11g | protein: 4g | carbs: 12g | fiber: 3g | sodium: 607mg

Lemony Orzo

Prep time: 5 minutes | Cook time: 5 minutes | Yield 2 cups

1 cup dry orzo
1 cup halved grape tomatoes
1 (6-ounce / 170-g) bag baby spinach
2 tablespoons extra-virgin olive
oil
¼ teaspoon salt
Freshly ground black pepper
¾ cup crumbled feta cheese
1 lemon, juiced and zested

1. Bring a medium pot of water to a boil. Stir in the orzo and cook uncovered for 8 minutes. Drain the water, then return the orzo to medium heat. 2. Add in the tomatoes and spinach and cook until the spinach is wilted. Add the oil, salt, and pepper and mix well. Top the dish with feta, lemon juice, and lemon zest, then toss one or two more times and enjoy!

Per Serving:

½ cup: calories: 273 | fat: 13g | protein: 10g | carbs: 32g | fiber: 6g | sodium: 445mg

Braised Eggplant and Tomatoes

Prep time: 10 minutes | Cook time: 40 minutes | Serves 4

1 large eggplant, peeled and diced
Pinch sea salt
1 (15-ounce / 425-g) can chopped tomatoes and juices
1 cup chicken broth
2 garlic cloves, smashed
1 tablespoon Italian seasoning
1 bay leaf
Sea salt and freshly ground pepper, to taste

1. Cut the eggplant, and salt both sides to remove bitter juices. Let the eggplant sit for 20 minutes before rinsing and patting dry. 2. Dice eggplant. 3. Put eggplant, tomatoes, chicken broth, garlic, seasoning, and bay leaf in a large saucepot. 4. Bring to a boil and reduce heat to simmer. 5. Cover and simmer for about 30–40 minutes until eggplant is tender. Remove garlic cloves and bay leaf, season to taste, and serve.

Per Serving:

calories: 70 | fat: 1g | protein: 4g | carbs: 14g | fiber: 6g | sodium: 186mg

Chapter ⑧
Vegetarian Mains

Baked Mediterranean Tempeh with Tomatoes and Garlic

Prep time: 25 minutes | Cook time: 35 minutes | Serves 4

For the Tempeh:	oil
12 ounces (340 g) tempeh	1 onion, diced
¼ cup white wine	3 garlic cloves, minced
2 tablespoons extra-virgin olive oil	1 (14½-ounce / 411-g) can no-salt-added crushed tomatoes
2 tablespoons lemon juice	1 beefsteak tomato, diced
Zest of 1 lemon	1 dried bay leaf
¼ teaspoon kosher salt	1 teaspoon white wine vinegar
¼ teaspoon freshly ground black pepper	1 teaspoon lemon juice
For the Tomatoes and Garlic Sauce:	1 teaspoon dried oregano
	1 teaspoon dried thyme
1 tablespoon extra-virgin olive	¾ teaspoon kosher salt
	¼ cup basil, cut into ribbons

Make the Tempeh: 1. Place the tempeh in a medium saucepan. Add enough water to cover it by 1 to 2 inches. Bring to a boil over medium-high heat, cover, and lower heat to a simmer. Cook for 10 to 15 minutes. Remove the tempeh, pat dry, cool, and cut into 1-inch cubes. 2. In a large bowl, combine the white wine, olive oil, lemon juice, lemon zest, salt, and black pepper. Add the tempeh, cover the bowl, and put in the refrigerator for 4 hours, or up to overnight. 3. Preheat the oven to 375ºF (190ºC). Place the marinated tempeh and the marinade in a baking dish and cook for 15 minutes. Make the Tomatoes and Garlic Sauce: 4. Heat the olive oil in a large skillet over medium heat. Add the onion and sauté until transparent, 3 to 5 minutes. Add the garlic and sauté for 30 seconds. Add the crushed tomatoes, beefsteak tomato, bay leaf, vinegar, lemon juice, oregano, thyme, and salt. Mix well. Simmer for 15 minutes. 5. Add the baked tempeh to the tomato mixture and gently mix together. Garnish with the basil.

Per Serving:

calories: 330 | fat: 20g | protein: 18g | carbs: 22g | fiber: 4g | sodium: 305mg

Cheese Stuffed Zucchini

Prep time: 20 minutes | Cook time: 8 minutes | Serves 4

1 large zucchini, cut into four pieces	1 heaping tablespoon coriander, minced
2 tablespoons olive oil	2 ounces (57 g) Cheddar cheese, preferably freshly grated
1 cup Ricotta cheese, room temperature	
2 tablespoons scallions, chopped	1 teaspoon celery seeds
1 heaping tablespoon fresh parsley, roughly chopped	½ teaspoon salt
	½ teaspoon garlic pepper

1. Cook your zucchini in the air fryer basket for approximately 10 minutes at 350ºF (177ºC). Check for doneness and cook for 2-3 minutes longer if needed. 2. Meanwhile, make the stuffing by mixing the other items. 3. When your zucchini is thoroughly cooked, open them up. Divide the stuffing among all zucchini pieces and bake an additional 5 minutes.

Per Serving:

calories: 242 | fat: 20g | protein: 12g | carbs: 5g | fiber: 1g | sodium: 443mg

Quinoa with Almonds and Cranberries

Prep time: 15 minutes | Cook time: 0 minutes | Serves 4

2 cups cooked quinoa	½ teaspoon ground cumin
⅓ teaspoon cranberries or currants	½ teaspoon turmeric
¼ cup sliced almonds	¼ teaspoon ground cinnamon
2 garlic cloves, minced	¼ teaspoon freshly ground black pepper
1¼ teaspoons salt	

1. In a large bowl, toss the quinoa, cranberries, almonds, garlic, salt, cumin, turmeric, cinnamon, and pepper and stir to combine. Enjoy alone or with roasted cauliflower.

Per Serving:

calories: 194 | fat: 6g | protein: 7g | carbs: 31g | fiber: 4g | sodium: 727mg

Turkish Red Lentil and Bulgur Kofte

Prep time: 10 minutes | Cook time: 45 minutes | Serves 4

⅓ cup olive oil, plus 2 tablespoons, divided, plus more for brushing	2 tablespoons tomato paste
	1 teaspoon ground cumin
1 cup red lentils	¼ cup finely chopped flat-leaf parsley
½ cup bulgur	3 scallions, thinly sliced
1 teaspoon salt	Juice of ½ lemon
1 medium onion, finely diced	

1. Preheat the oven to 400ºF(205ºC). 2. Brush a large, rimmed baking sheet with olive oil. 3. In a medium saucepan, combine the lentils with 2 cups water and bring to a boil. Reduce the heat to low and cook, stirring occasionally, for about 15 minutes, until the lentils are tender and have soaked up most of the liquid. Remove from the heat, stir in the bulgur and salt, cover, and let sit for 15 minutes or so, until the bulgur is tender. 4. Meanwhile, heat ⅓ cup olive oil in a medium skillet over medium-high heat. Add the onion and cook, stirring frequently, until softened, about 5 minutes. Stir in the tomato paste and cook for 2 minutes more. Remove from the heat and stir in the cumin. 5. Add the cooked onion mixture to the lentil-bulgur mixture and stir to combine. Add the parsley, scallions, and lemon juice and stir to mix well. 6. Shape the mixture into walnut-sized balls and place them on the prepared baking sheet. Brush the balls with the remaining 2 tablespoons of olive oil and bake for 15 to 20 minutes, until golden brown. Serve hot.

Per Serving:

calories: 460 | fat: 25g | protein: 16g | carbs: 48g | fiber: 19g | sodium: 604mg

Cauliflower Steak with Gremolata

Prep time: 15 minutes | Cook time: 25 minutes | Serves 4

2 tablespoons olive oil	Gremolata:
1 tablespoon Italian seasoning	1 bunch Italian parsley (about 1
1 large head cauliflower, outer	cup packed)
leaves removed and sliced	2 cloves garlic
lengthwise through the core into	Zest of 1 small lemon, plus 1 to
thick "steaks"	2 teaspoons lemon juice
Salt and freshly ground black	½ cup olive oil
pepper, to taste	Salt and pepper, to taste
¼ cup Parmesan cheese	

1. Preheat the air fryer to 400ºF (204ºC). 2. In a small bowl, combine the olive oil and Italian seasoning. Brush both sides of each cauliflower "steak" generously with the oil. Season to taste with salt and black pepper. 3. Working in batches if necessary, arrange the cauliflower in a single layer in the air fryer basket. Pausing halfway through the cooking time to turn the "steaks," air fry for 15 to 20 minutes until the cauliflower is tender and the edges begin to brown. Sprinkle with the Parmesan and air fry for 5 minutes longer. 4. To make the gremolata: In a food processor fitted with a metal blade, combine the parsley, garlic, and lemon zest and juice. With the motor running, add the olive oil in a steady stream until the mixture forms a bright green sauce. Season to taste with salt and black pepper. Serve the cauliflower steaks with the gremolata spooned over the top.

Per Serving:

calories: 336 | fat: 30g | protein: 7g | carbs: 15g | fiber: 5g | sodium: 340mg

Fava Bean Purée with Chicory

Prep time: 5 minutes | Cook time: 2 hours 10 minutes | Serves 4

½ pound (227 g) dried fava	¼ cup olive oil
beans, soaked in water	1 small onion, chopped
overnight and drained	1 clove garlic, minced
1 pound (454 g) chicory leaves	Salt

1. In a saucepan, cover the fava beans by at least an inch of water and bring to a boil over medium-high heat. Reduce the heat to low, cover, and simmer until very tender, about 2 hours. Check the pot from time to time to make sure there is enough water and add more as needed. 2. Drain off any excess water and then mash the beans with a potato masher. 3. While the beans are cooking, bring a large pot of salted water to a boil. Add the chicory and cook for about 3 minutes, until tender. Drain. 4. In a medium skillet, heat the olive oil over medium-high heat. Add the onion and a pinch of salt and cook, stirring frequently, until softened and beginning to brown, about 5 minutes. Add the garlic and cook, stirring, for another minute. Transfer half of the onion mixture, along with the oil, to the bowl with the mashed beans and stir to mix. Taste and add salt as needed. 5. Serve the purée topped with some of the remaining onions and oil, with the chicory leaves on the side.

Per Serving:

calories: 336 | fat: 14g | protein: 17g | carbs: 40g | fiber: 19g | sodium: 59mg

Eggplant Parmesan

Prep time: 15 minutes | Cook time: 17 minutes | Serves 4

1 medium eggplant, ends	1 ounce (28 g) 100% cheese
trimmed, sliced into ½-inch	crisps, finely crushed
rounds	½ cup low-carb marinara sauce
¼ teaspoon salt	½ cup shredded Mozzarella
2 tablespoons coconut oil	cheese
½ cup grated Parmesan cheese	

1. Sprinkle eggplant rounds with salt on both sides and wrap in a kitchen towel for 30 minutes. Press to remove excess water, then drizzle rounds with coconut oil on both sides. 2. In a medium bowl, mix Parmesan and cheese crisps. Press each eggplant slice into mixture to coat both sides. 3. Place rounds into ungreased air fryer basket. Adjust the temperature to 350ºF (177ºC) and air fry for 15 minutes, turning rounds halfway through cooking. They will be crispy around the edges when done. 4. Spoon marinara over rounds and sprinkle with Mozzarella. Continue cooking an additional 2 minutes at 350ºF (177ºC) until cheese is melted. Serve warm.

Per Serving:

calories: 208 | fat: 13g | protein: 12g | carbs: 13g | fiber: 5g | sodium: 531mg

Balsamic Marinated Tofu with Basil and Oregano

Prep time: 10 minutes | Cook time: 30 minutes | Serves 4

¼ cup extra-virgin olive oil	½ teaspoon dried sage
¼ cup balsamic vinegar	¼ teaspoon kosher salt
2 tablespoons low-sodium soy	¼ teaspoon freshly ground black
sauce or gluten-free tamari	pepper
3 garlic cloves, grated	¼ teaspoon red pepper flakes
2 teaspoons pure maple syrup	(optional)
Zest of 1 lemon	1 (16-ounce / 454-g) block extra
1 teaspoon dried basil	firm tofu, drained and patted
1 teaspoon dried oregano	dry, cut into ½-inch or 1-inch
½ teaspoon dried thyme	cubes

1. In a bowl or gallon zip-top bag, mix together the olive oil, vinegar, soy sauce, garlic, maple syrup, lemon zest, basil, oregano, thyme, sage, salt, black pepper, and red pepper flakes, if desired. Add the tofu and mix gently. Put in the refrigerator and marinate for 30 minutes, or up to overnight if you desire. 2. Preheat the oven to 425ºF (220ºC). Line a baking sheet with parchment paper or foil. Arrange the marinated tofu in a single layer on the prepared baking sheet. Bake for 20 to 30 minutes, turning over halfway through, until slightly crispy on the outside and tender on the inside.

Per Serving:

calories: 225 | fat: 16g | protein: 13g | carbs: 9g | fiber: 2g | sodium: 265mg

Root Vegetable Soup with Garlic Aioli

Prep time: 10 minutes | Cook time 25 minutes | Serves 4

For the Soup:	1 pound (454 g) turnips, peeled
8 cups vegetable broth	and cut into 1-inch cubes
½ teaspoon salt	1 red bell pepper, cut into strips
1 medium leek, cut into thick	2 tablespoons fresh oregano
rounds	For the Aioli:
1 pound (454 g) carrots, peeled	5 garlic cloves, minced
and diced	¼ teaspoon salt
1 pound (454 g) potatoes,	⅔ cup olive oil
peeled and diced	1 drop lemon juice

1. Bring the broth and salt to a boil and add the vegetables one at a time, letting the water return to a boil after each addition. Add the carrots first, then the leeks, potatoes, turnips, and finally the red bell peppers. Let the vegetables cook for about 3 minutes after adding the green beans and bringing to a boil. The process will take about 20 minutes in total. 2. Meanwhile, make the aioli. In a mortar and pestle, grind the garlic to a paste with the salt. Using a whisk and whisking constantly, add the olive oil in a thin stream. Continue whisking until the mixture thickens to the consistency of mayonnaise. Add the lemon juice. 3. Serve the vegetables in the broth, dolloped with the aioli and garnished with the fresh oregano.

Per Serving:

calories: 538 | fat: 37g | protein: 5g | carbs: 50g | fiber: 9g | sodium: 773mg

Moroccan Vegetable Tagine

Prep time: 20 minutes | Cook time: 1 hour | Serves 6

½ cup extra-virgin olive oil	2 medium zucchini, cut into
2 medium yellow onions, sliced	½-inch-thick semicircles
6 celery stalks, sliced into	2 cups cauliflower florets
¼-inch crescents	1 (13¾-ounce / 390-g) can
6 garlic cloves, minced	artichoke hearts, drained and
1 teaspoon ground cumin	quartered
1 teaspoon ginger powder	1 cup halved and pitted green
1 teaspoon salt	olives
½ teaspoon paprika	½ cup chopped fresh flat-leaf
½ teaspoon ground cinnamon	parsley, for garnish
¼ teaspoon freshly ground black	½ cup chopped fresh cilantro
pepper	leaves, for garnish
2 cups vegetable stock	Greek yogurt, for garnish
1 medium eggplant, cut into	(optional)
1-inch cubes	

1. In a large, thick soup pot or Dutch oven, heat the olive oil over medium-high heat. Add the onion and celery and sauté until softened, 6 to 8 minutes. Add the garlic, cumin, ginger, salt, paprika, cinnamon, and pepper and sauté for another 2 minutes. 2. Add the stock and bring to a boil. Reduce the heat to low and add the eggplant, zucchini, and cauliflower. Simmer on low heat, covered, until the vegetables are tender, 30 to 35 minutes. Add the artichoke hearts and olives, cover, and simmer for another 15 minutes. 3. Serve garnished with parsley, cilantro, and Greek yogurt (if using).

Per Serving:

calories: 265 | fat: 21g | protein: 5g | carbs: 19g | fiber: 9g | sodium: 858mg

One-Pan Mushroom Pasta with Mascarpone

Prep time: 10 minutes | Cook time: 20 minutes | Serves 2

2 tablespoons olive oil	stock
1 large shallot, minced	6 ounces (170 g) dry
8 ounces (227 g) baby bella	pappardelle pasta
(cremini) mushrooms, sliced	2 tablespoons mascarpone
¼ cup dry sherry	cheese
1 teaspoon dried thyme	Salt
2 cups low-sodium vegetable	Freshly ground black pepper

1. Heat olive oil in a large sauté pan over medium-high heat. Add the shallot and mushrooms and sauté for 10 minutes, or until the mushrooms have given up much of their liquid. 2. Add the sherry, thyme, and vegetable stock. Bring the mixture to a boil. 3. Add the pasta, breaking it up as needed so it fits into the pan and is covered by the liquid. Return the mixture to a boil. Cover, and reduce the heat to medium-low. Let the pasta cook for 10 minutes, or until al dente. Stir it occasionally so it doesn't stick. If the sauce gets too dry, add some water or additional chicken stock. 4. When the pasta is tender, stir in the mascarpone cheese and season with salt and pepper. 5. The sauce will thicken up a bit when it's off the heat.

Per Serving:

calories: 517 | fat: 18g | protein: 16g | carbs: 69g | fiber: 3g | sodium: 141mg

Stuffed Portobellos

Prep time: 10 minutes | Cook time: 8 minutes | Serves 4

3 ounces (85 g) cream cheese,	leaves
softened	4 large portobello mushrooms,
½ medium zucchini, trimmed	stems removed
and chopped	2 tablespoons coconut oil,
¼ cup seeded and chopped red	melted
bell pepper	½ teaspoon salt
1½ cups chopped fresh spinach	

1. In a medium bowl, mix cream cheese, zucchini, pepper, and spinach. 2. Drizzle mushrooms with coconut oil and sprinkle with salt. Scoop ¼ zucchini mixture into each mushroom. 3. Place mushrooms into ungreased air fryer basket. Adjust the temperature to 400ºF (204ºC) and air fry for 8 minutes. Portobellos will be tender and tops will be browned when done. Serve warm.

Per Serving:

calories: 151 | fat: 13g | protein: 4g | carbs: 6g | fiber: 2g | sodium: 427mg

Roasted Veggie Bowl

Prep time: 10 minutes | Cook time: 15 minutes | Serves 2

1 cup broccoli florets	seeded and sliced ¼ inch thick
1 cup quartered Brussels sprouts	1 tablespoon coconut oil
½ cup cauliflower florets	2 teaspoons chili powder
¼ medium white onion, peeled and sliced ¼ inch thick	½ teaspoon garlic powder
½ medium green bell pepper,	½ teaspoon cumin

1. Toss all ingredients together in a large bowl until vegetables are fully coated with oil and seasoning. 2. Pour vegetables into the air fryer basket. 3. Adjust the temperature to 360ºF (182ºC) and roast for 15 minutes. 4. Shake two or three times during cooking. Serve warm.

Per Serving:

calories: 112 | fat: 8g | protein: 4g | carbs: 11g | fiber: 5g | sodium: 106mg

Asparagus and Mushroom Farrotto

Prep time: 20 minutes | Cook time: 45 minutes | Serves 2

1½ ounces (43 g) dried porcini mushrooms	ounces / 113-g)
1 cup hot water	¾ cup farro
3 cups low-sodium vegetable stock	½ cup dry white wine
2 tablespoons olive oil	½ teaspoon dried thyme
½ large onion, minced (about 1 cup)	4 ounces (113 g) asparagus, cut into ½-inch pieces (about 1 cup)
1 garlic clove	2 tablespoons grated Parmesan cheese
1 cup diced mushrooms (about 4	Salt

1. Soak the dried mushrooms in the hot water for about 15 minutes. When they're softened, drain the mushrooms, reserving the liquid. (I like to strain the liquid through a coffee filter in case there's any grit.) Mince the porcini mushrooms. 2. Add the mushroom liquid and vegetable stock to a medium saucepan and bring it to a boil. Reduce the heat to low just to keep it warm. 3. Heat the olive oil in a Dutch oven over high heat. Add the onion, garlic, and mushrooms, and sauté for 10 minutes. 4. Add the farro to the Dutch oven and sauté it for 3 minutes to toast. 5. Add the wine, thyme, and one ladleful of the hot mushroom and chicken stock. Bring it to a boil while stirring the farro. Do not cover the pot while the farro is cooking. 6. Reduce the heat to medium. When the liquid is absorbed, add another ladleful or two at a time to the pot, stirring occasionally, until the farro is cooked through. Keep an eye on the heat, to make sure it doesn't cook too quickly. 7. When the farro is al dente, add the asparagus and another ladleful of stock. Cook for another 3 to 5 minutes, or until the asparagus is softened. 8. Stir in Parmesan cheese and season with salt.

Per Serving:

calories: 341 | fat: 16g | protein: 13g | carbs: 26g | fiber: 5g | sodium: 259mg

Moroccan Red Lentil and Pumpkin Stew

Prep time: 10 minutes | Cook time: 30 minutes | Serves 4

2 tablespoons olive oil	1 pound (454 g) pumpkin, peeled, seeded, and cut into 1-inch dice
1 teaspoon ground cumin	1 red bell pepper, seeded and diced
1 teaspoon ground turmeric	
1 tablespoon curry powder	
1 large onion, diced	1½ cups red lentils, rinsed
1 teaspoon salt	6 cups vegetable broth
2 tablespoons minced fresh ginger	¼ cup chopped cilantro, for garnish
4 cloves garlic, minced	

1. Heat the olive oil in a stockpot over medium heat. Add the cumin, turmeric, and curry powder and cook, stirring, for 1 minute, until fragrant. Add the onion and salt and cook, stirring frequently, until softened, about 5 minutes. Add the ginger and garlic and cook, stirring frequently, for 2 more minutes. Stir in the pumpkin and bell pepper, and then the lentils and broth and bring to a boil. 2. Reduce the heat to low and simmer, uncovered, for about 20 minutes, until the lentils are very tender. Serve hot, garnished with cilantro.

Per Serving:

calories: 405 | fat: 9g | protein: 20g | carbs: 66g | fiber: 11g | sodium: 594mg

Linguine and Brussels Sprouts

Prep time: 10 minutes | Cook time: 25 minutes | Serves 4

8 ounces (227 g) whole-wheat linguine	sprouts, chopped
	½ cup chicken stock, as needed
⅓ cup, plus 2 tablespoons extra-virgin olive oil, divided	⅓ cup dry white wine
1 medium sweet onion, diced	½ cup shredded Parmesan cheese
2 to 3 garlic cloves, smashed	
8 ounces (227 g) Brussels	1 lemon, cut in quarters

1. Bring a large pot of water to a boil and cook the pasta according to package directions. Drain, reserving 1 cup of the pasta water. Mix the cooked pasta with 2 tablespoons of olive oil, then set aside. 2. In a large sauté pan or skillet, heat the remaining ⅓ cup of olive oil on medium heat. Add the onion to the pan and cook for about 5 minutes, until softened. Add the smashed garlic cloves and cook for 1 minute, until fragrant. 3. Add the Brussels sprouts and cook covered for 15 minutes. Add chicken stock as needed to prevent burning. Once Brussels sprouts have wilted and are fork-tender, add white wine and cook down for about 7 minutes, until reduced. 4. Add the pasta to the skillet and add the pasta water as needed. 5. Serve with the Parmesan cheese and lemon for squeezing over the dish right before eating.

Per Serving:

calories: 502 | fat: 31g | protein: 15g | carbs: 50g | fiber: 9g | sodium: 246mg

Mozzarella and Sun-Dried Portobello Mushroom Pizza

Prep time: 10 minutes | Cook time: 10 minutes | Serves 4

4 large portobello mushroom caps	4 sun-dried tomatoes
3 tablespoons extra-virgin olive oil	1 cup mozzarella cheese, divided
Salt	½ to ¾ cup low-sodium tomato sauce
Freshly ground black pepper	

1. Preheat the broiler on high. 2. On a baking sheet, drizzle the mushroom caps with the olive oil and season with salt and pepper. Broil the portobello mushrooms for 5 minutes on each side, flipping once, until tender. 3. Fill each mushroom cap with 1 sun-dried tomato, 2 tablespoons of cheese, and 2 to 3 tablespoons of sauce. Top each with 2 tablespoons of cheese. Place the caps back under the broiler for a final 2 to 3 minutes, then quarter the mushrooms and serve.

Per Serving:

calories: 218| fat: 16g | protein: 11g | carbs: 12g | fiber: 2g | sodium: 244mg

Cauliflower Rice-Stuffed Peppers

Prep time: 10 minutes | Cook time: 15 minutes | Serves 4

2 cups uncooked cauliflower rice	cheese
¾ cup drained canned petite diced tomatoes	¼ teaspoon salt
2 tablespoons olive oil	¼ teaspoon ground black pepper
1 cup shredded Mozzarella	4 medium green bell peppers, tops removed, seeded

1. In a large bowl, mix all ingredients except bell peppers. Scoop mixture evenly into peppers. 2. Place peppers into ungreased air fryer basket. Adjust the temperature to 350ºF (177ºC) and air fry for 15 minutes. Peppers will be tender and cheese will be melted when done. Serve warm.

Per Serving:

calories: 144 | fat: 7g | protein: 11g | carbs: 11g | fiber: 5g | sodium: 380mg

Vegetable Burgers

Prep time: 10 minutes | Cook time: 12 minutes | Serves 4

8 ounces (227 g) cremini mushrooms	yellow onion
2 large egg yolks	1 clove garlic, peeled and finely minced
½ medium zucchini, trimmed and chopped	½ teaspoon salt
¼ cup peeled and chopped	¼ teaspoon ground black pepper

1. Place all ingredients into a food processor and pulse twenty times until finely chopped and combined. 2. Separate mixture into four equal sections and press each into a burger shape. Place burgers into ungreased air fryer basket. Adjust the temperature to 375ºF (191ºC) and air fry for 12 minutes, turning burgers halfway through cooking. Burgers will be browned and firm when done. 3. Place burgers on a large plate and let cool 5 minutes before serving.

Per Serving:

calories: 50 | fat: 3g | protein: 3g | carbs: 4g | fiber: 1g | sodium: 299mg

Tangy Asparagus and Broccoli

Prep time: 25 minutes | Cook time: 22 minutes | Serves 4

½ pound (227 g) asparagus, cut into 1½-inch pieces	Salt and white pepper, to taste
½ pound (227 g) broccoli, cut into 1½-inch pieces	½ cup vegetable broth
2 tablespoons olive oil	2 tablespoons apple cider vinegar

1. Place the vegetables in a single layer in the lightly greased air fryer basket. Drizzle the olive oil over the vegetables. 2. Sprinkle with salt and white pepper. 3. Cook at 380ºF (193ºC) for 15 minutes, shaking the basket halfway through the cooking time. 4. Add ½ cup of vegetable broth to a saucepan; bring to a rapid boil and add the vinegar. Cook for 5 to 7 minutes or until the sauce has reduced by half. 5. Spoon the sauce over the warm vegetables and serve immediately. Bon appétit!

Per Serving:

calories: 93 | fat: 7g | protein: 3g | carbs: 6g | fiber: 3g | sodium: 89mg

Cauliflower Steaks with Olive Citrus Sauce

Prep time: 15 minutes | Cook time: 30 minutes | Serves 4

1 or 2 large heads cauliflower (at least 2 pounds / 907 g, enough for 4 portions)	Zest of 1 orange
⅓ cup extra-virgin olive oil	¼ cup black olives, pitted and chopped
¼ teaspoon kosher salt	1 tablespoon Dijon or grainy mustard
⅛ teaspoon ground black pepper	1 tablespoon red wine vinegar
Juice of 1 orange	½ teaspoon ground coriander

1. Preheat the oven to 400ºF (205ºC). Line a baking sheet with parchment paper or foil. 2. Cut off the stem of the cauliflower so it will sit upright. Slice it vertically into four thick slabs. Place the cauliflower on the prepared baking sheet. Drizzle with the olive oil, salt, and black pepper. Bake for about 30 minutes, turning over once, until tender and golden brown. 3. In a medium bowl, combine the orange juice, orange zest, olives, mustard, vinegar, and coriander; mix well. 4. Serve the cauliflower warm or at room temperature with the sauce.

Per Serving:

calories: 265 | fat: 21g | protein: 5g | carbs: 19g | fiber: 4g | sodium: 310mg

Pistachio Mint Pesto Pasta

Prep time: 10 minutes | Cook time: 10 minutes | Serves 4

8 ounces (227 g) whole-wheat pasta	shelled
1 cup fresh mint	1 garlic clove, peeled
½ cup fresh basil	½ teaspoon kosher salt
⅓ cup unsalted pistachios,	Juice of ½ lime
	⅓ cup extra-virgin olive oil

1. Cook the pasta according to the package directions. Drain, reserving ½ cup of the pasta water, and set aside. 2. In a food processor, add the mint, basil, pistachios, garlic, salt, and lime juice. Process until the pistachios are coarsely ground. Add the olive oil in a slow, steady stream and process until incorporated. 3. In a large bowl, mix the pasta with the pistachio pesto; toss well to incorporate. If a thinner, more saucy consistency is desired, add some of the reserved pasta water and toss well.

Per Serving:

calories: 420 | fat: 3g | protein: 11g | carbs: 48g | fiber: 2g | sodium: 150mg

Cheesy Cauliflower Pizza Crust

Prep time: 15 minutes | Cook time: 11 minutes | Serves 2

1 (12 ounces / 340 g) steamer bag cauliflower	2 tablespoons blanched finely ground almond flour
½ cup shredded sharp Cheddar cheese	1 teaspoon Italian blend seasoning
1 large egg	

1. Cook cauliflower according to package instructions. Remove from bag and place into cheesecloth or paper towel to remove excess water. Place cauliflower into a large bowl. 2. Add cheese, egg, almond flour, and Italian seasoning to the bowl and mix well. 3. Cut a piece of parchment to fit your air fryer basket. Press cauliflower into 6-inch round circle. Place into the air fryer basket. 4. Adjust the temperature to 360ºF (182ºC) and air fry for 11 minutes. 5. After 7 minutes, flip the pizza crust. 6. Add preferred toppings to pizza. Place back into air fryer basket and cook an additional 4 minutes or until fully cooked and golden. Serve immediately.

Per Serving:

calories: 251 | fat: 17g | protein: 15g | carbs: 12g | fiber: 5g | sodium: 375mg

Pesto Vegetable Skewers

Prep time: 30 minutes | Cook time: 8 minutes | Makes 8 skewers

1 medium zucchini, trimmed and cut into ½-inch slices	squares
½ medium yellow onion, peeled and cut into 1-inch squares	16 whole cremini mushrooms
1 medium red bell pepper, seeded and cut into 1-inch	⅓ cup basil pesto
	½ teaspoon salt
	¼ teaspoon ground black pepper

1. Divide zucchini slices, onion, and bell pepper into eight even portions. Place on 6-inch skewers for a total of eight kebabs. Add 2 mushrooms to each skewer and brush kebabs generously with pesto. 2. Sprinkle each kebab with salt and black pepper on all sides, then place into ungreased air fryer basket. Adjust the temperature to 375ºF (191ºC) and air fry for 8 minutes, turning kebabs halfway through cooking. Vegetables will be browned at the edges and tender-crisp when done. Serve warm.

Per Serving:

calories: 75 | fat: 6g | protein: 3g | carbs: 4g | fiber: 1g | sodium: 243mg

Parmesan Artichokes

Prep time: 10 minutes | Cook time: 10 minutes | Serves 4

2 medium artichokes, trimmed and quartered, center removed	Parmesan cheese
2 tablespoons coconut oil	¼ cup blanched finely ground almond flour
1 large egg, beaten	½ teaspoon crushed red pepper flakes
½ cup grated vegetarian	

1. In a large bowl, toss artichokes in coconut oil and then dip each piece into the egg. 2. Mix the Parmesan and almond flour in a large bowl. Add artichoke pieces and toss to cover as completely as possible, sprinkle with pepper flakes. Place into the air fryer basket. 3. Adjust the temperature to 400ºF (204ºC) and air fry for 10 minutes. 4. Toss the basket two times during cooking. Serve warm.

Per Serving:

calories: 207 | fat: 13g | protein: 10g | carbs: 15g | fiber: 5g | sodium: 211mg

Pesto Spinach Flatbread

Prep time: 10 minutes | Cook time: 8 minutes | Serves 4

1 cup blanched finely ground almond flour	cheese
2 ounces (57 g) cream cheese	1 cup chopped fresh spinach leaves
2 cups shredded Mozzarella	2 tablespoons basil pesto

1. Place flour, cream cheese, and Mozzarella in a large microwave-safe bowl and microwave on high 45 seconds, then stir. 2. Fold in spinach and microwave an additional 15 seconds. Stir until a soft dough ball forms. 3. Cut two pieces of parchment paper to fit air fryer basket. Separate dough into two sections and press each out on ungreased parchment to create 6-inch rounds. 4. Spread 1 tablespoon pesto over each flatbread and place rounds on parchment into ungreased air fryer basket. Adjust the temperature to 350ºF (177ºC) and air fry for 8 minutes, turning crusts halfway through cooking. Flatbread will be golden when done. 5. Let cool 5 minutes before slicing and serving.

Per Serving:

calories: 387 | fat: 28g | protein: 28g | carbs: 10g | fiber: 5g | sodium: 556mg

Grilled Eggplant Stacks

Prep time: 20 minutes | Cook time: 10 minutes | Serves 2

1 medium eggplant, cut crosswise into 8 slices	2 tablespoons olive oil
¼ teaspoon salt	1 large tomato, cut into 4 slices
1 teaspoon Italian herb seasoning mix	4 (1-ounce / 28-g) slices of buffalo mozzarella
	Fresh basil, for garnish

1. Place the eggplant slices in a colander set in the sink or over a bowl. Sprinkle both sides with the salt. Let the eggplant sit for 15 minutes. 2. While the eggplant is resting, heat the grill to medium-high heat (about 350ºF / 180ºC). 3. Pat the eggplant dry with paper towels and place it in a mixing bowl. Sprinkle it with the Italian herb seasoning mix and olive oil. Toss well to coat. 4. Grill the eggplant for 5 minutes, or until it has grill marks and is lightly charred. Flip each eggplant slice over, and grill on the second side for another 5 minutes. 5. Flip the eggplant slices back over and top four of the slices with a slice of tomato and a slice of mozzarella. Top each stack with one of the remaining four slices of eggplant. 6. Turn the grill down to low and cover it to let the cheese melt. Check after 30 seconds and remove when the cheese is soft and mostly melted. 7. Sprinkle with fresh basil slices.

Per Serving:

calories: 354 | fat: 29g | protein: 13g | carbs: 19g | fiber: 9g | sodium: 340mg

Kate's Warm Mediterranean Farro Bowl

Prep time: 15 minutes | Cook time: 10 minutes | Serves 4 to 6

⅓ cup extra-virgin olive oil	Salt
½ cup chopped red bell pepper	Freshly ground black pepper
⅓ cup chopped red onions	¼ cup sliced olives, for serving (optional)
2 garlic cloves, minced	
1 cup zucchini, cut in ½-inch slices	½ cup crumbled feta cheese, for serving (optional)
½ cup canned chickpeas, drained and rinsed	2 tablespoons fresh basil, chiffonade, for serving (optional)
½ cup coarsely chopped artichokes	
3 cups cooked farro	3 tablespoons balsamic reduction, for serving (optional)

1. In a large sauté pan or skillet, heat the oil over medium heat and sauté the pepper, onions, and garlic for about 5 minutes, until tender. 2. Add the zucchini, chickpeas, and artichokes, then stir and continue to sauté vegetables, approximately 5 more minutes, until just soft. 3. Stir in the cooked farro, tossing to combine and cooking enough to heat through. Season with salt and pepper and remove from the heat. 4. Transfer the contents of the pan into the serving vessels or bowls.

5. Top with olives, feta, and basil (if using). Drizzle with balsamic reduction (if using) to finish.

Per Serving:

calories: 367 | fat: 20g | protein: 9g | carbs: 51g | fiber: 9g | sodium: 87mg

Herbed Ricotta–Stuffed Mushrooms

Prep time: 10 minutes | Cook time: 30 minutes | Serves 4

6 tablespoons extra-virgin olive oil, divided	(such as basil, parsley, rosemary, oregano, or thyme)
4 portobello mushroom caps, cleaned and gills removed	2 garlic cloves, finely minced
	½ teaspoon salt
1 cup whole-milk ricotta cheese	¼ teaspoon freshly ground black pepper
⅓ cup chopped fresh herbs	

1. Preheat the oven to 400ºF (205ºC). 2. Line a baking sheet with parchment or foil and drizzle with 2 tablespoons olive oil, spreading evenly. Place the mushroom caps on the baking sheet, gill-side up. 3. In a medium bowl, mix together the ricotta, herbs, 2 tablespoons olive oil, garlic, salt, and pepper. Stuff each mushroom cap with one-quarter of the cheese mixture, pressing down if needed. Drizzle with remaining 2 tablespoons olive oil and bake until golden brown and the mushrooms are soft, 30 to 35 minutes, depending on the size of the mushrooms.

Per Serving:

calories: 308 | fat: 29g | protein: 9g | carbs: 6g | fiber: 1g | sodium: 351mg

Tortellini in Red Pepper Sauce

Prep time: 15 minutes | Cook time: 10 minutes | Serves 4

1 (16-ounce / 454-g) container fresh cheese tortellini (usually green and white pasta)	1 teaspoon garlic powder
	¼ cup tahini
	1 tablespoon red pepper oil (optional)
1 (16-ounce / 454-g) jar roasted red peppers, drained	

1. Bring a large pot of water to a boil and cook the tortellini according to package directions. 2. In a blender, combine the red peppers with the garlic powder and process until smooth. Once blended, add the tahini until the sauce is thickened. If the sauce gets too thick, add up to 1 tablespoon red pepper oil (if using). 3. Once tortellini are cooked, drain and leave pasta in colander. Add the sauce to the bottom of the empty pot and heat for 2 minutes. Then, add the tortellini back into the pot and cook for 2 more minutes. Serve and enjoy!

Per Serving:

calories: 350 | fat: 11g | protein: 12g | carbs: 46g | fiber: 4g | sodium: 192mg

Chapter 9
Snacks and Appetizers

Italian Crepe with Herbs and Onion

Prep time: 15 minutes | Cook time: 20 minutes per crepe | Serves 6

2 cups cold water	olive oil, divided
1 cup chickpea flour	½ onion, julienned
½ teaspoon kosher salt	½ cup fresh herbs, chopped
¼ teaspoon freshly ground black	(thyme, sage, and rosemary
pepper	are all nice on their own or as
3½ tablespoons extra-virgin	a mix)

1. In a large bowl, whisk together the water, flour, salt, and black pepper. Add 2 tablespoons of the olive oil and whisk. Let the batter sit at room temperature for at least 30 minutes. 2. Preheat the oven to 450ºF (235ºC). Place a 12-inch cast-iron pan or oven-safe skillet in the oven to warm as the oven comes to temperature. 3. Remove the hot pan from the oven carefully, add ½ tablespoon of the olive oil and one-third of the onion, stir, and place the pan back in the oven. Cook, stirring occasionally, until the onions are golden brown, 5 to 8 minutes. 4. Remove the pan from the oven and pour in one-third of the batter (about 1 cup), sprinkle with one-third of the herbs, and put it back in the oven. Bake for 10 minutes, or until firm and the edges are set. 5. Increase the oven setting to broil and cook 3 to 5 minutes, or until golden brown. Slide the crepe onto the cutting board and repeat twice more. Halve the crepes and cut into wedges. Serve warm or at room temperature.

Per Serving:

calories: 135 | fat: 9g | protein: 4g | carbs: 11g | fiber: 2g | sodium: 105mg

Grilled North African Spice-Kissed Sweet Potatoes

Prep time: 5 minutes | Cook time: 20 minutes | Serves 8

¼ cup olive oil	2 pounds (907 g) sweet
3 cloves garlic, mashed to a	potatoes, scrubbed and cut into
paste	½'-thick wedges
1 teaspoon kosher salt	¼ cup finely chopped fresh flat-
1 teaspoon ground cumin	leaf parsley
½ teaspoon ground coriander	¼ cup pitted kalamata olives,
¼ teaspoon ground cinnamon	slivered
Pinch of cayenne pepper	

1. Coat a grill rack or grill pan with olive oil and prepare the grill to medium-high heat. 2. In a large bowl, combine the oil, garlic, salt, cumin, coriander, cinnamon, and pepper. Toss in the sweet potato wedges until completely coated. 3. Grill the sweet potatoes until pronounced grill marks form on all sides and the wedges are completely tender, 3 to 6 minutes per side. 4. Transfer to a serving platter. Pour any remaining oil from the bowl over the potatoes and top with the parsley and olives.

Per Serving:

calories: 179 | fat: 10g | protein: 2g | carbs: 22g | fiber: 4g | sodium: 466mg

Roasted Pepper Bruschetta with Capers and Basil

Prep time: 10 minutes | Cook time: 15 minutes | Serves 6 to 8

2 red bell peppers	3 tablespoons red wine vinegar
2 yellow bell peppers	1 teaspoon Dijon mustard
2 orange bell peppers	1 clove garlic, minced
2 tablespoons olive oil, plus ¼	2 tablespoons capers, drained
cup	¼ cup chopped fresh basil
¾ teaspoon salt, divided	leaves, divided
½ teaspoon freshly ground black	1 whole-wheat baguette or other
pepper, divided	crusty bread, thinly sliced

1. Preheat the broiler to high and line a large baking sheet with aluminum foil. 2. Brush the peppers all over with 2 tablespoons of the olive oil and sprinkle with ½ teaspoon of the salt and ¼ teaspoon of the pepper. 3. Broil the peppers, turning every 3 minutes or so, until the skin is charred on all sides. Place them in a bowl, cover with plastic wrap, and let steam for 10 minutes. Slip the skins off and discard them. Seed and dice the peppers. 4. In a large bowl, whisk together the vinegar, mustard, garlic, the remaining ¼ teaspoon salt, and the remaining ¼ teaspoon of pepper. Still whisking, slowly add the remaining ¼ cup oil in a thin stream until the dressing is emulsified. Stir in the capers, 2 tablespoons of the basil, and the diced peppers. 5. Toast the bread slices and then spoon the pepper mixture over them, drizzling with extra dressing. Garnish with the remaining basil and serve immediately.

Per Serving:

calories: 243 | fat: 6g | protein: 8g | carbs: 39g | fiber: 4g | sodium: 755mg

Spanish Home Fries with Spicy Tomato Sauce

Prep time: 5 minutes | Cook time: 1 hour | Serves 6

4 russet potatoes, peeled, cut	1 teaspoon hot smoked paprika
into large dice	1 serrano chile, seeded and
¼ cup olive oil plus 1	chopped
tablespoon, divided	½ teaspoon salt
½ cup crushed tomatoes	¼ teaspoon freshly ground black
1½ teaspoons red wine	pepper

1. Preheat the oven to 425°F(220ºC). 2. Toss the potatoes with ¼ cup of olive oil and spread on a large baking sheet. Season with salt and pepper and roast in the preheated oven for about 50 to 60 minutes, turning once in the middle, until the potatoes are golden brown and crisp. 3. Meanwhile, make the sauce by combining the tomatoes, the remaining 1 tablespoon olive oil, wine, paprika, chile, salt, and pepper in a food processor or blender and process until smooth. 4. Serve the potatoes hot with the sauce on the side for dipping or spooned over the top.

Per Serving:

calories: 201 | fat: 11g | protein: 3g | carbs: 25g | fiber: 4g | sodium: 243mg

Fig-Pecan Energy Bites

Prep time: 20 minutes |Cook time: 0 minutes| Serves: 6

¾ cup diced dried figs (6 to 8)	or wheat germ (flaxseed for gluten-free)
½ cup chopped pecans	
¼ cup rolled oats (old-fashioned or quick oats)	2 tablespoons powdered or regular peanut butter
2 tablespoons ground flaxseed	2 tablespoons honey

1. In a medium bowl, mix together the figs, pecans, oats, flaxseed, and peanut butter. Drizzle with the honey, and mix everything together. A wooden spoon works well to press the figs and nuts into the honey and powdery ingredients. (If you're using regular peanut butter instead of powdered, the dough will be stickier to handle, so freeze the dough for 5 minutes before making the bites.) 2. Divide the dough evenly into four sections in the bowl. Dampen your hands with water—but don't get them too wet or the dough will stick to them. Using your hands, roll three bites out of each of the four sections of dough, making 12 total energy bites. 3. Enjoy immediately or chill in the freezer for 5 minutes to firm up the bites before serving. The bites can be stored in a sealed container in the refrigerator for up to 1 week.

Per Serving:

calories: 196 | fat: 10g | protein: 4g | carbs: 26g | fiber: 4g | sodium: 13mg

Fried Baby Artichokes with Lemon-Garlic Aioli

Prep time: 5 minutes | Cook time: 50 minutes | Serves 10

Artichokes:	2 cloves garlic, chopped
15 baby artichokes	1 tablespoon fresh lemon juice
½ lemon	½ teaspoon Dijon mustard
3 cups olive oil	½ cup olive oil
Kosher salt, to taste	Kosher salt and ground black pepper, to taste
Aioli:	
1 egg	

1. Make the Artichokes: Wash and drain the artichokes. With a paring knife, strip off the coarse outer leaves around the base and stalk, leaving the softer leaves on. Carefully peel the stalks and trim off all but 2' below the base. Slice off the top ½' of the artichokes. Cut each artichoke in half. Rub the cut surfaces with a lemon half to keep from browning. 2. In a medium saucepan fitted with a deep-fry thermometer over medium heat, warm the oil to about 280°F(138°C). Working in batches, cook the artichokes in the hot oil until tender, about 15 minutes. Using a slotted spoon, remove and drain on a paper towel–lined plate. Repeat with all the artichoke halves. 3. Increase the heat of the oil to 375°F(190°C). In batches, cook the precooked baby artichokes until browned at the edges and crisp, about 1 minute. Transfer to a paper towel–lined plate. Season with the salt to taste. Repeat with the remaining artichokes. 4. Make the aioli: In a blender, pulse together the egg, garlic, lemon juice, and mustard until combined. With the blender running, slowly drizzle in the oil a few drops at a time until the mixture thickens like mayonnaise, about 2 minutes. Transfer to a bowl and season to taste with the salt and pepper. 5. Serve the warm artichokes with the aioli on the side.

Per Serving:

calories: 236 | fat: 17g | protein: 6g | carbs: 21g | fiber: 10g | sodium: 283mg

Vegetable Pot Stickers

Prep time: 12 minutes | Cook time: 11 to 18 minutes | Makes 12 pot stickers

1 cup shredded red cabbage	2 garlic cloves, minced
¼ cup chopped button mushrooms	2 teaspoons grated fresh ginger
¼ cup grated carrot	12 gyoza/pot sticker wrappers
2 tablespoons minced onion	2½ teaspoons olive oil, divided

1. In a baking pan, combine the red cabbage, mushrooms, carrot, onion, garlic, and ginger. Add 1 tablespoon of water. Place in the air fryer and air fry at 370°F (188°C) for 3 to 6 minutes, until the vegetables are crisp-tender. Drain and set aside. 2. Working one at a time, place the pot sticker wrappers on a work surface. Top each wrapper with a scant 1 tablespoon of the filling. Fold half of the wrapper over the other half to form a half circle. Dab one edge with water and press both edges together. 3. To another pan, add 1¼ teaspoons of olive oil. Put half of the pot stickers, seam-side up, in the pan. Air fry for 5 minutes, or until the bottoms are light golden brown. Add 1 tablespoon of water and return the pan to the air fryer. 4. Air fry for 4 to 6 minutes more, or until hot. Repeat with the remaining pot stickers, remaining 1¼ teaspoons of oil, and another tablespoon of water. Serve immediately.

Per Serving:

1 pot stickers: calories: 36 | fat: 1g | protein: 1g | carbs: 6g | fiber: 0g | sodium: 49mg

Greek Street Tacos

Prep time: 10 minutes | Cook time: 3 minutes | Makes 8 small tacos

8 small flour tortillas (4-inch diameter)	cheese
8 tablespoons hummus	4 tablespoons chopped kalamata or other olives (optional)
4 tablespoons crumbled feta	Olive oil for misting

1. Place 1 tablespoon of hummus or tapenade in the center of each tortilla. Top with 1 teaspoon of feta crumbles and 1 teaspoon of chopped olives, if using. 2. Using your finger or a small spoon, moisten the edges of the tortilla all around with water. 3. Fold tortilla over to make a half-moon shape. Press center gently. Then press the edges firmly to seal in the filling. 4. Mist both sides with olive oil. 5. Place in air fryer basket very close but try not to overlap. 6. Air fry at 390°F (199°C) for 3 minutes, just until lightly browned and crispy.

Per Serving:

1 taco: calories: 127 | fat: 4g | protein: 4g | carbs: 19g | fiber: 1g | sodium: 292mg

Buffalo Bites

Prep time: 15 minutes | Cook time: 11 to 12 minutes per batch | Makes 16 meatballs

1½ cups cooked jasmine or sushi rice	sauce
¼ teaspoon salt	2 ounces (57 g) Gruyère cheese, cut into 16 cubes
1 pound (454 g) ground chicken	1 tablespoon maple syrup
8 tablespoons buffalo wing	

1. Mix 4 tablespoons buffalo wing sauce into all the ground chicken. 2. Shape chicken into a log and divide into 16 equal portions. 3. With slightly damp hands, mold each chicken portion around a cube of cheese and shape into a firm ball. When you have shaped 8 meatballs, place them in air fryer basket. 4. Air fry at 390°F (199°C) for approximately 5 minutes. Shake basket, reduce temperature to 360°F (182°C), and cook for 5 to 6 minutes longer. 5. While the first batch is cooking, shape remaining chicken and cheese into 8 more meatballs. 6. Repeat step 4 to cook second batch of meatballs. 7. In a medium bowl, mix the remaining 4 tablespoons of buffalo wing sauce with the maple syrup. Add all the cooked meatballs and toss to coat. 8. Place meatballs back into air fryer basket and air fry at 390°F (199°C) for 2 to 3 minutes to set the glaze. Skewer each with a toothpick and serve.

Per Serving:

calories: 85 | fat: 4g | protein: 7g | carbs: 6g | fiber: 0g | sodium: 236mg

Pea and Arugula Crostini with Pecorino Romano

Prep time: 10 minutes | Cook time: 15 minutes | Serves 6 to 8

1½ cups fresh or frozen peas	½ teaspoon salt
1 loaf crusty whole-wheat bread, cut into thin slices	¼ teaspoon freshly ground black pepper
3 tablespoons olive oil, divided	1 cup (packed) baby arugula
1 small garlic clove, finely mined or pressed	¼ cup thinly shaved Pecorino Romano
Juice of ½ lemon	

1. Preheat the oven to 350°F(180°C). 2. Fill a small saucepan with about ½ inch of water. Bring to a boil over medium-high heat. Add the peas and cook for 3 to 5 minutes, until tender. Drain and rinse with cold water. 3. Arrange the bread slices on a large baking sheet and brush the tops with 2 tablespoons olive oil. Bake in the preheated oven for about 8 minutes, until golden brown. 4. Meanwhile, in a medium bowl, mash the peas gently with the back of a fork. They should be smashed but not mashed into a paste. Add the remaining 1 tablespoon olive oil, lemon juice, garlic, salt, and pepper and stir to mix. 5. Spoon the pea mixture onto the toasted bread slices and top with the arugula and cheese. Serve immediately.

Per Serving:

calories: 301 | fat: 13g | protein: 14g | carbs: 32g | fiber: 6g | sodium: 833mg

Marinated Olives

Prep time: 5 minutes | Cook time: 5 minutes | Serves 8 to 10

3 tablespoons olive oil	1 cup pitted Kalamata olives
Zest and juice of 1 lemon	1 cup pitted green olives, such as Castelvetrano
½ teaspoon Aleppo pepper or red pepper flakes	2 tablespoons finely chopped fresh parsley
¼ teaspoon ground sumac	

1. In a medium skillet, heat the olive oil over medium heat. Add the lemon zest, Aleppo pepper, and sumac and cook for 1 to 2 minutes, occasionally stirring, until fragrant. Remove from the heat and stir in the olives, lemon juice, and parsley. 2. Transfer the olives to a bowl and serve immediately, or let cool, then transfer to an airtight container and store in the refrigerator for up to 1 week. The flavor will continue to develop and is best after 8 to 12 hours.

Per Serving:

1 cup: calories: 59 | fat: 6g | protein: 0g | carbs: 1g | fiber: 1g | sodium: 115mg

Loaded Vegetable Pita Pizzas with Tahini Sauce

Prep time: 5 minutes | Cook time: 12 minutes | Serves 2

2 (6-inch) pita breads	2 teaspoons extra virgin olive oil
4 canned artichoke hearts, chopped	Pinch of kosher salt
¼ cup chopped tomato (any variety)	Juice of 1 lemon
¼ cup chopped onion (any variety)	Tahini Sauce:
4 Kalamata olives, pitted and sliced	2 tablespoons tahini
	2 tablespoons fresh lemon juice
	1 tablespoon water
4 green olives, pitted and sliced	1 garlic clove, minced
2 teaspoons pine nuts	Pinch of freshly ground black pepper

1. Preheat the oven to 400°F (205°C) and line a large baking sheet with wax paper. 2. Make the tahini sauce by combining the tahini and lemon juice in a small bowl. While stirring rapidly, begin adding the water, garlic, and black pepper. Continue stirring rapidly until the ingredients are well combined and smooth. 3. Place the pita breads on the prepared baking sheet. Spread about 1 tablespoon of the tahini sauce over the top of each pita and then top each pita with the chopped artichoke hearts, 2 tablespoons of the tomatoes, 2 tablespoons of the onions, half of the sliced Kalamata olives, half of the green olives, and 1 teaspoon of the pine nuts. 4. Transfer the pizzas to the oven and bake for 12 minutes or until the edges of the pita breads turn golden and crunchy. 5. Drizzle 1 teaspoon of the olive oil over each pizza, then sprinkle a pinch of kosher salt over the top followed by a squeeze of lemon. Cut the pizzas into quarters. Store covered in the refrigerator for up to 2 days.

Per Serving:

calories: 381 | fat: 17g | protein: 15g | carbs: 52g | fiber: 19g | sodium: 553mg

Mexican Potato Skins

Prep time: 10 minutes | Cook time: 55 minutes | Serves 6

Olive oil	beans
6 medium russet potatoes, scrubbed	1 tablespoon taco seasoning
	½ cup salsa
Salt and freshly ground black pepper, to taste	¾ cup reduced-fat shredded Cheddar cheese
1 cup fat-free refried black	

1. Spray the air fryer basket lightly with olive oil. 2. Spray the potatoes lightly with oil and season with salt and pepper. Pierce each potato a few times with a fork. 3. Place the potatoes in the air fryer basket. Air fry at 400ºF (204ºC) until fork-tender, 30 to 40 minutes. The cooking time will depend on the size of the potatoes. You can cook the potatoes in the microwave or a standard oven, but they won't get the same lovely crispy skin they will get in the air fryer. 4. While the potatoes are cooking, in a small bowl, mix together the beans and taco seasoning. Set aside until the potatoes are cool enough to handle. 5. Cut each potato in half lengthwise. Scoop out most of the insides, leaving about ¼ inch in the skins so the potato skins hold their shape. 6. Season the insides of the potato skins with salt and black pepper. Lightly spray the insides of the potato skins with oil. You may need to cook them in batches. 7. Place them into the air fryer basket, skin-side down, and air fry until crisp and golden, 8 to 10 minutes. 8. Transfer the skins to a work surface and spoon ½ tablespoon of seasoned refried black beans into each one. Top each with 2 teaspoons salsa and 1 tablespoon shredded Cheddar cheese. 9. Place filled potato skins in the air fryer basket in a single layer. Lightly spray with oil. 10. Air fry until the cheese is melted and bubbly, 2 to 3 minutes.

Per Serving:

calories: 239 | fat: 2g | protein: 10g | carbs: 46g | fiber: 5g | sodium: 492mg

Cheese-Stuffed Dates

Prep time: 10 minutes | Cook time: 10 minutes | Serves 4

2 ounces (57 g) low-fat cream cheese, at room temperature	¼ teaspoon kosher salt
	⅛ teaspoon ground black pepper
2 tablespoons sweet pickle relish	Dash of hot sauce
	2 tablespoons pistachios, chopped
1 tablespoon low-fat plain Greek yogurt	8 Medjool dates, pitted and halved
1 teaspoon finely chopped fresh chives	

1. In a small bowl, stir together the cream cheese, relish, yogurt, chives, salt, pepper, and hot sauce. 2. Put the pistachios on a clean plate. Put the cream cheese mixture into a resealable plastic bag, and snip off 1 corner of the bag. Pipe the cream cheese mixture into the date halves and press the tops into the pistachios to coat.

Per Serving:

calories: 196 | fat: 4g | protein: 3g | carbs: 41g | fiber: 4g | sodium:

294mg

Spicy Roasted Potatoes

Prep time: 20 minutes | Cook time: 25 minutes | Serves 5

1½ pounds (680 g) red potatoes or gold potatoes	½ cup fresh cilantro, chopped
3 tablespoons garlic, minced	½ teaspoon freshly ground black pepper
1½ teaspoons salt	¼ teaspoon cayenne pepper
¼ cup extra-virgin olive oil	3 tablespoons lemon juice

1. Preheat the oven to 450°F(235ºC). 2. Scrub the potatoes and pat dry. 3. Cut the potatoes into ½-inch pieces and put them into a bowl. 4. Add the garlic, salt, and olive oil and toss everything together to evenly coat. 5. Pour the potato mixture onto a baking sheet, spread the potatoes out evenly, and put them into the oven, roasting for 25 minutes. Halfway through roasting, turn the potatoes with a spatula; continue roasting for the remainder of time until the potato edges start to brown. 6. Remove the potatoes from the oven and let them cool on the baking sheet for 5 minutes. 7. Using a spatula, remove the potatoes from the pan and put them into a bowl. 8. Add the cilantro, black pepper, cayenne, and lemon juice to the potatoes and toss until well mixed. 9. Serve warm.

Per Serving:

calories: 203 | fat: 11g | protein: 3g | carbs: 24g | fiber: 3g | sodium: 728mg

Sardine and Herb Bruschetta

Prep time: 5 minutes | Cook time: 10 minutes | Serves 4

8 (1-inch) thick whole-grain baguette slices	2 tablespoons capers, drained
	3 tablespoons finely chopped onion (any variety)
1½ tablespoons extra virgin olive oil	½ teaspoon dried oregano
4 ounces (113 g) olive oil–packed sardines	1 tablespoon finely chopped fresh mint
2 tablespoons fresh lemon juice	1 garlic clove, halved
1 teaspoon red wine vinegar	

1. Preheat the oven to 400°F (205ºC). 2. Place the baguette slices on a large baking sheet and brush them with the olive oil. Transfer to the oven and toast until the slices are golden, about 10 minutes. 3. While the baguette slices are toasting, make the sardine topping by combining the sardines, lemon juice, and vinegar in a medium bowl. Mash with a fork. Add the capers, onions, oregano, and mint, and stir to combine. 4. When the baguette slices are done toasting, remove them from the oven and rub them with the garlic. 5. Transfer the slices to a serving platter. Place 1 heaping tablespoon of the topping onto each baguette slice. Store the sardine topping in the refrigerator for up to 3 days.

Per Serving:

calories: 249 | fat: 11g | protein: 14g | carbs: 24g | fiber: 4g | sodium: 387mg

Burrata Caprese Stack

Prep time: 5 minutes | Cook time: 0 minutes | Serves 4

1 large organic tomato, preferably heirloom	cheese
½ teaspoon salt	8 fresh basil leaves, thinly sliced
¼ teaspoon freshly ground black pepper	2 tablespoons extra-virgin olive oil
1 (4 ounces / 113 g) ball burrata	1 tablespoon red wine or balsamic vinegar

1. Slice the tomato into 4 thick slices, removing any tough center core and sprinkle with salt and pepper. Place the tomatoes, seasoned-side up, on a plate. 2. On a separate rimmed plate, slice the burrata into 4 thick slices and place one slice on top of each tomato slice. Top each with one-quarter of the basil and pour any reserved burrata cream from the rimmed plate over top. 3. Drizzle with olive oil and vinegar and serve with a fork and knife.

Per Serving:

calories: 109 | fat: 7g | protein: 9g | carbs: 3g | fiber: 1g | sodium: 504mg

Salmon Niçoise Salad with Dijon-Chive Dressing

Prep time: 10 minutes | Cook time: 20 minutes | Serves 4

1 pound (454 g) baby or fingerling potatoes	1 tablespoon, plus 1 teaspoon finely chopped fresh chives
½ pound (227 g) green beans	1 head romaine lettuce, sliced cross-wise
6 tablespoons olive oil	2 hard-boiled eggs, quartered
4 (4-ounce / 113-g) salmon fillets	¼ cup Niçoise or other small black olives
¼ teaspoon freshly ground black pepper	1 cup cherry tomatoes, quartered
2 teaspoons Dijon mustard	
3 tablespoons red wine vinegar	

1. Put potatoes in a large saucepan and add cold water to cover. Bring the water to a boil, then reduce the heat to maintain a simmer and cook for 12 to 15 minutes, until fork-tender. Drain and set aside until cool enough to handle, then cut into cubes. Set aside. 2. Meanwhile, bring a medium saucepan of water to a boil. Add the green beans and cook for 3 minutes. Drain and rinse with cold water to stop the cooking. Set aside. 3. In a large skillet, heat 1 tablespoon of the olive oil over medium-high heat. Season the salmon with pepper. Add the salmon to the pan and cook for 4 to 5 minutes on each side. Transfer to a platter; keep warm. 4. In a small bowl, whisk together the mustard, vinegar, 1 tablespoon of chives, and remaining 5 tablespoons olive oil. 5. Divide the lettuce evenly among four plates. Add 1 salmon fillet to each plate. Divide the potatoes, green beans, eggs, olives, and tomatoes among the plates and drizzle with the dressing. 6.Sprinkle with the remaining 1 teaspoon chives and serve.

Per Serving:

1 cup: calories: 398 | fat: 25g | protein: 15g | carbs: 30g | fiber: 8g | sodium: 173mg

Croatian Red Pepper Dip

Prep time: 10 minutes | Cook time: 30 minutes | Serves 4 to 6

4 or 5 medium red bell peppers	½ teaspoon freshly ground black pepper, divided
1 medium eggplant (about ¾ pound / 340 g)	4 cloves garlic, minced
¼ cup olive oil, divided	1 tablespoon white vinegar
1 teaspoon salt, divided	

1. Preheat the broiler to high. 2. Line a large baking sheet with aluminum foil. 3. Brush the peppers and eggplant all over with 2 tablespoons of the olive oil and sprinkle with ½ teaspoon of the salt and ¼ teaspoon of the pepper. Place the peppers and the eggplant on the prepared baking sheet and broil, turning every few minutes, until the skins are charred on all sides. The peppers will take about 10 minutes and the eggplant will take about 20 minutes. 4. When the peppers are fully charred, remove them from the baking sheet, place them in a bowl, cover with plastic wrap, and let them steam while the eggplant continues to cook. When the eggplant is fully charred and soft in the center, remove it from the oven and set aside to cool. 5. When the peppers are cool enough to handle, slip the charred skins off. Discard the charred skins. Seed the peppers and place them in a food processor. 6. Add the garlic to the food processor and pulse until the vegetables are coarsely chopped. Add the rest of the olive oil, the vinegar, and remaining ½ teaspoon of salt and process to a smooth purée. 7. Transfer the vegetable mixture to a medium saucepan and bring to a simmer over medium-high heat. Lower the heat to medium-low and let simmer, stirring occasionally, for 30 minutes. Remove from the heat and cool to room temperature. Serve at room temperature.

Per Serving:

calories: 144 | fat: 11g | protein: 2g | carbs: 12g | fiber: 5g | sodium: 471mg

Black Bean Corn Dip

Prep time: 10 minutes | Cook time: 10 minutes | Serves 4

½ (15 ounces / 425 g) can black beans, drained and rinsed	¼ cup shredded reduced-fat Cheddar cheese
½ (15 ounces / 425 g) can corn, drained and rinsed	½ teaspoon ground cumin
¼ cup chunky salsa	½ teaspoon paprika
2 ounces (57 g) reduced-fat cream cheese, softened	Salt and freshly ground black pepper, to taste

1. Preheat the air fryer to 325°F (163°C). 2. In a medium bowl, mix together the black beans, corn, salsa, cream cheese, Cheddar cheese, cumin, and paprika. Season with salt and pepper and stir until well combined. 3. Spoon the mixture into a baking dish. 4. Place baking dish in the air fryer basket and bake until heated through, about 10 minutes. 5. Serve hot.

Per Serving:

calories: 119 | fat: 2g | protein: 8g | carbs: 19g | fiber: 6g | sodium: 469mg

Sfougato

Prep time: 10 minutes | Cook time: 8 minutes | Serves 4

½ cup crumbled feta cheese
¼ cup bread crumbs
1 medium onion, peeled and minced
4 tablespoons all-purpose flour
2 tablespoons minced fresh mint

½ teaspoon salt
½ teaspoon ground black pepper
1 tablespoon dried thyme
6 large eggs, beaten
1 cup water

1. In a medium bowl, mix cheese, bread crumbs, onion, flour, mint, salt, pepper, and thyme. Stir in eggs. 2. Spray an 8" round baking dish with nonstick cooking spray. Pour egg mixture into dish. 3. Place rack in the Instant Pot® and add water. Fold a long piece of foil in half lengthwise. Lay foil over rack to form a sling and top with dish. Cover loosely with foil. Close lid, set steam release to Sealing, press the Manual button, and set time to 8 minutes. 4. When the timer beeps, quick-release the pressure until the float valve drops. Open lid. Let stand 5 minutes, then remove dish from pot.

Per Serving:
calories: 226 | fat: 12g | protein: 14g | carbs: 15g | fiber: 1g | sodium: 621mg

Sea Salt Potato Chips

Prep time: 30 minutes | Cook time: 27 minutes | Serves 4

Oil, for spraying
4 medium yellow potatoes

1 tablespoon oil
⅛ to ¼ teaspoon fine sea salt

1. Line the air fryer basket with parchment and spray lightly with oil. 2. Using a mandoline or a very sharp knife, cut the potatoes into very thin slices. 3. Place the slices in a bowl of cold water and let soak for about 20 minutes. 4. Drain the potatoes, transfer them to a plate lined with paper towels, and pat dry. 5. Drizzle the oil over the potatoes, sprinkle with the salt, and toss to combine. Transfer to the prepared basket. 6. Air fry at 200°F (93°C) for 20 minutes. Toss the chips, increase the heat to 400°F (204°C), and cook for another 5 to 7 minutes, until crispy.

Per Serving:
calories: 194 | fat: 4g | protein: 4g | carbs: 37g | fiber: 5g | sodium: 90mg

Eggplant Fries

Prep time: 10 minutes | Cook time: 7 to 8 minutes per batch | Serves 4

1 medium eggplant
1 teaspoon ground coriander
1 teaspoon cumin
1 teaspoon garlic powder
½ teaspoon salt

1 cup crushed panko bread crumbs
1 large egg
2 tablespoons water
Oil for misting or cooking spray

1. Peel and cut the eggplant into fat fries, ⅜- to ½-inch thick. 2. Preheat the air fryer to 390°F (199°C). 3. In a small cup, mix together the coriander, cumin, garlic, and salt. 4. Combine 1 teaspoon of the seasoning mix and panko crumbs in a shallow dish. 5. Place eggplant fries in a large bowl, sprinkle with remaining seasoning, and stir well to combine. 6. Beat eggs and water together and pour over eggplant fries. Stir to coat. 7. Remove eggplant from egg wash, shaking off excess, and roll in panko crumbs. 8. Spray with oil. 9. Place half of the fries in air fryer basket. You should have only a single layer, but it's fine if they overlap a little. 10. Cook for 5 minutes. Shake basket, mist lightly with oil, and cook 2 to 3 minutes longer, until browned and crispy. 11. Repeat step 10 to cook remaining eggplant.

Per Serving:
calories: 163 | fat: 3g | protein: 7g | carbs: 28g | fiber: 6g | sodium: 510mg

Cream Cheese Wontons

Prep time: 15 minutes | Cook time: 6 minutes | Makes 20 wontons

Oil, for spraying
20 wonton wrappers

4 ounces (113 g) cream cheese

1. Line the air fryer basket with parchment and spray lightly with oil. 2. Pour some water in a small bowl. 3. Lay out a wonton wrapper and place 1 teaspoon of cream cheese in the center. 4. Dip your finger in the water and moisten the edge of the wonton wrapper. Fold over the opposite corners to make a triangle and press the edges together. 5. Pinch the corners of the triangle together to form a classic wonton shape. Place the wonton in the prepared basket. Repeat with the remaining wrappers and cream cheese. You may need to work in batches, depending on the size of your air fryer. 6. Air fry at 400°F (204°C) for 6 minutes, or until golden brown around the edges.

Per Serving:
1 wonton: calories: 43 | fat: 2g | protein: 1g | carbs: 5g | fiber: 0g | sodium: 66mg

Garlic-Lemon Hummus

Prep time: 15 minutes | Cook time: 0 minutes | Serves 6

1 (15-ounce / 425-g) can chickpeas, drained and rinsed
4 to 5 tablespoons tahini (sesame seed paste)
4 tablespoons extra-virgin olive

oil, divided
2 lemons, juice
1 lemon, zested, divided
1 tablespoon minced garlic
Pinch salt

1. In a food processor, combine the chickpeas, tahini, 2 tablespoons of olive oil, lemon juice, half of the lemon zest, and garlic and blend for up to 1 minute. After 30 seconds of blending, stop and scrape the sides down with a spatula, before blending for another 30 seconds. At this point, you've made hummus! Taste and add salt as desired. Feel free to add 1 teaspoon of water at a time to help thin the hummus to a better consistency. 2. Scoop the hummus into a bowl, then drizzle with the remaining 2 tablespoons of olive oil and remaining lemon zest.

Per Serving:
calories: 216 | fat: 15g | protein: 5g | carbs: 17g | fiber: 5g | sodium: 12mg

Smoky Baba Ghanoush

Prep time: 50 minutes | Cook time: 40 minutes | Serves 6

2 large eggplants, washed	½ cup tahini paste
¼ cup lemon juice	3 tablespoons extra-virgin olive
1 teaspoon garlic, minced	oil
1 teaspoon salt	

1. Grill the whole eggplants over a low flame using a gas stovetop or grill. Rotate the eggplant every 5 minutes to make sure that all sides are cooked evenly. Continue to do this for 40 minutes. 2. Remove the eggplants from the stove or grill and put them onto a plate or into a bowl; cover with plastic wrap. Let sit for 5 to 10 minutes. 3. Using your fingers, peel away and discard the charred skin of the eggplants. Cut off the stem. 4. Put the eggplants into a food processor fitted with a chopping blade. Add the lemon juice, garlic, salt, and tahini paste, and pulse the mixture 5 to 7 times. 5. Pour the eggplant mixture onto a serving plate. Drizzle with the olive oil. Serve chilled or at room temperature.

Per Serving:

calories: 230 | fat: 18g | protein: 5g | carbs: 16g | fiber: 7g | sodium: 416mg

Cheesy Dates

Prep time: 15 minutes | Cook time: 10 minutes | Serves 12 to 15

1 cup pecans, shells removed	mascarpone cheese
1 (8-ounce / 227-g) container	20 Medjool dates

1. Preheat the oven to 350°F(180°C). Put the pecans on a baking sheet and bake for 5 to 6 minutes, until lightly toasted and aromatic. Take the pecans out of the oven and let cool for 5 minutes. 2. Once cooled, put the pecans in a food processor fitted with a chopping blade and chop until they resemble the texture of bulgur wheat or coarse sugar. 3. Reserve ¼ cup of ground pecans in a small bowl. Pour the remaining chopped pecans into a larger bowl and add the mascarpone cheese. 4. Using a spatula, mix the cheese with the pecans until evenly combined. 5. Spoon the cheese mixture into a piping bag. 6. Using a knife, cut one side of the date lengthwise, from the stem to the bottom. Gently open and remove the pit. 7. Using the piping bag, squeeze a generous amount of the cheese mixture into the date where the pit used to be. Close up the date and repeat with the remaining dates. 8. Dip any exposed cheese from the stuffed dates into the reserved chopped pecans to cover it up. 9. Set the dates on a serving plate; serve immediately or chill in the fridge until you are ready to serve.

Per Serving:

calories: 253 | fat: 4g | protein: 2g | carbs: 31g | fiber: 4g | sodium: 7mg

Crispy Spiced Chickpeas

Prep time: 5 minutes | Cook time: 25 minutes | Serves 6

3 cans (15 ounces / 425 g each) chickpeas, drained and rinsed	½ teaspoon ground cumin
	½ teaspoon kosher salt
1 cup olive oil	¼ teaspoon ground cinnamon
1 teaspoon paprika	¼ teaspoon ground black pepper

1. Spread the chickpeas on paper towels and pat dry. 2. In a large saucepan over medium-high heat, warm the oil until shimmering. Add 1 chickpea; if it sizzles right away, the oil is hot enough to proceed. 3. Add enough chickpeas to form a single layer in the saucepan. Cook, occasionally gently shaking the saucepan until golden brown, about 8 minutes. With a slotted spoon, transfer to a paper towel–lined plate to drain. Repeat with the remaining chickpeas until all the chickpeas are fried. Transfer to a large bowl. 4. In a small bowl, combine the paprika, cumin, salt, cinnamon, and pepper. Sprinkle all over the fried chickpeas and toss to coat. The chickpeas will crisp as they cool.

Per Serving:

calories: 175 | fat: 9g | protein: 6g | carbs: 20g | fiber: 5g | sodium: 509mg

Rosemary-Grape Focaccia

Prep time: 5 minutes | Cook time: 45 minutes | Serves 8

1 pound (454 g) whole wheat pizza dough	½ teaspoon kosher salt
	1 cup red or black seedless grapes, halved
3 tablespoons olive oil or grapeseed oil, divided	2 tablespoons pine nuts
1 tablespoon fresh rosemary, chopped	Generous pinch of flaky sea salt, such as Maldon (optional)

1. Preheat the oven to 400°F(205°C). Set out the dough at room temperature for 10 minutes. 2. Meanwhile, in a small saucepan over medium-low heat, combine 2 tablespoons of the oil, the rosemary, and kosher salt and warm for 5 minutes. Remove from the heat and set aside to steep. 3. Brush a rimmed baking sheet with the remaining 1 tablespoon oil. Press the dough into the baking sheet, stretching it out 10' to 12' in diameter. With your fingers, make dimples in the dough, and brush it with some of the rosemary oil. Sprinkle the grapes and pine nuts over the dough, pushing the grapes in a little bit. Generously brush the top with the remaining rosemary oil. Sprinkle with the flaky sea salt, if using. 4. Bake until the dough is golden, 20 to 25 minutes. Cool 10 minutes before cutting and serving.

Per Serving:

calories: 192 | fat: 9g | protein: 4g | carbs: 28g | fiber: 4g | sodium: 369mg

Lebanese Muhammara

Prep time: 15 minutes | Cook time: 15 minutes | Serves 6

2 large red bell peppers
¼ cup plus 2 tablespoons extra-virgin olive oil
1 cup walnut halves
1 tablespoon agave nectar or honey
1 teaspoon fresh lemon juice

1 teaspoon ground cumin
1 teaspoon kosher salt
1 teaspoon red pepper flakes
Raw vegetables (such as cucumber, carrots, zucchini slices, or cauliflower) or toasted pita chips, for serving

1. Drizzle the peppers with 2 tablespoons of the olive oil and place in the air fryer basket. Set the air fryer to 400°F (204°C) for 10 minutes. 2. Add the walnuts to the basket, arranging them around the peppers. Set the air fryer to 400°F (204°C) for 5 minutes. 3. Remove the peppers, seal in a resealable plastic bag, and let rest for 5 to 10 minutes. Transfer the walnuts to a plate and set aside to cool. 4. Place the softened peppers, walnuts, agave, lemon juice, cumin, salt, and ½ teaspoon of the pepper flakes in a food processor and purée until smooth. 5. Transfer the dip to a serving bowl and make an indentation in the middle. Pour the remaining ¼ cup olive oil into the indentation. Garnish the dip with the remaining ½ teaspoon pepper flakes. 6. Serve with vegetables or toasted pita chips.

Per Serving:
calories: 219 | fat: 20g | protein: 3g | carbs: 9g | fiber: 2g | sodium: 391mg

Chapter 10
Pizzas, Wraps, and Sandwiches

Cucumber Basil Sandwiches

Prep time: 10 minutes | Cook time: 0 minutes | Serves 2

Cucumber Basil Sandwiches	1 large cucumber, thinly sliced
4 slices whole-grain bread	4 whole basil leaves
¼ cup hummus	

1. Spread the hummus on 2 slices of bread, and layer the cucumbers onto it. Top with the basil leaves and close the sandwiches. 2. Press down lightly and serve immediately.

Per Serving:

calories: 209 | fat: 5g | protein: 9g | carbs: 32g | fiber: 6g | sodium: 275mg

Mediterranean-Pita Wraps

Prep time: 5 minutes | Cook time: 14 minutes | Serves 4

1 pound (454 g) mackerel fish fillets	Sea salt and freshly ground black pepper, to taste
2 tablespoons olive oil	2 ounces (57 g) feta cheese, crumbled
1 tablespoon Mediterranean seasoning mix	4 tortillas
½ teaspoon chili powder	

1. Toss the fish fillets with the olive oil; place them in the lightly oiled air fryer basket. 2. Air fry the fish fillets at 400ºF (204ºC) for about 14 minutes, turning them over halfway through the cooking time. 3. Assemble your pitas with the chopped fish and remaining ingredients and serve warm.

Per Serving:

calories: 275 | fat: 13g | protein: 27g | carbs: 13g | fiber: 2g | sodium: 322mg

Sautéed Mushroom, Onion, and Pecorino Romano Panini

Prep time: 10 minutes | Cook time: 20 minutes | Serves 4

3 tablespoons olive oil, divided	¼ teaspoon freshly ground black pepper
1 small onion, diced	4 crusty Italian sandwich rolls
10 ounces (283 g) button or cremini mushrooms, sliced	4 ounces (113 g) freshly grated Pecorino Romano
½ teaspoon salt	

1. Heat 1 tablespoon of the olive oil in a skillet over medium-high heat. Add the onion and cook, stirring, until it begins to soften, about 3 minutes. Add the mushrooms, season with salt and pepper, and cook, stirring, until they soften and the liquid they release evaporates, about 7 minutes. 2. To make the panini, heat a skillet or grill pan over high heat and brush with 1 tablespoon olive oil. Brush the inside of the rolls with the remaining 1 tablespoon olive oil. Divide the mushroom mixture evenly among the rolls and top each with ¼ of the grated cheese. 3. Place the sandwiches in the hot pan and place another heavy pan, such as a cast-iron skillet, on top

to weigh them down. Cook for about 3 to 4 minutes, until crisp and golden on the bottom, and then flip over and repeat on the second side, cooking for an additional 3 to 4 minutes until golden and crisp. Slice each sandwich in half and serve hot.

Per Serving:

calories: 348 | fat: 20g | protein: 14g | carbs: 30g | fiber: 2g | sodium: 506mg

Grilled Chicken Salad Pita

Prep time: 15 minutes | Cook time: 16 minutes | Serves 1

1 boneless, skinless chicken breast	½ small red onion, thinly sliced
Sea salt and freshly ground pepper, to taste	½ small cucumber, chopped
	1 tablespoon olive oil
1 cup baby spinach	Juice of 1 lemon
1 roasted red pepper, sliced	1 whole-wheat pita pocket
1 tomato, chopped	2 tablespoons crumbled feta cheese

1. Preheat a gas or charcoal grill to medium-high heat. 2. Season the chicken breast with sea salt and freshly ground pepper, and grill until cooked through, about 7–8 minutes per side. 3. Allow chicken to rest for 5 minutes before slicing into strips. 4. While the chicken is cooking, put all the chopped vegetables into a medium-mixing bowl and season with sea salt and freshly ground pepper. 5. Chop the chicken into cubes and add to salad. Add the olive oil and lemon juice and toss well. 6. Stuff the mixture onto a pita pocket and top with the feta cheese. Serve immediately.

Per Serving:

calories: 653 | fat: 26g | protein: 71g | carbs: 34g | fiber: 6g | sodium: 464mg

Jerk Chicken Wraps

Prep time: 30 minutes | Cook time: 15 minutes | Serves 4

1 pound (454 g) boneless, skinless chicken tenderloins	1 cup julienned carrots
1 cup jerk marinade	1 cup peeled cucumber ribbons
Olive oil	1 cup shredded lettuce
4 large low-carb tortillas	1 cup mango or pineapple chunks

1. In a medium bowl, coat the chicken with the jerk marinade, cover, and refrigerate for 1 hour. 2. Spray the air fryer basket lightly with olive oil. 3. Place the chicken in the air fryer basket in a single layer and spray lightly with olive oil. You may need to cook the chicken in batches. Reserve any leftover marinade. 4. Air fry at 375ºF (191ºC) for 8 minutes. Turn the chicken over and brush with some of the remaining marinade. Cook until the chicken reaches an internal temperature of at least 165ºF (74ºC), an additional 5 to 7 minutes. 5. To assemble the wraps, fill each tortilla with ¼ cup carrots, ¼ cup cucumber, ¼ cup lettuce, and ¼ cup mango. Place one quarter of the chicken tenderloins on top and roll up the tortilla. These are great served warm or cold.

Per Serving:

calories: 241 | fat: 4g | protein: 28g | carbs: 23g | fiber: 4g | sodium: 85mg

Moroccan Lamb Flatbread with Pine Nuts, Mint, and Ras Al Hanout

Prep time: 10 minutes | Cook time: 20 minutes | Serves 4

1⅓ cups plain Greek yogurt	leaves
Juice of 1½ lemons, divided	Freshly ground black pepper
1¼ teaspoons salt, divided	4 Middle Eastern-style flatbread
1 pound (454 g) ground lamb	rounds
1 medium red onion, diced	2 tablespoons toasted pine nuts
1 clove garlic, minced	16 cherry tomatoes, halved
1 tablespoon ras al hanout	2 tablespoons chopped cilantro
¼ cup chopped fresh mint	

1. Preheat the oven to 450°F(235°C). 2. In a small bowl, stir together the yogurt, the juice of ½ lemon, and ¼ teaspoon salt. 3. Heat a large skillet over medium-high heat. Add the lamb and cook, stirring frequently, until browned, about 5 minutes. Drain any excess rendered fat from the pan and then stir in the onion and garlic and cook, stirring, until softened, about 3 minutes more. Stir in the ras al hanout, mint, the remaining teaspoon of salt, and pepper. 4. Place the flatbread rounds on a baking sheet (or two if necessary) and top with the lamb mixture, pine nuts, and tomatoes, dividing equally. Bake in the preheated oven until the crust is golden brown and the tomatoes have softened, about 10 minutes. Scatter the cilantro over the flatbreads and squeeze the remaining lemon juice over them. Cut into wedges and serve dolloped with the yogurt sauce.

Per Serving:

calories: 463 | fat: 22g | protein: 34g | carbs: 34g | fiber: 3g | sodium: 859mg

Margherita Open-Face Sandwiches

Prep time: 10 minutes |Cook time: 5 minutes| Serves: 4

2 (6- to 7-inch) whole-wheat submarine or hoagie rolls, sliced open horizontally	¼ teaspoon dried oregano
	1 cup fresh mozzarella (about 4 ounces / 113 g), patted dry and
1 tablespoon extra-virgin olive oil	sliced
	¼ cup lightly packed fresh basil
1 garlic clove, halved	leaves, torn into small pieces
1 large ripe tomato, cut into 8 slices	¼ teaspoon freshly ground black pepper

1. Preheat the broiler to high with the rack 4 inches under the heating element. 2. Place the sliced bread on a large, rimmed baking sheet. Place under the broiler for 1 minute, until the bread is just lightly toasted. Remove from the oven. 3. Brush each piece of the toasted bread with the oil, and rub a garlic half over each piece. 4. Place the toasted bread back on the baking sheet. Evenly distribute the tomato slices on each piece, sprinkle with the oregano, and layer the cheese on top. 5. Place the baking sheet under the broiler. Set the timer for 1½ minutes, but check after 1 minute. When the cheese

is melted and the edges are just starting to get dark brown, remove the sandwiches from the oven (this can take anywhere from 1½ to 2 minutes). 6. Top each sandwich with the fresh basil and pepper.

Per Serving:

calories: 176 | fat: 9g | protein: 10g | carbs: 14g | fiber: 2g | sodium: 119mg

Pesto Chicken Mini Pizzas

Prep time: 5 minutes | Cook time: 10 minutes | Serves 4

2 cups shredded cooked chicken	2 cups shredded Mozzarella
¾ cup pesto	cheese
4 English muffins, split	

1. In a medium bowl, toss the chicken with the pesto. Place one-eighth of the chicken on each English muffin half. Top each English muffin with ¼ cup of the Mozzarella cheese. 2. Put four pizzas at a time in the air fryer and air fry at 350°F (177°C) for 5 minutes. Repeat this process with the other four pizzas.

Per Serving:

calories: 617 | fat: 36g | protein: 45g | carbs: 29g | fiber: 3g | sodium: 544mg

Bocadillo with Herbed Tuna and Piquillo Peppers

Prep time: 5 minutes | Cook time: 20 minutes | Serves 4

2 tablespoons olive oil, plus more for brushing	3 tablespoons sherry vinegar
	1 carrot, finely diced
1 medium onion, finely chopped	2 (8-ounce / 227-g) jars Spanish
2 leeks, white and tender green parts only, finely chopped	tuna in olive oil
	4 crusty whole-wheat sandwich
1 teaspoon chopped thyme	rolls, split
½ teaspoon dried marjoram	1 ripe tomato, grated on the
½ teaspoon salt	large holes of a box grater
¼ teaspoon freshly ground black pepper	4 piquillo peppers, cut into thin strips

1. Heat 2 tablespoons olive oil in a medium skillet over medium heat. Add the onion, leeks, thyme, marjoram, salt, and pepper. Stir frequently until the onions are softened, about 10 minutes. Stir in the vinegar and carrot and cook until the liquid has evaporated, 5 minutes. Transfer the mixture to a bowl and let cool to room temperature or refrigerate for 15 minutes or so. 2. In a medium bowl, combine the tuna, along with its oil, with the onion mixture, breaking the tuna chunks up with a fork. 3. Brush the rolls lightly with oil and toast under the broiler until lightly browned, about 2 minutes. Spoon the tomato pulp onto the bottom half of each roll, dividing equally and spreading it with the back of the spoon. Divide the tuna mixture among the rolls and top with the piquillo pepper slices. Serve immediately.

Per Serving:

calories: 416 | fat: 18g | protein: 35g | carbs: 30g | fiber: 5g | sodium: 520mg

Roasted Vegetable Bocadillo with Romesco Sauce

Prep time: 10 minutes | Cook time: 20 minutes | Serves 4

2 small yellow squash, sliced lengthwise
2 small zucchini, sliced lengthwise
1 medium red onion, thinly sliced
4 large button mushrooms, sliced
2 tablespoons olive oil
1 teaspoon salt, divided
½ teaspoon freshly ground black

pepper, divided
2 roasted red peppers from a jar, drained
2 tablespoons blanched almonds
1 tablespoon sherry vinegar
1 small clove garlic
4 crusty multigrain rolls
4 ounces (113 g) goat cheese, at room temperature
1 tablespoon chopped fresh basil

1. Preheat the oven to 400°F(205ºC). 2. In a medium bowl, toss the yellow squash, zucchini, onion, and mushrooms with the olive oil, ½ teaspoon salt, and ¼ teaspoon pepper. Spread on a large baking sheet. Roast the vegetables in the oven for about 20 minutes, until softened. 3. Meanwhile, in a food processor, combine the roasted peppers, almonds, vinegar, garlic, the remaining ½ teaspoon salt, and the remaining ¼ teaspoon pepper and process until smooth. 4. Split the rolls and spread ¼ of the goat cheese on the bottom of each. Place the roasted vegetables on top of the cheese, dividing equally. Top with chopped basil. Spread the top halves of the rolls with the roasted red pepper sauce and serve immediately.

Per Serving:

calories: 379 | fat: 21g | protein: 17g | carbs: 32g | fiber: 4g | sodium: 592mg

Croatian Double-Crust Pizza with Greens and Garlic

Prep time: 15 minutes | Cook time: 20 minutes | Serves 4

4½ cups all-purpose flour
1¼ teaspoons salt, divided
1½ cups olive oil, plus 3 tablespoons, divided
1 cup warm water
1 pound (454 g) Swiss chard or kale, tough center ribs removed,

leaves julienned
¼ small head of green cabbage, thinly sliced
¼ teaspoon freshly ground black pepper
4 cloves garlic, minced

1. In a medium bowl, combine the flour and 1 teaspoon salt. Add 1½ cups olive oil and the warm water and stir with a fork until the mixture comes together and forms a ball. Wrap the ball in plastic wrap and refrigerate for at least 30 minutes. 2. While the dough is chilling, in a large bowl, toss together the greens, cabbage, 2 tablespoons olive oil, the remaining ¼ teaspoon salt, and the pepper. 3. Preheat the oven to 400°F(205ºC). 4. Halve the dough and place the halves on two sheets of lightly floured parchment paper. Roll or pat the dough out into two ¼-inch-thick, 11-inch-diameter rounds. 5. Spread the greens mixture over one of the dough rounds, leaving about an inch

clear around the edge. Place the second dough round over the greens and fold the edges together to seal the two rounds together. Bake in the preheated oven until the crust is golden brown, about 20 minutes. 6. While the pizza is in the oven, combine 1 tablespoon of olive oil with the garlic. When the pizza is done, remove it from the oven and immediately brush the garlic-oil mixture over the crust. Cut into wedges and serve hot.

Per Serving:

calories: 670 | fat: 45g | protein: 10g | carbs: 62g | fiber: 5g | sodium: 504mg

Beans and Greens Pizza

Prep time: 11 minutes | Cook time: 14 to 19 minutes | Serves 4

¾ cup whole-wheat pastry flour
½ teaspoon low-sodium baking powder
1 tablespoon olive oil, divided
1 cup chopped kale
2 cups chopped fresh baby spinach

1 cup canned no-salt-added cannellini beans, rinsed and drained
½ teaspoon dried thyme
1 piece low-sodium string cheese, torn into pieces

1. In a small bowl, mix the pastry flour and baking powder until well combined. 2. Add ¼ cup of water and 2 teaspoons of olive oil. Mix until a dough forms. 3. On a floured surface, press or roll the dough into a 7-inch round. Set aside while you cook the greens. 4. In a baking pan, mix the kale, spinach, and remaining teaspoon of the olive oil. Air fry at 350ºF (177ºC) for 3 to 5 minutes, until the greens are wilted. Drain well. 5. Put the pizza dough into the air fryer basket. Top with the greens, cannellini beans, thyme, and string cheese. Air fry for 11 to 14 minutes, or until the crust is golden brown and the cheese is melted. Cut into quarters to serve.

Per Serving:

calories: 181 | fat: 6g | protein: 8g | carbs: 27g | fiber: 6g | sodium: 103mg

Chicken and Goat Cheese Pizza

Prep time: 10 minutes | Cook time: 10 minutes | Serves 4

All-purpose flour, for dusting
1 pound (454 g) premade pizza dough
2 tablespoons olive oil
1 cup shredded cooked chicken

3 ounces (85 g) goat cheese, crumbled
Sea salt
Freshly ground black pepper

1. Preheat the oven to 475°F (245°C). 2. On a floured surface, roll out the dough to a 12-inch round and place it on a lightly floured pizza pan or baking sheet. Drizzle the dough with the olive oil and spread it out evenly. Top the dough with the chicken and goat cheese. 3. Bake the pizza for 8 to 10 minutes, until the crust is cooked through and golden. 4. Season with salt and pepper and serve.

Per Serving:

calories: 555 | fat: 23g | protein: 24g | carbs: 60g | fiber: 2g | sodium: 660mg

Flatbread Pizza with Roasted Cherry Tomatoes, Artichokes, and Feta

Prep time: 5 minutes | Cook time: 20 minutes | Serves 4

1½ pounds (680 g) cherry or grape tomatoes, halved	1 can artichoke hearts, rinsed, well drained, and cut into thin wedges
3 tablespoons olive oil, divided	
½ teaspoon salt	8 ounces (227 g) crumbled feta cheese
½ teaspoon freshly ground black pepper	
4 Middle Eastern–style flatbread rounds	¼ cup chopped fresh Greek oregano

1. Preheat the oven to 500°F(260°C). 2. In a medium bowl, toss the tomatoes with 1 tablespoon olive oil, the salt, and the pepper. Spread out on a large baking sheet. Roast in the preheated oven until the tomato skins begin to blister and crack, about 10 to 12 minutes. Remove the tomatoes from the oven and reduce the heat to 450°F(235°C). 3. Place the flatbreads on a large baking sheet (or two baking sheets if necessary) and brush the tops with the remaining 2 tablespoons of olive oil. Top with the artichoke hearts, roasted tomatoes, and cheese, dividing equally. 4. Bake the flatbreads in the oven for about 8 to 10 minutes, until the edges are lightly browned and the cheese is melted. Sprinkle the oregano over the top and serve immediately.

Per Serving:

calories: 436 | fat: 27g | protein: 16g | carbs: 34g | fiber: 6g | sodium: 649mg

Grilled Eggplant and Chopped Greek Salad Wraps

Prep time: 10 minutes | Cook time: 20 minutes | Serves 4

15 small tomatoes, such as cherry or grape tomatoes, halved	2 tablespoons olive oil, plus 2 teaspoons, divided
	¾ teaspoon salt, divided
10 pitted Kalamata olives, chopped	1 medium cucumber, peeled, halved lengthwise, seeded, and diced
1 medium red onion, halved and thinly sliced	
¾ cup crumbled feta cheese (about 4 ounces / 113 g)	1 large eggplant, sliced ½-inch thick
2 tablespoons balsamic vinegar	½ teaspoon freshly ground black pepper
1 tablespoon chopped fresh parsley	4 whole-wheat sandwich wraps or whole-wheat flour tortillas
1 clove garlic, minced	

1. In a medium bowl, toss together the tomatoes, olives, onion, cheese, vinegar, parsley, garlic, 2 teaspoons olive oil, and ¼ teaspoon of salt. Let sit at room temperature for 20 minutes. Add the cucumber, toss to combine, and let sit another 10 minutes. 2. While the salad is resting, grill the eggplant. Heat a grill or grill pan to high heat. Brush the remaining 2 tablespoons olive oil onto both sides of the eggplant slices. Grill for about 8 to 10 minutes per side, until grill marks appear and the eggplant is tender and cooked through. Transfer to a plate and season with the remaining ½ teaspoon of salt and the pepper. 3. Heat the wraps in a large, dry skillet over medium heat just until warm and soft, about 1 minute on each side. Place 2 or 3 eggplant slices down the center of each wrap. Spoon some of the salad mixture on top of the eggplant, using a slotted spoon so that any excess liquid is drained off. Fold in the sides of the wrap and roll up like a burrito. Serve immediately.

Per Serving:

calories: 233 | fat: 10g | protein: 8g | carbs: 29g | fiber: 7g | sodium: 707mg

Za'atar Pizza

Prep time: 10 minutes | Cook time: 15 minutes | Serves 4 to 6

1 sheet puff pastry	⅓ cup za'atar seasoning
¼ cup extra-virgin olive oil	

1. Preheat the oven to 350°F(180°C). 2. Put the puff pastry on a parchment-lined baking sheet. Cut the pastry into desired slices. 3. Brush the pastry with olive oil. Sprinkle with the za'atar. 4. Put the pastry in the oven and bake for 10 to 12 minutes or until edges are lightly browned and puffed up. Serve warm or at room temperature.

Per Serving:

calories: 374 | fat: 30g | protein: 3g | carbs: 20g | fiber: 1g | sodium: 166mg

Greek Salad Wraps

Prep time: 15 minutes |Cook time: 0 minutes| Serves: 4

1½ cups seedless cucumber, peeled and chopped (about 1 large cucumber)	2 tablespoons extra-virgin olive oil
	1 tablespoon red wine vinegar
1 cup chopped tomato (about 1 large tomato)	¼ teaspoon freshly ground black pepper
½ cup finely chopped fresh mint	¼ teaspoon kosher or sea salt
1 (2¼ ounces / 64 g) can sliced black olives (about ½ cup), drained	½ cup crumbled goat cheese (about 2 ounces / 57 g)
¼ cup diced red onion (about ¼ onion)	4 whole-wheat flatbread wraps or soft whole-wheat tortillas

1. In a large bowl, mix together the cucumber, tomato, mint, olives, and onion until well combined. 2. In a small bowl, whisk together the oil, vinegar, pepper, and salt. Drizzle the dressing over the salad, and mix gently. 3. With a knife, spread the goat cheese evenly over the four wraps. Spoon a quarter of the salad filling down the middle of each wrap. 4. Fold up each wrap: Start by folding up the bottom, then fold one side over and fold the other side over the top. Repeat with the remaining wraps and serve.

Per Serving:

calories: 217 | fat: 14g | protein: 7g | carbs: 17g | fiber: 3g | sodium: 329mg

Mediterranean Tuna Salad Sandwiches

Prep time: 10 minutes | Cook time: 5 minutes | Serves 2

1 can white tuna, packed in water or olive oil, drained	1 tablespoon flat-leaf parsley, chopped
1 roasted red pepper, diced	Juice of 1 lemon
½ small red onion, diced	Sea salt and freshly ground pepper, to taste
10 low-salt olives, pitted and finely chopped	4 whole-grain pieces of bread
¼ cup plain Greek yogurt	

1. In a small bowl, combine all of the ingredients except the bread, and mix well. 2. Season with sea salt and freshly ground pepper to taste. Toast the bread or warm in a pan. 3. Make the sandwich and serve immediately.

Per Serving:

calories. 307 | fat: 7g | protein: 30g | carbs: 31g | fiber: 5g | sodium: 564mg

Barbecue Chicken Pita Pizza

Prep time: 5 minutes | Cook time: 5 to 7 minutes per batch | Makes 4 pizzas

1 cup barbecue sauce, divided	cheese
4 pita breads	½ small red onion, thinly sliced
2 cups shredded cooked chicken	2 tablespoons finely chopped fresh cilantro
2 cups shredded Mozzarella	

1. Measure ½ cup of the barbecue sauce in a small measuring cup. Spread 2 tablespoons of the barbecue sauce on each pita. 2. In a medium bowl, mix together the remaining ½ cup of barbecue sauce and chicken. Place ½ cup of the chicken on each pita. Top each pizza with ½ cup of the Mozzarella cheese. Sprinkle the tops of the pizzas with the red onion. 3. Place one pizza in the air fryer. Air fry at 400°F (204°C) for 5 to 7 minutes. Repeat this process with the remaining pizzas. 4. Top the pizzas with the cilantro.

Per Serving:

calories: 530 | fat: 19g | protein: 40g | carbs: 47g | fiber: 2g | sodium: 672mg

Turkey and Provolone Panini with Roasted Peppers and Onions

Prep time: 15 minutes | Cook time: 1 hour 5 minutes | Serves 4

For the peppers and onions	pepper
2 red bell pepper, seeded and quartered	For the panini
2 red onions, peeled and quartered	2 tablespoons olive oil
2 tablespoons olive oil	8 slices whole-wheat bread
½ teaspoon salt	8 ounces (227 g) thinly sliced provolone cheese
½ teaspoon freshly ground black	8 ounces (227 g) sliced roasted turkey or chicken breast

1. Preheat the oven to 375°F(190°C). 2. To roast the peppers and onions, toss them together with the olive oil, salt, and pepper on a large, rimmed baking sheet. Spread them out in a single layer and then bake in the preheated oven for 45 to 60 minutes, turning occasionally, until they are tender and beginning to brown. Remove the peppers and onions from the oven and let them cool for a few minutes until they are cool enough to handle. Skin the peppers and thinly slice them. Thinly slice the onions. 3. Preheat a skillet or grill pan over medium-high heat. 4. To make the panini, brush one side of each of the 8 slices of bread with olive oil. Place 4 of the bread slices, oiled side down, on your work surface. Top each with ¼ of the cheese and ¼ of the turkey, and top with some of the roasted peppers and onions. Place the remaining 4 bread slices on top of the sandwiches, oiled side up. 5. Place the sandwiches in the skillet or grill pan (you may have to cook them in two batches), cover the pan, and cook until the bottoms have golden brown grill marks and the cheese is beginning to melt, about 2 minutes. Turn the sandwiches over and cook, covered, until the second side is golden brown and the cheese is melted, another 2 minutes or so. Cut each sandwich in half and serve immediately.

Per Serving:

calories: 603 | fat: 32g | protein: 41g | carbs: 37g | fiber: 6g | sodium: 792mg

Chapter 11

Salads

Red Pepper, Pomegranate, and Walnut Salad

Prep time: 5 minutes | Cook time: 40 minutes | Serves 4

2 red bell peppers, halved and seeded	¼ teaspoon kosher salt
1 teaspoon plus 2 tablespoons olive oil	⅛ teaspoon ground black pepper
4 teaspoons pomegranate molasses, divided	4 plum tomatoes, halved, seeded, and chopped
2 teaspoons fresh lemon juice	¼ cup walnut halves, chopped
	¼ cup chopped fresh flat-leaf parsley

1. Preheat the oven to 450°F(235°C). 2. Brush the bell peppers all over with 1 teaspoon of the oil and place cut side up on a large rimmed baking sheet. Drizzle 2 teaspoons of the pomegranate molasses in the cavities of the bell peppers. Roast the bell peppers until they have softened and the skins have charred, turning once during cooking, 30 to 40 minutes. Remove from the oven and cool to room temperature. Remove the skins and chop the peppers coarsely. 3. In a large bowl, whisk together the lemon juice, salt, black pepper, the remaining 2 tablespoons oil, and the remaining 2 teaspoons pomegranate molasses. Add the bell peppers, tomatoes, walnuts, and parsley and toss gently to combine. Serve at room temperature.

Per Serving:

calories: 166 | fat: 13g | protein: 2g | carbs: 11g | fiber: 3g | sodium: 153mg

Pipirrana (Spanish Summer Salad)

Prep time: 15 minutes | Cook time: 0 minutes | Serves 2

1 medium red onion, diced	Pinch of ground cumin
2 large tomatoes, cut into small cubes	½ teaspoon salt plus a pinch for the garlic paste
1 large Persian or mini cucumber, cut into small cubes	3 tablespoons extra virgin olive oil plus a few drops for the garlic paste
1 large green bell pepper, seeded and diced	2 tablespoons red wine vinegar
2 garlic cloves, minced	

1. Place the onions in a small bowl filled with water. Set aside to soak. 2. Place the tomatoes, cucumber, and bell pepper in a medium bowl. Drain the onions and then combine them with the rest of the vegetables. Mix well. 3. In a mortar or small bowl, combine the garlic, cumin, a pinch of salt, and a few drops of olive oil, then roll or mash the ingredients until a paste is formed. 4. In another small bowl, combine 3 tablespoons of the olive oil, vinegar, and ½ teaspoon of the salt. Add the garlic paste and mix well. 5. Add the dressing to the salad and mix well. 6. Cover and refrigerate for 30 minutes before serving. Store in the refrigerator for up to 2 days.

Per Serving:

calories: 274 | fat: 21g | protein: 4g | carbs: 20g | fiber: 6g | sodium: 600mg

Arugula Spinach Salad with Shaved Parmesan

Prep time: 10 minutes | Cook time: 2 minutes | Serves 3

3 tablespoons raw pine nuts	For the Dressing:
3 cups arugula	4 teaspoons balsamic vinegar
3 cups baby leaf spinach	1 teaspoon Dijon mustard
5 dried figs, pitted and chopped	1 teaspoon honey
2½ ounces (71 g) shaved Parmesan cheese	5 tablespoons extra virgin olive oil

1. In a small pan over low heat, toast the pine nuts for 2 minutes or until they begin to brown. Promptly remove them from the heat and transfer to a small bowl. 2. Make the dressing by combining the balsamic vinegar, Dijon mustard, and honey in a small bowl. Using a fork to whisk, gradually add the olive oil while continuously mixing. 3. In a large bowl, toss the arugula and baby spinach and then top with the figs, Parmesan cheese, and toasted pine nuts. Drizzle the dressing over the top and toss until the ingredients are thoroughly coated with the dressing. Serve promptly. (This salad is best served fresh.)

Per Serving:

calories: 416 | fat: 35g | protein: 10g | carbs: 18g | fiber: 3g | sodium: 478mg

Bacalhau and Black-Eyed Pea Salad

Prep time: 10 minutes | Cook time: 10 minutes | Serves 4

1 pound (454 g) bacalhau (salt cod) fillets	pepper
¼ cup olive oil, plus 1 tablespoon, divided	1 (15-ounce / 425-g) can black-eyed peas, drained and rinsed
3 tablespoons white wine vinegar	1 small yellow onion, halved and thinly sliced crosswise
1 teaspoon salt	1 small clove garlic, minced
¼ teaspoon freshly ground black	¼ cup chopped fresh flat-leaf parsley leaves, divided

1. Rinse the cod under cold running water to remove any surface salt. Place the fish pieces in a large nonreactive pot, cover with water and refrigerate (covered) for 24 hours, changing the water several times. 2. Pour off the water, refill the pot with clean water and gently boil the cod until it flakes easily with a fork, about 7 to 10 minutes (or longer), depending on the thickness. Drain and set aside to cool. 3. To make the dressing, whisk together the oil, vinegar, salt, and pepper in a small bowl. 4. In a large bowl, combine the beans, onion, garlic, and ¾ of the parsley. Add the dressing and mix to coat well. Stir in the salt cod, cover, and chill in the refrigerator for at least 2 hours to let the flavors meld. Let sit on the countertop for 30 minutes before serving. 5. Serve garnished with the remaining parsley.

Per Serving:

calories: 349 | fat: 18g | protein: 32g | carbs: 16g | fiber: 4g | sodium: 8mg

Arugula and Fennel Salad with Fresh Basil

Prep time: 5 minutes | Cook time: 0 minutes | Serves 4

3 tablespoons olive oil	sliced
3 tablespoons lemon juice	2 cups arugula
1 teaspoon honey	¼ cup toasted pine nuts
½ teaspoon salt	½ cup crumbled feta cheese
1 medium bulb fennel, very	¼ cup julienned fresh basil
thinly sliced	leaves
1 small cucumber, very thinly	

1. In a medium bowl, whisk together the olive oil, lemon juice, honey, and salt. Add the fennel and cucumber and toss to coat and let sit for 10 minutes or so. 2. Put the arugula in a large salad bowl. Add the marinated cucumber and fennel, along with the dressing, to the bowl and toss well. Serve immediately, sprinkled with pine nuts, feta cheese, and basil.

Per Serving:

calories: 237 | fat: 21g | protein: 6g | carbs: 11g | fiber: 3g | sodium: 537mg

Zucchini and Ricotta Salad

Prep time: 5 minutes | Cook time: 2 minutes | Serves 1

2 teaspoons raw pine nuts	mandoline slicer
5 ounces (142 g) whole-milk	Pinch of freshly ground black
ricotta cheese	pepper
1 tablespoon chopped fresh mint	For the Dressing:
1 teaspoon chopped fresh basil	1½ tablespoons extra virgin
1 tablespoon chopped fresh	olive oil
parsley	1 tablespoon fresh lemon juice
Pinch of fine sea salt	Pinch of fine sea salt
1 medium zucchini, very thinly	Pinch of freshly ground black
sliced horizontally with a	pepper

1. Add the pine nuts to a small pan placed over medium heat. Toast the nuts, turning them frequently, for 2 minutes or until golden. Set aside. 2. In a food processor, combine the ricotta, mint, basil, parsley, and a pinch of sea salt. Process until smooth and then set aside. 3. Make the dressing by combining the olive oil and lemon juice in a small bowl. Use a fork to stir rapidly until the mixture thickens, then add a pinch of sea salt and a pinch of black pepper. Stir again. 4. Place the sliced zucchini in a medium bowl. Add half of the dressing, and toss to coat the zucchini. 5. To serve, place half of the ricotta mixture in the center of a serving plate, then layer the zucchini in a circle, covering the cheese. Add the rest of the cheese in the center and on top of the zucchini, then sprinkle the toasted pine nuts over the top. Drizzle the remaining dressing over the top, and finish with a pinch of black pepper. Store covered in the refrigerator for up to 1 day.

Per Serving:

calories: 504 | fat: 43g | protein: 19g | carbs: 13g | fiber: 3g | sodium: 136mg

Tossed Green Mediterranean Salad

Prep time: 15 minutes | Cook time: 0 minutes | Serves 4

1 medium head romaine lettuce, washed, dried, and chopped into bite-sized pieces	½ cup finely chopped fresh dill
	⅓ cup extra virgin olive oil
	2 tablespoons fresh lemon juice
2 medium cucumbers, peeled and sliced	¼ teaspoon fine sea salt
	4 ounces (113 g) crumbled feta
3 spring onions (white parts only), sliced	7 Kalamata olives, pitted

1. Add the lettuce, cucumber, spring onions, and dill to a large bowl. Toss to combine. 2. In a small bowl, whisk together the olive oil and lemon juice. Pour the dressing over the salad, toss, then sprinkle the sea salt over the top. 3. Sprinkle the feta and olives over the top and then gently toss the salad one more time. Serve promptly. (This recipe is best served fresh.)

Per Serving:

calories: 284 | fat: 25g | protein: 7g | carbs: 10g | fiber: 5g | sodium: 496mg

Caprese Salad with Fresh Mozzarella

Prep time: 10 minutes | Cook time: 0 minutes | Serves 6 to 8

For the Pesto:	Freshly ground black pepper
2 cups (packed) fresh basil leaves, plus more for garnish	For the Salad:
	4 to 6 large, ripe tomatoes, cut into thick slices
⅓ cup pine nuts	
3 garlic cloves, minced	1 pound (454 g) fresh
½ cup (about 2 ounces / 57 g) freshly grated Parmesan cheese	mozzarella, cut into thick slices
	3 tablespoons balsamic vinegar
½ cup extra-virgin olive oil	Salt
Salt	Freshly ground black pepper

1. To make the pesto, in a food processor combine the basil, pine nuts, and garlic and pulse several times to chop. Add the Parmesan cheese and pulse again until well combined. With the food processor running, add the olive oil in a slow, steady stream. Transfer to a small bowl, taste, and add salt and pepper as needed. Slice, quarter, or halve the tomatoes, based on your preferred salad presentation. 2. To make the salad, on a large serving platter arrange the tomato slices and cheese slices, stacking them like fallen dominoes. 3. Dollop the pesto decoratively on top of the tomato and cheese slices. (You will likely have extra pesto. Refrigerate the extra in a tightly sealed container and use within 3 days, or freeze it for up to 3 months.) 4. Drizzle the balsamic vinegar over the top, garnish with basil leaves, sprinkle with salt and pepper to taste, and serve immediately.

Per Serving:

calories: 398 | fat: 32g | protein: 23g | carbs: 8g | fiber: 1g | sodium: 474mg

Valencia-Inspired Salad

Prep time: 5 minutes | Cook time: 0 minutes | Serves 4

2 small oranges, peeled, thinly sliced, and pitted	1 small shallot, thinly sliced (optional)
1 small blood orange, peeled, thinly sliced, and pitted	¼ cup raw hulled pumpkin seeds
1 (7-ounce / 198-g) bag butter lettuce	8 slices Manchego cheese, roughly broken
½ English cucumber, thinly sliced into rounds	2 to 3 tablespoons extra-virgin olive oil
1 (6-ounce / 170-g) can pitted black olives, halved	Juice of 1 orange

1. In a large bowl, toss together the oranges, lettuce, cucumber, olives, shallot (if desired), pumpkin seeds, and cheese until well mixed. Evenly divide the mixture among four plates. 2. Drizzle the salads with the olive oil and orange juice. Serve.

Per Serving:

calories: 419 | fat: 31g | protein: 17g | carbs: 22g | fiber: 5g | sodium: 513mg

Raw Zucchini Salad

Prep time: 15 minutes | Cook time: 0 minutes | Serves 2

1 medium zucchini, shredded or sliced paper thin	Sea salt and freshly ground pepper, to taste
6 cherry tomatoes, halved	3–4 basil leaves, thinly sliced
3 tablespoons olive oil	2 tablespoons freshly grated, low-fat Parmesan cheese
Juice of 1 lemon	

1. Layer the zucchini slices on 2 plates in even layers. Top with the tomatoes. 2. Drizzle with the olive oil and lemon juice. Season to taste. 3. Top with the basil and sprinkle with cheese before serving.

Per Serving:

calories: 256 | fat: 21g | protein: 2g | carbs: 19g | fiber: 3g | sodium: 3mg

Sicilian Salad

Prep time: 5 minutes | Cook time: 0 minutes | Serves 2

2 tablespoons extra virgin olive oil	sliced
1 tablespoon red wine vinegar	2 tablespoons capers, drained
2 medium tomatoes (preferably beefsteak variety), sliced	6 green olives, halved
½ medium red onion, thinly	1 teaspoon dried oregano
	Pinch of fine sea salt

1. Make the dressing by combining the olive oil and vinegar in a small bowl. Use a fork to whisk until the mixture thickens slightly. Set aside. 2. Arrange the sliced tomatoes on a large plate and then scatter the onions, capers, and olives over the tomatoes. 3. Sprinkle the oregano and sea salt over the top, then drizzle the dressing over

the salad. Serve promptly. (This salad is best served fresh, but can be stored covered in the refrigerator for up to 1 day.)

Per Serving:

calories: 169 | fat: 15g | protein: 2g | carbs: 8g | fiber: 3g | sodium: 336mg

Mediterranean Potato Salad

Prep time: 10 minutes |Cook time: 20 minutes| Serves: 6

2 pounds (907 g) Yukon Gold baby potatoes, cut into 1-inch cubes	¼ teaspoon kosher or sea salt
	1 (2¼-ounce / 35-g) can sliced olives (about ½ cup)
3 tablespoons freshly squeezed lemon juice (from about 1 medium lemon)	1 cup sliced celery (about 2 stalks) or fennel
3 tablespoons extra-virgin olive oil	2 tablespoons chopped fresh oregano
1 tablespoon olive brine	2 tablespoons torn fresh mint

1. In a medium saucepan, cover the potatoes with cold water until the waterline is one inch above the potatoes. Set over high heat, bring the potatoes to a boil, then turn down the heat to medium-low. Simmer for 12 to 15 minutes, until the potatoes are just fork tender. 2. While the potatoes are cooking, in a small bowl, whisk together the lemon juice, oil, olive brine, and salt. 3. Drain the potatoes in a colander and transfer to a serving bowl. Immediately pour about 3 tablespoons of the dressing over the potatoes. Gently mix in the olives and celery. 4. Before serving, gently mix in the oregano, mint, and the remaining dressing.

Per Serving:

calories: 192 | fat: 8g | protein: 3g | carbs: 28g | fiber: 4g | sodium: 195mg

Tuscan Kale Salad with Anchovies

Prep time: 15 minutes | Cook time: 0 minutes | Serves 4

1 large bunch lacinato or dinosaur kale	chopped
¼ cup toasted pine nuts	2 to 3 tablespoons freshly squeezed lemon juice (from 1 large lemon)
1 cup shaved or coarsely shredded fresh Parmesan cheese	2 teaspoons red pepper flakes (optional)
¼ cup extra-virgin olive oil	
8 anchovy fillets, roughly	

1. Remove the rough center stems from the kale leaves and roughly tear each leaf into about 4-by-1-inch strips. Place the torn kale in a large bowl and add the pine nuts and cheese. 2. In a small bowl, whisk together the olive oil, anchovies, lemon juice, and red pepper flakes (if using). Drizzle over the salad and toss to coat well. Let sit at room temperature 30 minutes before serving, tossing again just prior to serving.

Per Serving:

calories: 333 | fat: 27g | protein: 16g | carbs: 12g | fiber: 4g | sodium: 676mg

Powerhouse Arugula Salad

Prep time: 10 minutes | Cook time: 0 minutes | Serves 4

4 tablespoons extra-virgin olive oil	¼ teaspoon freshly ground black pepper
Zest and juice of 2 clementines or 1 orange (2 to 3 tablespoons)	8 cups baby arugula
1 tablespoon red wine vinegar	1 cup coarsely chopped walnuts
½ teaspoon salt	1 cup crumbled goat cheese
	½ cup pomegranate seeds

1. In a small bowl, whisk together the olive oil, zest and juice, vinegar, salt, and pepper and set aside. 2. To assemble the salad for serving, in a large bowl, combine the arugula, walnuts, goat cheese, and pomegranate seeds. Drizzle with the dressing and toss to coat.

Per Serving:

calories: 448 | fat: 41g | protein: 11g | carbs: 13g | fiber: 4g | sodium: 647mg

Greek Black-Eyed Pea Salad

Prep time: 10 minutes | Cook time: 0 minutes | Serves 4

2 tablespoons olive oil	1 shallot, finely chopped
Juice of 1 lemon (about 2 tablespoons)	2 scallions (green onions), chopped
1 garlic clove, minced	2 tablespoons chopped fresh dill
1 teaspoon ground cumin	¼ cup chopped fresh parsley
1 (15½-ounce / 439-g) can no-salt-added black-eyed peas, drained and rinsed	½ cup pitted Kalamata olives, sliced
1 red bell pepper, seeded and chopped	½ cup crumbled feta cheese (optional)

1. In a large bowl, whisk together the olive oil, lemon juice, garlic, and cumin. 2. Add the black-eyed peas, bell pepper, shallot, scallions, dill, parsley, olives, and feta (if using) and toss to combine. Serve.

Per Serving:

calories: 213 | fat: 14g | protein: 7g | carbs: 16g | fiber: 5g | sodium: 426mg

Asparagus Salad

Prep time: 10 minutes | Cook time: 0 minutes | Serves 4

1 pound (454 g) asparagus	4 tablespoons olive oil
Sea salt and freshly ground pepper, to taste	1 tablespoon balsamic vinegar
	1 tablespoon lemon zest

1. Either roast the asparagus or, with a vegetable peeler, shave it into thin strips. 2. Season to taste. 3. Toss with the olive oil and vinegar, garnish with a sprinkle of lemon zest, and serve.

Per Serving:

calories: 146 | fat: 14g | protein: 3g | carbs: 5g | fiber: 3g | sodium: 4mg

Panzanella (Tuscan Tomato and Bread Salad)

Prep time: 1 hour 5 minutes | Cook time: 0 minutes | Serves 2

3 tablespoons white wine vinegar, divided	1 large Persian (or mini) cucumber, sliced
1 small red onion, thinly sliced	¼ cup chopped fresh basil
4 ounces (113 g) stale, dense bread, such as French baguette or Italian (Vienna-style)	2 tablespoons extra virgin olive oil, divided
1 large tomato (any variety), chopped into bite-sized pieces	Pinch of kosher salt
	⅛ teaspoon freshly ground black pepper

1. Add 2 tablespoons of the vinegar to a small bowl filled with water. Add the onion and then set aside. 2. In a medium bowl, combine the remaining tablespoon of vinegar and 2 cups of water. Add the bread to the bowl and soak for 2–3 minutes (depending on how hard the bread is) until the bread has softened on the outside but is not falling apart. Place the bread in a colander and gently squeeze out any excess water and then chop into bite-sized pieces. Arrange the bread pieces on a large plate. 3. Drain the onion and add it to plate with the bread. Add the tomato, cucumber, basil, 1 tablespoon of the olive oil, kosher salt, and black pepper. Toss the ingredients carefully, then cover and transfer to the refrigerator to chill for a minimum of 1 hour. 4. When ready to serve, drizzle the remaining 1 tablespoon of olive oil over the top of the salad and serve promptly. This salad can be stored in the refrigerator for up to 5 hours, but should be consumed on the same day it is prepared.

Per Serving:

calories: 325 | fat: 16g | protein: 7g | carbs: 38g | fiber: 4g | sodium: 358mg

Citrus Fennel Salad

Prep time: 15 minutes | Cook time: 0 minutes | Serves 2

For the Dressing:	2 cups packed baby kale
2 tablespoons fresh orange juice	1 medium navel or blood orange, segmented
3 tablespoons olive oil	½ small fennel bulb, stems and leaves removed, sliced into matchsticks
1 tablespoon blood orange vinegar, other orange vinegar, or cider vinegar	3 tablespoons toasted pecans, chopped
1 tablespoon honey	2 ounces (57 g) goat cheese, crumbled
Salt	
Freshly ground black pepper	
For the Salad:	

Make the Dressing: Combine the orange juice, olive oil, vinegar, and honey in a small bowl and whisk to combine. Season with salt and pepper. Set the dressing aside. Make the Salad: 1. Divide the baby kale, orange segments, fennel, pecans, and goat cheese evenly between two plates. 2. Drizzle half of the dressing over each salad.

Per Serving:

calories: 502 | fat: 39g | protein: 13g | carbs: 31g | fiber: 6g | sodium: 158mg

Orange-Tarragon Chicken Salad Wrap

Prep time: 15 minutes | Cook time: 0 minutes | Serves 4

½ cup plain whole-milk Greek yogurt
2 tablespoons Dijon mustard
2 tablespoons extra-virgin olive oil
2 tablespoons chopped fresh tarragon or 1 teaspoon dried tarragon
½ teaspoon salt
¼ teaspoon freshly ground black

pepper
2 cups cooked shredded chicken
½ cup slivered almonds
4 to 8 large Bibb lettuce leaves, tough stem removed
2 small ripe avocados, peeled and thinly sliced
Zest of 1 clementine, or ½ small orange (about 1 tablespoon)

1. In a medium bowl, combine the yogurt, mustard, olive oil, tarragon, orange zest, salt, and pepper and whisk until creamy. 2. Add the shredded chicken and almonds and stir to coat. 3. To assemble the wraps, place about ½ cup chicken salad mixture in the center of each lettuce leaf and top with sliced avocados.

Per Serving:
calories: 491 | fat: 38g | protein: 28g | carbs: 14g | fiber: 9g | sodium: 454mg

Dakos (Cretan Salad)

Prep time: 7 minutes | Cook time: 00 minutes | Serves 1

1 medium ripe tomato (any variety)
2 whole-grain crispbreads or rusks (or 1 slice toasted whole-grain, wheat, or barley bread)
1 tablespoon plus 1 teaspoon

extra virgin olive oil
Pinch of kosher salt
1½ ounces (43 g) crumbled feta
2 teaspoons capers, drained
2 Kalamata olives, pitted
Pinch of dried oregano

1. Slice a thin round off the bottom of the tomato. Hold the tomato from the stem side and begin grating the tomato over a plate, using the largest holes of the grater. Grate until only the skin of the tomato remains, then discard the skin. Use a fine mesh strainer to drain the liquid from the grated tomato. 2. Place the crisps on a plate, one next to the other, and sprinkle with a few drops of water. Drizzle 1 tablespoon of the olive oil over the crisps and then top the crisps with the grated tomato, ensuring the crisps are thoroughly covered with the tomato. 3. Sprinkle the kosher salt over the tomato, then layer the crumbled feta over the top. Top with the capers and olives, and sprinkle the oregano over the top and drizzle with the remaining 1 teaspoon of olive oil. Serve promptly. (This salad is best served fresh.)

Per Serving:
calories: 346 | fat: 24g | protein: 12g | carbs: 21g | fiber: 4g | sodium: 626mg

Traditional Greek Salad

Prep time: 10 minutes | Cook time: 0 minutes | Serves 4

2 large English cucumbers
4 Roma tomatoes, quartered
1 green bell pepper, cut into 1- to 1½-inch chunks
¼ small red onion, thinly sliced
4 ounces (113 g) pitted Kalamata olives
¼ cup extra-virgin olive oil
2 tablespoons freshly squeezed

lemon juice
1 tablespoon red wine vinegar
1 tablespoon chopped fresh oregano or 1 teaspoon dried oregano
¼ teaspoon freshly ground black pepper
4 ounces (113 g) crumbled traditional feta cheese

1. Cut the cucumbers in half lengthwise and then into ½-inch-thick half-moons. Place in a large bowl. 2. Add the quartered tomatoes, bell pepper, red onion, and olives. 3. In a small bowl, whisk together the olive oil, lemon juice, vinegar, oregano, and pepper. Drizzle over the vegetables and toss to coat. 4. Divide between salad plates and top each with 1 ounce (28 g) of feta.

Per Serving:
calories: 256 | fat: 22g | protein: 6g | carbs: 11g | fiber: 3g | sodium: 476mg

Simple Insalata Mista (Mixed Salad) with Honey Balsamic Dressing

Prep time: 15 minutes | Cook time: 0 minutes | Serves 2

For the Dressing:
¼ cup balsamic vinegar
¼ cup olive oil
1 tablespoon honey
1 teaspoon Dijon mustard
¼ teaspoon salt, plus more to taste
¼ teaspoon garlic powder
Pinch freshly ground black pepper
For the Salad:

4 cups chopped red leaf lettuce
½ cup cherry or grape tomatoes, halved
½ English cucumber, sliced in quarters lengthwise and then cut into bite-size pieces
Any combination fresh, torn herbs (parsley, oregano, basil, chives, etc.)
1 tablespoon roasted sunflower seeds

Make the Dressing: Combine the vinegar, olive oil, honey, mustard, salt, garlic powder, and pepper in a jar with a lid. Shake well. Make the Salad: 1. In a large bowl, combine the lettuce, tomatoes, cucumber, and herbs. 2. Toss well to combine. 3. Pour all or as much dressing as desired over the tossed salad and toss again to coat the salad with dressing. 4. Top with the sunflower seeds.

Per Serving:
calories: 339 | fat: 26g | protein: 4g | carbs: 24g | fiber: 3g | sodium: 171mg

Cauliflower Tabbouleh Salad

Prep time: 15 minutes | Cook time: 0 minutes | Serves 4

¼ cup extra-virgin olive oil
¼ cup lemon juice
Zest of 1 lemon
¾ teaspoon kosher salt
½ teaspoon ground turmeric
¼ teaspoon ground coriander
¼ teaspoon ground cumin

¼ teaspoon black pepper
⅛ teaspoon ground cinnamon
1 pound (454 g) riced cauliflower
1 English cucumber, diced
12 cherry tomatoes, halved
1 cup fresh parsley, chopped
½ cup fresh mint, chopped

1. In a large bowl, whisk together the olive oil, lemon juice, lemon zest, salt, turmeric, coriander, cumin, black pepper, and cinnamon. 2. Add the riced cauliflower to the bowl and mix well. Add in the cucumber, tomatoes, parsley, and mint and gently mix together.

Per Serving:

calories: 180 | fat: 15g | protein: 4g | carbs: 12g | fiber: 5g | sodium:260 mg

Flank Steak Spinach Salad

Prep time: 15 minutes | Cook time: 10 minutes | Serves 4

1 pound (454 g) flank steak
1 teaspoon extra-virgin olive oil
1 tablespoon garlic powder
½ teaspoon salt
½ teaspoon freshly ground black pepper

4 cups baby spinach leaves
10 cherry tomatoes, halved
10 cremini or white mushrooms, sliced
1 small red onion, thinly sliced
½ red bell pepper, thinly sliced

1. Preheat the broiler. Line a baking sheet with aluminum foil. 2. Rub the top of the flank steak with the olive oil, garlic powder, salt, and pepper and let sit for 10 minutes before placing under the broiler. Broil for 5 minutes on each side for medium rare. Allow the meat to rest on a cutting board for 10 minutes. 3. Meanwhile, in a large bowl, combine the spinach, tomatoes, mushrooms, onion, and bell pepper and toss well. 4. To serve, divide the salad among 4 dinner plates. Slice the steak on the diagonal and place 4 to 5 slices on top of each salad. Serve with your favorite vinaigrette.

Per Serving:

calories: 211 | fat: 7g | protein: 28g | carbs: 9g | fiber: 2g | sodium: 382mg

Tuna Niçoise

Prep time: 15 minutes | Cook time: 20 minutes | Serves 4

1 pound (454 g) small red or fingerling potatoes, halved
1 pound (454 g) green beans or haricots verts, trimmed
1 head romaine lettuce, chopped or torn into bite-size pieces
½ pint cherry tomatoes, halved
8 radishes, thinly sliced

½ cup olives, pitted (any kind you like)
2 (5-ounce / 142-g) cans no-salt-added tuna packed in olive oil, drained
8 anchovies (optional)

1. Fill a large pot fitted with a steamer basket with 2 to 3 inches of water. Put the potatoes in the steamer basket and lay the green beans on top of the potatoes. Bring the water to a boil over high heat, lower the heat to low and simmer, cover, and cook for 7 minutes, or until the green beans are tender but crisp. Remove the green beans and continue to steam the potatoes for an additional 10 minutes. 2. Place the romaine lettuce on a serving platter. Group the potatoes, green beans, tomatoes, radishes, olives, and tuna in different areas of the platter. If using the anchovies, place them around the platter.

Per Serving:

calories: 315 | fat: 9g | protein: 28g | carbs: 33g | fiber: 9g | sodium: 420mg

Chapter 12
Desserts

Greek Yogurt with Honey and Pomegranates

Prep time: 5 minutes | Cook time: 0 minutes | Serves 4

4 cups plain full-fat Greek yogurt	¼ cup honey
½ cup pomegranate seeds	Sugar, for topping (optional)

1. Evenly divide the yogurt among four bowls. Evenly divide the pomegranate seeds among the bowls and drizzle each with the honey. 2. Sprinkle each bowl with a pinch of sugar, if desired, and serve.

Per Serving:
calories: 232 | fat: 8g | protein: 9g | carbs: 33g | fiber: 1g | sodium: 114mg

Lemon Coconut Cake

Prep time: 5 minutes | Cook time: 40 minutes | Serves 9

Base:	Optional: low-carb sweetener, to taste
6 large eggs, separated	
⅓ cup melted ghee or virgin coconut oil	Topping:
1 tablespoon fresh lemon juice	½ cup unsweetened large coconut flakes
Zest of 2 lemons	1 cup heavy whipping cream or coconut cream
2 cups almond flour	
½ cup coconut flour	¼ cup mascarpone, more heavy whipping cream, or coconut cream
¼ cup collagen powder	
1 teaspoon baking soda	
1 teaspoon vanilla powder or 1 tablespoon unsweetened vanilla extract	½ teaspoon vanilla powder or 1½ teaspoons unsweetened vanilla extract

1. Preheat the oven to 285°F (140°C) fan assisted or 320°F (160°C) conventional. Line a baking tray with parchment paper (or use a silicone tray). A square 8 × 8–inch (20 × 20 cm) or a rectangular tray of similar size will work best. 2. To make the base: Whisk the egg whites in a bowl until stiff peaks form. In a separate bowl, whisk the egg yolks, melted ghee, lemon juice, and lemon zest. In a third bowl, mix the almond flour, coconut flour, collagen, baking soda, vanilla and optional sweetener. 3. Add the whisked egg yolk–ghee mixture into the dry mixture and combine well. Gently fold in the egg whites, trying not to deflate them. 4. Pour into the baking tray. Bake for 35 to 40 minutes, until lightly golden on top and set inside. Remove from the oven and let cool completely before adding the topping. 5. To make the topping: Preheat the oven to 350°F (175°C) fan assisted or 380°F (195°C) conventional. Place the coconut flakes on a baking tray and bake for 2 to 3 minutes. Remove from the oven and set aside to cool. 6. Once the cake is cool, place the cream, mascarpone, and vanilla in a bowl. Whip until soft peaks form. Spread on top of the cooled cake and top with the toasted coconut flakes. 7. To store, refrigerate for up to 5 days or freeze for up to 3 months. Coconut flakes will soften in the fridge. If you want to keep them crunchy, sprinkle on top of each slice before serving.

Per Serving:
calories: 342 | fat: 31g | protein: 9g | carbs: 10g | fiber: 4g | sodium: 208mg

Chocolate-Dipped Fruit Bites

Prep time: 10 minutes | Cook time: 0 minutes | Serves 4 to 6

½ cup semisweet chocolate chips	2 kiwis, peeled and sliced
¼ cup low-fat milk	1 cup honeydew melon chunks (about 2-inch chunks)
½ teaspoon pure vanilla extract	1 pound (454 g) whole strawberries
½ teaspoon ground nutmeg	
¼ teaspoon salt	

1. Place the chocolate chips in a small bowl. 2. In another small bowl, microwave the milk until hot, about 30 seconds. Pour the milk over the chocolate chips and let sit for 1 minute, then whisk until the chocolate is melted and smooth. Stir in the vanilla, nutmeg, and salt and allow to cool for 5 minutes. 3. Line a baking sheet with wax paper. Dip each piece of fruit halfway into the chocolate, tap gently to remove excess chocolate, and place the fruit on the baking sheet. 4. Once all the fruit has been dipped, allow it to sit until dry, about 30 minutes. Arrange on a platter and serve.

Per Serving:
calories: 125 | fat: 5g | protein: 2g | carbs: 21g | fiber: 3g | sodium: 110mg

Chocolate Turtle Hummus

Prep time: 15 minutes | Cook time: 0 minutes | Serves 2

For the Caramel:	2 tablespoons unsweetened cocoa powder
2 tablespoons coconut oil	
1 tablespoon maple syrup	1 tablespoon maple syrup, plus more to taste
1 tablespoon almond butter	
Pinch salt	2 tablespoons almond milk, or more as needed, to thin
For the Hummus:	
½ cup chickpeas, drained and rinsed	Pinch salt
	2 tablespoons pecans

Make the caramel 1. put the coconut oil in a small microwave-safe bowl. If it's solid, microwave it for about 15 seconds to melt it. 2. Stir in the maple syrup, almond butter, and salt. 3. Place the caramel in the refrigerator for 5 to 10 minutes to thicken. Make the hummus 1. In a food processor, combine the chickpeas, cocoa powder, maple syrup, almond milk, and pinch of salt, and process until smooth. Scrape down the sides to make sure everything is incorporated. 2. If the hummus seems too thick, add another tablespoon of almond milk. 3. Add the pecans and pulse 6 times to roughly chop them. 4. Transfer the hummus to a serving bowl and when the caramel is thickened, swirl it into the hummus. Gently fold it in, but don't mix it in completely. 5. Serve with fresh fruit or pretzels.

Per Serving:
calories: 321 | fat: 22g | protein: 7g | carbs: 30g | fiber: 6g | sodium: 100mg

Mascarpone and Fig Crostini

Prep time: 10 minutes | Cook time: 10 minutes | Serves 6 to 8

1 long French baguette	1 (8-ounce / 227-g) tub
4 tablespoons (½ stick) salted	mascarpone cheese
butter, melted	1 (12-ounce / 340-g) jar fig jam

1. Preheat the oven to 350°F(180℃). 2. Slice the bread into ¼-inch-thick slices. 3. Arrange the sliced bread on a baking sheet and brush each slice with the melted butter. 4. Put the baking sheet in the oven and toast the bread for 5 to 7 minutes, just until golden brown. 5. Let the bread cool slightly. Spread about a teaspoon or so of the mascarpone cheese on each piece of bread. 6. Top with a teaspoon or so of the jam. Serve immediately.

Per Serving:
calories: 445 | fat: 24g | protein: 3g | carbs: 48g | fiber: 5g | sodium: 314mg

Karithopita (Greek Juicy Walnut Cake)

Prep time: 10 minutes | Cook time: 30 minutes | Serves 8

¼ cup extra virgin olive oil plus	¼ cup whole-wheat flour
1 teaspoon for brushing	¼ teaspoon baking powder
½ cup walnut halves	¼ teaspoon baking soda
¼ cup granulated sugar	¼ teaspoon ground cinnamon
¼ cup brown sugar	Syrup:
1 egg	⅓ cup water
1 tablespoon pure vanilla extract	¼ cup granulated sugar
¼ cup orange juice, strained	1 cinnamon stick
½ cup all-purpose flour	1 tablespoon orange juice

1. Preheat the oven to 350°F (180℃). Brush an 8 × 4-inch loaf pan with 1 teaspoon of the olive oil, and then line the pan with parchment paper. 2. Prepare the syrup by combining the water, sugar, and cinnamon stick in a small pan placed over medium heat. Bring to a boil and then boil for 2 minutes, then remove the pan from the heat. Remove the cinnamon stick, add the orange juice, then stir and set aside to cool. 3. Pulse the walnuts in a food processor until you achieve a cornmeal-like consistency. (Do not over-grind.) 4. In a large bowl, combine ¼ cup of the olive oil, the granulated sugar, and the brown sugar. Stir until the sugar is dissolved, then add the egg. Add the vanilla extract and orange juice. Mix well. 5. In a small bowl, combine the all-purpose flour and whole-wheat flour with the baking powder, baking soda, and cinnamon. 6. Add the flour mixture to the olive oil mixture and mix just until the flour has been incorporated. Add ¼ cup of the ground walnuts and mix until they are distributed throughout the batter. 7. Pour the batter into the prepared pan. Bake for 25–30 minutes or until a toothpick inserted into the cake comes out clean. 8. Use a toothpick to poke 8 holes across the top of the cake and then pour the syrup over the entire surface of the cake. Sprinkle the remaining ground walnuts over the top, and then set the cake aside to rest for 30 minutes before cutting it in equal-sized 1-inch slices. Store in an airtight container in the refrigerator for up to 5 days.

Per Serving:
calories: 240 | fat: 12g | protein: 3g | carbs: 30g | fiber: 1g | sodium: 52mg

Individual Meringues with Strawberries, Mint, and Toasted Coconut

Prep time: 25 minutes | Cook time: 1 hour 30 minutes | Serves 6

4 large egg whites	diced
1 teaspoon vanilla extract	¼ cup fresh mint, chopped
½ teaspoon cream of tartar	¼ cup unsweetened shredded
¾ cup sugar	coconut, toasted
8 ounces (227 g) strawberries,	

1. Preheat the oven to 225ºF (107℃). Line 2 baking sheets with parchment paper. 2. Place the egg whites, vanilla, and cream of tartar in the bowl of a stand mixer (or use a large bowl with an electric hand mixer); beat at medium speed until soft peaks form, about 2 to 3 minutes. Increase to high speed and gradually add the sugar, beating until stiff peaks form and the mixture looks shiny and smooth, about 2 to 3 minutes. 3. Using a spatula or spoon, drop ⅓ cup of meringue onto a prepared baking sheet; smooth out and make shapelier as desired. In total, make 12 dollops, 6 per sheet, leaving at least 1 inch between dollops. 4. Bake for 1½ hours, rotating baking sheets between top and bottom, front and back, halfway through. After 1½ hours, turn off the oven, but keep the door closed. Leave the meringues in the oven for an additional 30 minutes. You can leave the meringues in the oven even longer (or overnight), or you may let them finish cooling to room temperature. 5. Combine the strawberries, mint, and coconut in a medium bowl. Serve 2 meringues per person topped with the fruit mixture.

Per Serving:
calories: 150 | fat: 2g | protein: 3g | carbs: 29g | fiber: 1g | sodium: 40mg

Whipped Greek Yogurt with Chocolate

Prep time: 10 minutes | Cook time: 0 minutes | Serves 4

4 cups plain full-fat Greek	2 ounces (57 g) dark chocolate
yogurt	(at least 70% cacao), grated, for
½ cup heavy (whipping) cream	topping

1. In the bowl of a stand mixer fitted with the whisk attachment or in a large bowl using a handheld mixer, whip the yogurt and cream for about 5 minutes, or until peaks form. 2. Evenly divide the whipped yogurt mixture among bowls and top with the grated chocolate. Serve.

Per Serving:
calories: 337 | fat: 25g | protein: 10g | carbs: 19g | fiber: 2g | sodium: 127mg

Fresh Figs with Chocolate Sauce

Prep time: 5 minutes | Cook time: 0 minutes | Serves 4

¼ cup honey	8 fresh figs
2 tablespoons cocoa powder	

1. Combine the honey and cocoa powder in a small bowl, and mix well to form a syrup. 2. Cut the figs in half and place cut side up. Drizzle with the syrup and serve.

Per Serving:

calories: 112 | fat: 1g | protein: 1g | carbs: 30g | fiber: 3g | sodium: 3mg

Minty Watermelon Salad

Prep time: 10 minutes | Cook time: 0 minutes | Serves 6 to 8

1 medium watermelon	2 tablespoons lemon juice
1 cup fresh blueberries	⅓ cup honey
2 tablespoons fresh mint leaves	

1. Cut the watermelon into 1-inch cubes. Put them in a bowl. 2. Evenly distribute the blueberries over the watermelon. 3. Finely chop the mint leaves and put them into a separate bowl. 4. Add the lemon juice and honey to the mint and whisk together. 5. Drizzle the mint dressing over the watermelon and blueberries. Serve cold.

Per Serving:

calories: 238 | fat: 1g | protein: 4g | carbs: 61g | fiber: 3g | sodium: 11mg

Grilled Fruit Kebabs with Honey Labneh

Prep time: 15 minutes | Cook time: 10 minutes | Serves 2

⅔ cup prepared labneh, or, if making your own, ⅔ cup full-fat plain Greek yogurt	Pinch salt
	3 cups fresh fruit cut into 2-inch chunks (pineapple, cantaloupe, nectarines, strawberries, plums, or mango)
2 tablespoons honey	
1 teaspoon vanilla extract	

1. If making your own labneh, place a colander over a bowl and line it with cheesecloth. Place the Greek yogurt in the cheesecloth and wrap it up. Put the bowl in the refrigerator and let sit for at least 12 to 24 hours, until it's thick like soft cheese. 2. Mix honey, vanilla, and salt into labneh. Stir well to combine and set it aside. 3. Heat the grill to medium (about 300°F/ 150°C) and oil the grill grate. Alternatively, you can cook these on the stovetop in a heavy grill pan (cast iron works well). 4. Thread the fruit onto skewers and grill for 4 minutes on each side, or until fruit is softened and has grill marks on each side. 5. Serve the fruit with labneh to dip.

Per Serving:

calories: 292 | fat: 6g | protein: 5g | carbs: 60g | fiber: 4g | sodium: 131mg

Baklava and Honey

Prep time: 40 minutes | Cook time: 1 hour | Serves 6 to 8

2 cups very finely chopped walnuts or pecans	butter, melted
1 teaspoon cinnamon	1 (16-ounce / 454-g) package phyllo dough, thawed
1 cup (2 sticks) of unsalted	1 (12-ounce / 340-g) jar honey

1. Preheat the oven to 350°F(180°C). 2. In a bowl, combine the chopped nuts and cinnamon. 3. Using a brush, butter the sides and bottom of a 9-by-13-inch inch baking dish. 4. Remove the phyllo dough from the package and cut it to the size of the baking dish using a sharp knife. 5. Place one sheet of phyllo dough on the bottom of the dish, brush with butter, and repeat until you have 8 layers. 6. Sprinkle ⅓ cup of the nut mixture over the phyllo layers. Top with a sheet of phyllo dough, butter that sheet, and repeat until you have 4 sheets of buttered phyllo dough. 7. Sprinkle ⅓ cup of the nut mixture for another layer of nuts. Repeat the layering of nuts and 4 sheets of buttered phyllo until all the nut mixture is gone. The last layer should be 8 buttered sheets of phyllo. 8. Before you bake, cut the baklava into desired shapes; traditionally this is diamonds, triangles, or squares. 9. Bake the baklava for 1 hour or until the top layer is golden brown. 10. While the baklava is baking, heat the honey in a pan just until it is warm and easy to pour. 11. Once the baklava is done baking, immediately pour the honey evenly over the baklava and let it absorb it, about 20 minutes. Serve warm or at room temperature.

Per Serving:

calories: 1235 | fat: 89g | protein: 18g | carbs: 109g | fiber: 7g | sodium: 588mg

Peaches Poached in Rose Water

Prep time: 15 minutes | Cook time: 1 minute | Serves 6

1 cup water	1 teaspoon vanilla bean paste
1 cup rose water	6 large yellow peaches, pitted and quartered
¼ cup wildflower honey	
8 green cardamom pods, lightly crushed	½ cup chopped unsalted roasted pistachio meats

1. Add water, rose water, honey, cardamom, and vanilla to the Instant Pot®. Whisk well, then add peaches. Close lid, set steam release to Sealing, press the Manual button, and set time to 1 minute. 2. When the timer beeps, quick-release the pressure until the float valve drops. Press the Cancel button and open lid. Allow peaches to stand for 10 minutes. Carefully remove peaches from poaching liquid with a slotted spoon. 3. Slip skins from peach slices. Arrange slices on a plate and garnish with pistachios. Serve warm or at room temperature.

Per Serving:

calories: 145 | fat: 3g | protein: 2g | carbs: 28g | fiber: 2g | sodium: 8mg

Lemon Fool

Prep time: 25minutes |Cook time: 5 minutes| Serves: 4

1 cup 2% plain Greek yogurt	3½ tablespoons honey, divided
1 medium lemon	⅔ cup heavy (whipping) cream
¼ cup cold water	Fresh fruit and mint leaves, for
1½ teaspoons cornstarch	serving (optional)

1. Place a large glass bowl and the metal beaters from your electric mixer in the refrigerator to chill. Add the yogurt to a medium glass bowl, and place that bowl in the refrigerator to chill as well. 2. Using a Microplane or citrus zester, zest the lemon into a medium, microwave-safe bowl. Halve the lemon, and squeeze 1 tablespoon of lemon juice into the bowl. Add the water and cornstarch, and stir well. Whisk in 3 tablespoons of honey. Microwave the lemon mixture on high for 1 minute; stir and microwave for an additional 10 to 30 seconds, until the mixture is thick and bubbling. 3. Remove the bowl of yogurt from the refrigerator, and whisk in the warm lemon mixture. Place the yogurt back in the refrigerator. 4. Remove the large chilled bowl and the beaters from the refrigerator. Assemble your electric mixer with the chilled beaters. Pour the cream into the chilled bowl, and beat until soft peaks form—1 to 3 minutes, depending on the freshness of your cream. 5. Take the chilled yogurt mixture out of the refrigerator. Gently fold it into the whipped cream using a rubber scraper; lift and turn the mixture to prevent the cream from deflating. Chill until serving, at least 15 minutes but no longer than 1 hour. 6. To serve, spoon the lemon fool into four glasses or dessert dishes and drizzle with the remaining ½ tablespoon of honey. Top with fresh fruit and mint, if desired.

Per Serving:

calories: 172 | fat: 8g | protein: 4g | carbs: 22g | fiber: 1g | sodium: 52mg

Individual Apple Pockets

Prep time: 5 minutes | Cook time: 15 minutes | Serves 6

1 organic puff pastry, rolled out, at room temperature	⅛ teaspoon ground cinnamon
1 Gala apple, peeled and sliced	⅛ teaspoon ground cardamom
¼ cup brown sugar	Nonstick cooking spray
	Honey, for topping

1. Preheat the oven to 350°F(180°C). 2. Cut the pastry dough into 4 even discs. Peel and slice the apple. In a small bowl, toss the slices with brown sugar, cinnamon, and cardamom. 3. Spray a muffin tin very well with nonstick cooking spray. Be sure to spray only the muffin holders you plan to use. 4. Once sprayed, line the bottom of the muffin tin with the dough and place 1 or 2 broken apple slices on top. Fold the remaining dough over the apple and drizzle with honey. 5. Bake for 15 minutes or until brown and bubbly.

Per Serving:

calories: 250 | fat: 15g | protein: 3g | carbs: 30g | fiber: 1g | sodium: 98mg

Roasted Orange Rice Pudding

Prep time: 10 minutes |Cook time: 20 minutes| Serves: 6

Nonstick cooking spray	1 cup 100% orange juice
2 medium oranges	1 cup uncooked instant brown
2 teaspoons extra-virgin olive oil	rice
⅛ teaspoon kosher or sea salt	¼ cup honey
2 large eggs, beaten	½ teaspoon ground cinnamon
2 cups 2% milk	1 teaspoon vanilla extract

1. Preheat the oven to 450°F(235°C). Spray a large, rimmed baking sheet with nonstick cooking spray. Set aside. 2. Slice the unpeeled oranges into ¼-inch rounds. Brush with oil, and sprinkle with salt. Place the slices on the baking sheet and roast for 4 minutes. Flip the slices and roast for 4 more minutes, until they begin to brown. Remove from the oven and set aside. 3. Crack the eggs into a medium bowl near the stove. In a medium saucepan, mix together the milk, orange juice, rice, honey, and cinnamon. Bring to a boil over medium-high heat, stirring constantly. Reduce the heat to medium-low and simmer for 10 minutes, stirring occasionally. 4. Using a measuring cup, scoop out ½ cup of the hot rice mixture and whisk it into the eggs. Then, while constantly stirring the mixture in the pan, slowly pour the egg mixture back into the saucepan (to prevent the eggs from scrambling). Cook on low heat for 1 to 2 minutes, until thickened, stirring constantly; do not boil. Remove from the heat and stir in the vanilla. 5. Let the pudding stand for a few minutes for the rice to soften. The rice will be cooked but slightly chewy. For softer rice, let stand for another half hour. Serve warm or at room temperature, topped with the roasted oranges.

Per Serving:

calories: 289 | fat: 6g | protein: 8g | carbs: 52g | fiber: 4g | sodium: 118mg

Grilled Pineapple Dessert

Prep time: 5 minutes | Cook time: 12 minutes | Serves 4

Oil for misting or cooking spray	2 tablespoons slivered almonds, toasted
4½-inch-thick slices fresh pineapple, core removed	Vanilla frozen yogurt or coconut sorbet
1 tablespoon honey	
¼ teaspoon brandy	

1. Spray both sides of pineapple slices with oil or cooking spray. Place into air fryer basket. 2. Air fry at 390°F (199°C) for 6 minutes. Turn slices over and cook for an additional 6 minutes. 3. Mix together the honey and brandy. 4. Remove cooked pineapple slices from air fryer, sprinkle with toasted almonds, and drizzle with honey mixture. 5. Serve with a scoop of frozen yogurt or sorbet on the side.

Per Serving:

calories: 65 | fat: 2g | protein: 1g | carbs: 11g | fiber: 1g | sodium: 1mg

Vanilla-Poached Apricots

Prep time: 10 minutes | Cook time: 1 minute | Serves 6

1¼ cups water	1 teaspoon vanilla bean paste
¼ cup marsala wine	8 medium apricots, sliced in
¼ cup sugar	half and pitted

1. Place all ingredients in the Instant Pot®. Stir to combine. Close lid, set steam release to Sealing, press the Manual button, and set time to 1 minute. 2. When the timer beeps, quick-release the pressure until the float valve drops. Press the Cancel button and open lid. Let stand for 10 minutes. Carefully remove apricots from poaching liquid with a slotted spoon. Serve warm or at room temperature.

Per Serving:

calories: 62 | fat: 0g | protein: 2g | carbs: 14g | fiber: 1g | sodium: 10mg

Roasted Plums with Nut Crumble

Prep time: 5 minutes | Cook time: 25 minutes | Serves 4

¼ cup honey	1 tablespoon nuts, coarsely
¼ cup freshly squeezed orange juice	chopped (your choice; I like almonds, pecans, and walnuts)
4 large plums, halved and pitted	1½ teaspoons canola oil
¼ cup whole-wheat pastry flour	½ cup plain Greek yogurt
1 tablespoon pure maple sugar	

1. Preheat the oven to 400°F (205°C). Combine the honey and orange juice in a square baking dish. Place the plums, cut-side down, in the dish. Roast about 15 minutes, and then turn the plums over and roast an additional 10 minutes, or until tender and juicy. 2. In a medium bowl, combine the flour, maple sugar, nuts, and canola oil and mix well. Spread on a small baking sheet and bake alongside the plums, tossing once, until golden brown, about 5 minutes. Set aside until the plums have finished cooking. 3. Serve the plums drizzled with pan juices and topped with the nut crumble and a dollop of yogurt.

Per Serving:

calories: 175 | fat: 3g | protein: 4g | carbs: 36g | fiber: 2g | sodium: 10mg

Orange–Olive Oil Cupcakes

Prep time: 15 minutes | Cook time: 20 minutes | Makes 6 cupcakes

1 large egg	Zest of 1 orange
2 tablespoons powdered sugar-free sweetener (such as stevia or monk fruit extract)	1 cup almond flour
	¾ teaspoon baking powder
	⅛ teaspoon salt
½ cup extra-virgin olive oil	1 tablespoon freshly squeezed
1 teaspoon almond extract	orange juice

1. Preheat the oven to 350°F (180°C). Place muffin liners into 6 cups of a muffin tin. 2. In a large bowl, whisk together the egg and powdered sweetener. Add the olive oil, almond extract, and orange zest and whisk to combine well. 3. In a small bowl, whisk together the almond flour, baking powder, and salt. Add to wet ingredients along with the orange juice and stir until just combined. 4. Divide the batter evenly into 6 muffin cups and bake until a toothpick inserted in the center of the cupcake comes out clean, 15 to 18 minutes. 5. Remove from the oven and cool for 5 minutes in the tin before transferring to a wire rack to cool completely.

Per Serving:

1 cup cake: calories: 280 | fat: 27g | protein: 4g | carbs: 8g | fiber: 2g | sodium: 65mg

Ricotta with Balsamic Cherries and Black Pepper

Prep time: 10 minutes | Cook time: 0 minutes | Serves 4

1 cup (8 ounces/ 227 g) ricotta	1½ teaspoons aged balsamic vinegar
2 tablespoons honey	
1 teaspoon vanilla extract	Pinch of freshly ground black pepper
3 cups pitted sweet cherries (thawed if frozen), halved	

1. In a food processor, combine the ricotta, honey, and vanilla and process until smooth. Transfer the mixture to a medium bowl, cover, and refrigerate for 1 hour. 2. In a small bowl, combine the cherries, vinegar, and pepper and stir to mix well. Chill along with the ricotta mixture. 3. To serve, spoon the ricotta mixture into 4 serving bowls or glasses. Top with the cherries, dividing them equally and spooning a bit of the accumulated juice over the top of each bowl. Serve chilled.

Per Serving:

calories: 236 | fat: 5g | protein: 7g | carbs: 42g | fiber: 1g | sodium: 93mg

Red Grapefruit Granita

Prep time: 5 minutes | Cook time: 0 minutes | Serves 4 to 6

3 cups red grapefruit sections	1 tablespoon freshly squeezed lime juice
1 cup freshly squeezed red grapefruit juice	
	Fresh basil leaves for garnish
¼ cup honey	

1. Remove as much pith (white part) and membrane as possible from the grapefruit segments. 2. Combine all ingredients except the basil in a blender or food processor and pulse just until smooth. 3. Pour the mixture into a shallow glass baking dish and place in the freezer for 1 hour. Stir with a fork and freeze for another 30 minutes, then repeat. To serve, scoop into small dessert glasses and garnish with fresh basil leaves.

Per Serving:

calories: 94 | fat: 0g | protein: 1g | carbs: 24g | fiber: 1g | sodium: 1mg

Brown Betty Apple Dessert

Prep time: 15 minutes | Cook time: 10 minutes | Serves 8

2 cups dried bread crumbs	1 cup olive oil, divided
½ cup sugar	8 medium apples, peeled, cored,
1 teaspoon ground cinnamon	and diced
3 tablespoons lemon juice	2 cups water
1 tablespoon grated lemon zest	

1. Combine crumbs, sugar, cinnamon, lemon juice, lemon zest, and ½ cup oil in a medium mixing bowl. Set aside. 2. In a greased oven-safe dish that will fit in your cooker loosely, add a thin layer of crumbs, then one diced apple. Continue filling the container with alternating layers of crumbs and apples until all ingredients are finished. Pour remaining ½ cup oil on top. 3. Add water to the Instant Pot® and place rack inside. Make a foil sling by folding a long piece of foil in half lengthwise and lower the uncovered container into the pot using the sling. 4. Close lid, set steam release to Sealing, press the Manual button, and set time to 10 minutes. When the timer beeps, let pressure release naturally, about 20 minutes. Press the Cancel button and open lid. 5. Using the sling, remove the baking dish from the pot and let stand for 5 minutes before serving.

Per Serving:

calories: 422 | fat: 27g | protein: 0g | carbs: 40g | fiber: 4g | sodium: 474mg

Pears with Blue Cheese and Walnuts

Prep time: 10 minutes | Cook time: 0 minutes | Serves 1

1 to 2 pears, cored and sliced into 12 slices	12 walnut halves
	1 tablespoon honey
¼ cup blue cheese crumbles	

1. Lay the pear slices on a plate, and top with the blue cheese crumbles. Top each slice with 1 walnut, and drizzle with honey. 2. Serve and enjoy!

Per Serving:

calories: 420 | fat: 29g | protein: 12g | carbs: 35g | fiber: 6g | sodium: 389mg

Grilled Stone Fruit

Prep time: 15 minutes | Cook time: 6 minutes | Serves 2

2 peaches, halved and pitted	½ cup low-fat ricotta cheese
2 plums, halved and pitted	2 tablespoons honey
3 apricots, halved and pitted	

1. Heat grill to medium heat. 2. Oil the grates or spray with cooking spray. 3. Place the fruit cut side down on the grill, and grill for 2–3 minutes per side, until lightly charred and soft. 4. Serve warm with the ricotta and drizzle with honey.

Per Serving:

calories: 263 | fat: 6g | protein: 10g | carbs: 48g | fiber: 4g | sodium: 63mg

Spanish Cream

Prep time: 5 minutes | Cook time: 0 minutes | Serves 6

3 large eggs	tablespoon unsweetened vanilla
1¼ cups unsweetened almond milk, divided	extract
1 tablespoon gelatin powder	1 teaspoon cinnamon, plus more for dusting
1¼ cups goat's cream, heavy whipping cream, or coconut cream	½ ounce (14 g) grated 100% chocolate, for topping
1 teaspoon vanilla powder or 1	Optional: low-carb sweetener, to taste

1. Separate the egg whites from the egg yolks. Place ½ cup (120 ml) of the almond milk in a small bowl, then add the gelatin and let it bloom. 2. Place the yolks, cream, and the remaining ¾ cup (180 ml) almond milk in a heatproof bowl placed over a small saucepan filled with 1 cup (240 ml) of water, placed over medium heat, ensuring that the bottom of the bowl doesn't touch the water. Whisk while heating until the mixture is smooth and thickened. 3. Stir in the vanilla, cinnamon, sweetener (if using), and the bloomed gelatin. Cover with plastic wrap pressed to the surface, and chill for 30 minutes. At this point the mixture will look runny. Don't panic! This is absolutely normal. It will firm up. 4. In a bowl with a hand mixer, or in a stand mixer, whisk the egg whites until stiff, then fold them through the cooled custard. Divide among six serving glasses and chill until fully set, 3 to 4 hours. Sprinkle with the grated chocolate and, optionally, add the sweetener and a dusting of cinnamon. Store covered in the refrigerator for up to 5 days.

Per Serving:

calories: 172 | fat: 13g | protein: 5g | carbs: 7g | fiber: 1g | sodium: 83mg

Figs with Mascarpone and Honey

Prep time: 5 minutes | Cook time: 5 minutes | Serves 4

⅓ cup walnuts, chopped	1 tablespoon honey
8 fresh figs, halved	¼ teaspoon flaked sea salt
¼ cup mascarpone cheese	

1. In a skillet over medium heat, toast the walnuts, stirring often, 3 to 5 minutes. 2. Arrange the figs cut-side up on a plate or platter. Using your finger, make a small depression in the cut side of each fig and fill with mascarpone cheese. Sprinkle with a bit of the walnuts, drizzle with the honey, and add a tiny pinch of sea salt.

Per Serving:

calories: 200 | fat: 13g | protein: 3g | carbs: 24g | fiber: 3g | sodium: 105mg

Cinnamon-Stewed Dried Plums with Greek Yogurt

Prep time: 5 minutes | Cook time: 3 minutes | Serves 6

3 cups dried plums
2 cups water
2 tablespoons sugar

2 cinnamon sticks
3 cups low-fat plain Greek yogurt

1. Add dried plums, water, sugar, and cinnamon to the Instant Pot®. Close lid, set steam release to Sealing, press the Manual button, and set time to 3 minutes. 2. When the timer beeps, quick-release the pressure until the float valve drops. Press the Cancel button and open lid. Remove and discard cinnamon sticks. Serve warm over Greek yogurt.

Per Serving:

calories: 301 | fat: 2g | protein: 14g | carbs: 61g | fiber: 4g | sodium: 50mg

Chocolate Lava Cakes

Prep time: 5 minutes | Cook time: 15 minutes | Serves 2

2 large eggs, whisked
¼ cup blanched finely ground almond flour

½ teaspoon vanilla extract
2 ounces (57 g) low-carb chocolate chips, melted

1. In a medium bowl, mix eggs with flour and vanilla. Fold in chocolate until fully combined. 2. Pour batter into two ramekins greased with cooking spray. Place ramekins into air fryer basket. Adjust the temperature to 320ºF (160ºC) and bake for 15 minutes. Cakes will be set at the edges and firm in the center when done. Let cool 5 minutes before serving.

Per Serving:

calories: 313 | fat: 23g | protein: 11g | carbs: 16g | fiber: 5g | sodium: 77mg

Chapter 13

Pasta

Fresh Tomato Pasta Bowl

Prep time: 10 minutes | Cook time: 15 minutes | Serves 4

8 ounces (227 g) whole-grain linguine
1 tablespoon extra-virgin olive oil
2 garlic cloves, minced
¼ cup chopped yellow onion
1 teaspoon chopped fresh oregano
½ teaspoon salt
¼ teaspoon freshly ground black pepper
1 teaspoon tomato paste
8 ounces (227 g) cherry tomatoes, halved
½ cup grated Parmesan cheese
1 tablespoon chopped fresh parsley

1. Bring a large saucepan of water to a boil over high heat and cook the linguine according to the package instructions until al dente (still slightly firm). Drain, reserving ½ cup of the pasta water. Do not rinse the pasta. 2. In a large, heavy skillet, heat the olive oil over medium-high heat. Sauté the garlic, onion, and oregano until the onion is just translucent, about 5 minutes. 3. Add the salt, pepper, tomato paste, and ¼ cup of the reserved pasta water. Stir well and allow it to cook for 1 minute. 4. Stir in the tomatoes and cooked pasta, tossing everything well to coat. Add more pasta water if needed. 5. To serve, mound the pasta in shallow bowls and top with Parmesan cheese and parsley.

Per Serving:

calories: 310 | fat: 9g | protein: 10g | carbs: 49g | fiber: 7g | sodium: 305mg

Rotini with Walnut Pesto, Peas, and Cherry Tomatoes

Prep time: 10 minutes | Cook time: 4 minutes | Serves 8

1 cup packed fresh basil leaves
⅓ cup chopped walnuts
¼ cup grated Parmesan cheese
¼ cup plus 1 tablespoon extra-virgin olive oil, divided
1 clove garlic, peeled
1 tablespoon lemon juice
¼ teaspoon salt
1 pound (454 g) whole-wheat rotini pasta
4 cups water
1 pint cherry tomatoes
1 cup fresh or frozen green peas
½ teaspoon ground black pepper

1. In a food processor, add basil and walnuts. Pulse until finely chopped, about 12 pulses. Add cheese, ¼ cup oil, garlic, lemon juice, and salt, and pulse until a rough paste forms, about 10 pulses. Refrigerate until ready to use. 2. Add pasta, water, and remaining 1 tablespoon oil to the Instant Pot®. Close lid, set steam release to Sealing, press the Manual button, and set time to 4 minutes. 3. When the timer beeps, quick-release the pressure until the float valve drops and open lid. Drain off any excess liquid. Allow pasta to cool to room temperature, about 30 minutes. Stir in basil mixture until pasta is well coated. Add tomatoes, peas, and pepper and toss to coat. Refrigerate for 2 hours. Stir well before serving.

Per Serving:

calories: 371 | fat: 15g | protein: 12g | carbs: 47g | fiber: 7g | sodium: 205mg

Penne with Tuna and Green Olives

Prep time: 5 minutes | Cook time: 5 minutes | Serves 4

2 tablespoons olive oil
3 garlic cloves, minced
½ cup green olives
½ teaspoon salt
¼ teaspoon freshly ground black pepper
2 (6-ounce / 170-g) cans tuna in
olive oil (don't drain off the oil)
½ teaspoon wine vinegar
12 ounces (340 g) penne pasta, cooked according to package directions
2 tablespoons chopped flat-leaf parsley

1. Heat the olive oil in a medium skillet over medium heat. Add the garlic and cook, stirring, 2 to 3 minutes, just until the garlic begins to brown. Add the olives, salt, pepper, and the tuna along with its oil. Cook, stirring, for a minute or two to heat the ingredients through. Remove from the heat and stir in the vinegar. 2. Add the cooked pasta to the skillet and toss to combine the pasta with the sauce. Serve immediately, garnished with the parsley.

Per Serving:

calories: 511 | fat: 22g | protein: 31g | carbs: 52g | fiber: 1g | sodium: 826mg

Neapolitan Pasta and Zucchini

Prep time: 5 minutes | Cook time: 28 minutes | Serves 3

⅓ cup extra virgin olive oil
1 large onion (any variety), diced
1 teaspoon fine sea salt, divided
2 large zucchini, quartered lengthwise and cut into ½-inch pieces
10 ounces (283 g) uncooked
spaghetti, broken into 1-inch pieces
2 tablespoons grated Parmesan cheese
2 ounces (57 g) grated or shaved Parmesan cheese for serving
½ teaspoon freshly ground black pepper

1. Add the olive oil to a medium pot over medium heat. When the oil begins to shimmer, add the onions and ¼ teaspoon of the sea salt. Sauté for 3 minutes, add the zucchini, and continue sautéing for 3 more minutes. 2. Add 2 cups of hot water to the pot or enough to just cover the zucchini (the amount of water may vary depending on the size of the pot). Cover, reduce the heat to low, and simmer for 10 minutes. 3. Add the pasta to the pot, stir, then add 2 more cups of hot water. Continue simmering, stirring occasionally, until the pasta is cooked and the mixture has thickened, about 12 minutes. (If the pasta appears to be dry or undercooked, add small amounts of hot water to the pot to ensure the pasta is covered in the water.). When the pasta is cooked, remove the pot from the heat. Add 2 tablespoons of the grated Parmesan and stir. 4. Divide the pasta into three servings and then top each with 1 ounce (28 g) of the grated or shaved Parmesan. Sprinkle the remaining sea salt and black pepper over the top of each serving. Store covered in the refrigerator for up to 3 days.

Per Serving:

calories: 718 | fat: 33g | protein: 24g | carbs: 83g | fiber: 6g | sodium: 815mg

Rigatoni with Lamb Meatballs

Prep time: 15 minutes | Cook time: 3 to 5 hours | Serves 4

8 ounces (227 g) dried rigatoni pasta	1 pound (454 g) raw ground lamb
2 (28-ounce / 794-g) cans no-salt-added crushed tomatoes or no-salt-added diced tomatoes	1 large egg
	2 tablespoons bread crumbs
1 small onion, diced	1 tablespoon dried parsley
1 bell pepper, any color, seeded and diced	1 teaspoon dried oregano
	1 teaspoon sea salt
3 garlic cloves, minced, divided	½ teaspoon freshly ground black pepper

1. In a slow cooker, combine the pasta, tomatoes, onion, bell pepper, and 1 clove of garlic. Stir to mix well. 2. In a large bowl, mix together the ground lamb, egg, bread crumbs, the remaining 2 garlic cloves, parsley, oregano, salt, and black pepper until all of the ingredients are evenly blended. Shape the meat mixture into 6 to 9 large meatballs. Nestle the meatballs into the pasta and tomato sauce. 3. Cover the cooker and cook for 3 to 5 hours on Low heat, or until the pasta is tender.

Per Serving:

calories: 653 | fat: 29g | protein: 32g | carbs: 69g | fiber: 10g | sodium: 847mg

Toasted Orzo with Shrimp and Feta

Prep time: 10 minutes | Cook time: 15 minutes | Serves 4 to 6

1 pound (454 g) large shrimp (26 to 30 per pound), peeled and deveined	2 cups orzo
	2 cups chicken broth, plus extra as needed
1 tablespoon grated lemon zest plus 1 tablespoon juice	1¼ cups water
¼ teaspoon table salt	½ cup pitted kalamata olives, chopped coarse
¼ teaspoon pepper	
2 tablespoons extra-virgin olive oil, plus extra for serving	1 ounce (28 g) feta cheese, crumbled (¼ cup), plus extra for serving
1 onion, chopped fine	1 tablespoon chopped fresh dill
2 garlic cloves, minced	

1. Toss shrimp with lemon zest, salt, and pepper in bowl; refrigerate until ready to use. 2. Using highest sauté function, heat oil in Instant Pot until shimmering. Add onion and cook until softened, about 5 minutes. Stir in garlic and cook until fragrant, about 30 seconds. Add orzo and cook, stirring frequently, until orzo is coated with oil and lightly browned, about 5 minutes. Stir in broth and water, scraping up any browned bits. 3. Lock lid in place and close pressure release valve. Select high pressure cook function and cook for 2 minutes. Turn off Instant Pot and quick-release pressure. Carefully remove lid, allowing steam to escape away from you. 4. Stir shrimp, olives, and feta into orzo. Cover and let sit until shrimp are opaque throughout, 5 to 7 minutes. Adjust consistency with extra hot broth as needed. Stir in dill and lemon juice, and season with salt and pepper to taste.

Sprinkle individual portions with extra feta and drizzle with extra oil before serving.

Per Serving:

calories: 320 | fat: 8g | protein: 18g | carbs: 46g | fiber: 2g | sodium: 670mg

Creamy Spring Vegetable Linguine

Prep time: 10 minutes | Cook time: 10 minutes | Serves 4 to 6

1 pound (454 g) linguine	1 cup frozen peas, thawed
5 cups water, plus extra as needed	4 ounces (113 g) finely grated Pecorino Romano (2 cups), plus extra for serving
1 tablespoon extra-virgin olive oil	
1 teaspoon table salt	½ teaspoon pepper
1 cup jarred whole baby artichokes packed in water, quartered	2 teaspoons grated lemon zest
	2 tablespoons chopped fresh tarragon

1. Loosely wrap half of pasta in dish towel, then press bundle against corner of counter to break noodles into 6-inch lengths; repeat with remaining pasta. 2. Add pasta, water, oil, and salt to Instant Pot, making sure pasta is completely submerged. Lock lid in place and close pressure release valve. Select high pressure cook function and cook for 4 minutes. Turn off Instant Pot and quick-release pressure. Carefully remove lid, allowing steam to escape away from you. 3. Stir artichokes and peas into pasta, cover, and let sit until heated through, about 3 minutes. Gently stir in Pecorino and pepper until cheese is melted and fully combined, 1 to 2 minutes. Adjust consistency with extra hot water as needed. Stir in lemon zest and tarragon, and season with salt and pepper to taste. Serve, passing extra Pecorino separately.

Per Serving:

calories: 390 | fat: 8g | protein: 17g | carbs: 59g | fiber: 4g | sodium: 680mg

Spicy Broccoli Pasta Salad

Prep time: 10 minutes | Cook time: 10 minutes | Serves 2

8 ounces (227 g) whole-wheat pasta	¼ cup plain Greek yogurt
	Juice of 1 lemon
2 cups broccoli florets	1 teaspoon red pepper flakes
1 cup carrots, peeled and shredded	Sea salt and freshly ground pepper, to taste

1. Cook the pasta according to the package directions for al dente and drain well. 2. When the pasta is cool, combine it with the veggies, yogurt, lemon juice, and red pepper flakes in a large bowl, and stir thoroughly to combine. 3. Taste for seasoning, and add sea salt and freshly ground pepper as needed. 4. This dish can be served at room temperature or chilled.

Per Serving:

calories: 473 | fat: 2g | protein: 22g | carbs: 101g | fiber: 13g | sodium: 101mg

Meaty Baked Penne

Prep time: 10 minutes | Cook time: 40 minutes | Serves 8

1 pound (454 g) penne pasta	1 (1 pounds / 454 g) bag baby
1 pound (454 g) ground beef	spinach, washed
1 teaspoon salt	3 cups shredded mozzarella
1 (25 ounces / 709 g) jar	cheese, divided
marinara sauce	

1. Bring a large pot of salted water to a boil, add the penne, and cook for 7 minutes. Reserve 2 cups of the pasta water and drain the pasta. 2. Preheat the oven to 350°F(180°C). 3. In a large saucepan over medium heat, cook the ground beef and salt. Brown the ground beef for about 5 minutes. 4. Stir in marinara sauce, and 2 cups of pasta water. Let simmer for 5 minutes. 5. Add a handful of spinach at a time into the sauce, and cook for another 3 minutes. 6. To assemble, in a 9-by-13-inch baking dish, add the pasta and pour the pasta sauce over it. Stir in 1½ cups of the mozzarella cheese. Cover the dish with foil and bake for 20 minutes. 7. After 20 minutes, remove the foil, top with the rest of the mozzarella, and bake for another 10 minutes. Serve warm.

Per Serving:

calories: 454 | fat: 13g | protein: 31g | carbs: 55g | fiber: 9g | sodium: 408mg

Penne with Roasted Vegetables

Prep time: 20 minutes | Cook time: 25 to 30 minutes | Serves 6

1 large butternut squash, peeled	1 teaspoon paprika
and diced	½ teaspoon garlic powder
1 large zucchini, diced	1 pound (454 g) whole-grain
1 large yellow onion, chopped	penne
2 tablespoons extra-virgin olive	½ cup dry white wine or
oil	chicken stock
½ teaspoon salt	2 tablespoons grated Parmesan
½ teaspoon freshly ground black	cheese
pepper	

1. Preheat the oven to 400°F(205°C). Line a baking sheet with aluminum foil. 2. In a large bowl, toss the vegetables with the olive oil, then spread them out on the baking sheet. Sprinkle the vegetables with the salt, pepper, paprika, and garlic powder and bake just until fork-tender, 25 to 30 minutes. 3. Meanwhile, bring a large stockpot of water to a boil over high heat and cook the penne according to the package instructions until al dente (still slightly firm). Drain but do not rinse. 4. Place ½ cup of the roasted vegetables and the wine or stock in a blender or food processor and blend until smooth. 5. Place the purée in a large skillet and heat over medium-high heat. Add the pasta and cook, stirring, just until heated through. 6. Serve the pasta and sauce topped with the roasted vegetables. Sprinkle with Parmesan cheese.

Per Serving:

calories: 456 | fat: 7g | protein: 9g | carbs: 92g | fiber: 14g | sodium: 241mg

Mediterranean Pasta Salad

Prep time: 20 minutes | Cook time: 15 minutes | Serves 4

4 cups dried farfalle (bow-tie)	1 Roma (plum) tomato, diced
pasta	½ English cucumber, quartered
1 cup canned chickpeas, drained	lengthwise and cut into ½-inch
and rinsed	pieces
⅔ cup water-packed artichoke	⅓ cup extra-virgin olive oil
hearts, drained and diced	Juice of ½ lemon
½ red onion, thinly sliced	Sea salt
1 cup packed baby spinach	Freshly ground black pepper
½ red bell pepper, diced	½ cup crumbled feta cheese

1. Fill a large saucepan three-quarters full with water and bring to a boil over high heat. Add the pasta and cook according to the package directions until al dente, about 15 minutes. Drain the pasta and run it under cold water to stop the cooking process and cool. 2. While the pasta is cooking, in a large bowl, mix the chickpeas, artichoke hearts, onion, spinach, bell pepper, tomato, and cucumber. 3. Add the pasta to the bowl with the vegetables. Add the olive oil and lemon juice and season with salt and black pepper. Mix well. 4. Top the salad with the feta and serve.

Per Serving:

calories: 702 | fat: 25g | protein: 22g | carbs: 99g | fiber: 10g | sodium: 207mg

Greek Spaghetti with Meat Sauce

Prep time: 10 minutes | Cook time: 17 minutes | Serves 6

1 pound (454 g) spaghetti	¼ teaspoon ground black pepper
4 cups water	¼ cup white wine
3 tablespoons olive oil, divided	½ cup tomato sauce
1 medium white onion, peeled	1 cinnamon stick
and diced	2 bay leaves
½ pound (227 g) lean ground	1 clove garlic, peeled
veal	¼ cup grated aged myzithra or
½ teaspoon salt	Parmesan cheese

1. Add pasta, water, and 1 tablespoon oil to the Instant Pot®. Close lid, set steam release to Sealing, press the Manual button, and set time to 4 minutes. When the timer beeps, quick-release the pressure until the float valve drops, open lid, and drain. Press the Cancel button. Set aside. 2. Press the Sauté button and heat remaining 2 tablespoons oil. Add onion and cook until soft, about 3 minutes. Add veal and crumble well. Keep stirring until meat is browned, about 5 minutes. Add salt, pepper, wine, and tomato sauce, and mix well. 3. Stir in cinnamon stick, bay leaves, and garlic. Press the Cancel button. Close lid, set steam release to Sealing, press the Manual button, and set time to 5 minutes. When the timer beeps, quick-release the pressure until the float valve drops and open lid. Remove and discard cinnamon stick and bay leaves. 4. Place pasta in a large bowl. Sprinkle with cheese and spoon meat sauce over top. Serve immediately.

Per Serving:

calories: 447 | fat: 15g | protein: 18g | carbs: 60g | fiber: 4g | sodium: 394mg

Roasted Asparagus Caprese Pasta

Prep time: 10 minutes |Cook time: 15 minutes| Serves: 6

8 ounces (227 g) uncooked small pasta, like orecchiette (little ears) or farfalle (bow ties)	oil
	¼ teaspoon freshly ground black pepper
1½ pounds (680 g) fresh asparagus, ends trimmed and stalks chopped into 1-inch pieces (about 3 cups)	¼ teaspoon kosher or sea salt
	2 cups fresh mozzarella, drained and cut into bite-size pieces (about 8 ounces / 227 g)
1 pint grape tomatoes, halved (about 1½ cups)	⅓ cup torn fresh basil leaves
	2 tablespoons balsamic vinegar
2 tablespoons extra-virgin olive	

1. Preheat the oven to 400°F(205ºC). 2. In a large stockpot, cook the pasta according to the package directions. Drain, reserving about ¼ cup of the pasta water. 3. While the pasta is cooking, in a large bowl, toss the asparagus, tomatoes, oil, pepper, and salt together. Spread the mixture onto a large, rimmed baking sheet and bake for 15 minutes, stirring twice as it cooks. 4. Remove the vegetables from the oven, and add the cooked pasta to the baking sheet. Mix with a few tablespoons of pasta water to help the sauce become smoother and the saucy vegetables stick to the pasta. 5. Gently mix in the mozzarella and basil. Drizzle with the balsamic vinegar. Serve from the baking sheet or pour the pasta into a large bowl. 6. If you want to make this dish ahead of time or to serve it cold, follow the recipe up to step 4, then refrigerate the pasta and vegetables. When you are ready to serve, follow step 5 either with the cold pasta or with warm pasta that's been gently reheated in a pot on the stove.

Per Serving:
calories: 317 | fat: 12g | protein: 16g | carbs: 38g | fiber: 7g | sodium: 110mg

Rotini with Red Wine Marinara

Prep time: 10 minutes | Cook time: 25 minutes | Serves 6

1 pound (454 g) rotini	crushed tomatoes
4 cups water	½ cup red wine
1 tablespoon olive oil	1 teaspoon sugar
½ medium yellow onion, peeled and diced	2 tablespoons chopped fresh basil
3 cloves garlic, peeled and minced	½ teaspoon salt
1 (15-ounce / 425-g) can	¼ teaspoon ground black pepper

1. Add pasta and water to the Instant Pot®. Close lid, set steam release to Sealing, press the Manual button, and set time to 4 minutes. When the timer beeps, quick-release the pressure until the float valve drops and open the lid. Press the Cancel button. Drain pasta and set aside. 2. Clean pot and return to machine. Press the Sauté button and heat oil. Add onion and cook until it begins to caramelize, about 10 minutes. Add garlic and cook 30 seconds. Add tomatoes, red wine, and sugar, and simmer for 10 minutes. Add basil, salt, pepper, and

pasta. Serve immediately.

Per Serving:
calories: 320 | fat: 4g | protein: 10g | carbs: 59g | fiber: 4g | sodium: 215mg

Simple Pesto Pasta

Prep time: 10 minutes | Cook time: 10 minutes | Serves 4 to 6

1 pound (454 g) spaghetti	pepper
4 cups fresh basil leaves, stems removed	¼ cup lemon juice
	½ cup pine nuts, toasted
3 cloves garlic	½ cup grated Parmesan cheese
1 teaspoon salt	1 cup extra-virgin olive oil
½ teaspoon freshly ground black	

1. Bring a large pot of salted water to a boil. Add the spaghetti to the pot and cook for 8 minutes. 2. Put basil, garlic, salt, pepper, lemon juice, pine nuts, and Parmesan cheese in a food processor bowl with chopping blade and purée. 3. While the processor is running, slowly drizzle the olive oil through the top opening. Process until all the olive oil has been added. 4. Reserve ½ cup of the pasta water. Drain the pasta and put it into a bowl. Immediately add the pesto and pasta water to the pasta and toss everything together. Serve warm.

Per Serving:
calories: 1067 | fat: 72g | protein: 23g | carbs: 91g | fiber: 6g | sodium: 817mg

Whole-Wheat Spaghetti à la Puttanesca

Prep time: 5 minutes | Cook time: 20 minutes | Serves 6

1 pound (454 g) dried whole-wheat spaghetti	pepper
	1 (28-ounce / 794-g) can tomato purée
⅓ cup olive oil	
5 garlic cloves, minced or pressed	1 pint cherry tomatoes, halved
	½ cup pitted green olives, halved
4 anchovy fillets, chopped	
½ teaspoon red pepper flakes	2 tablespoons drained capers
1 teaspoon salt	¾ cup coarsely chopped basil
½ teaspoon freshly ground black	

1. Cook the pasta according to the package instructions. 2. Meanwhile, heat the oil in a large skillet over medium-high heat. Add the garlic, anchovies, red pepper flakes, salt, and pepper. Cook, stirring frequently, until the garlic just begins to turn golden brown, 2 to 3 minutes. Add the tomato purée, olives, cherry tomatoes, and capers and let the mixture simmer, reducing the heat if necessary, and stirring occasionally, until the pasta is done, about 10 minutes. 3. Drain the pasta in a colander and then add it to the sauce, tossing with tongs until the pasta is well coated. Serve hot, garnished with the basil.

Per Serving:
calories: 464 | fat: 17g | protein: 12g | carbs: 70g | fiber: 12g | sodium: 707mg

Pasta Salad with Tomato, Arugula, and Feta

Prep time: 10 minutes | Cook time: 4 minutes | Serves 8

1 pound (454 g) rotini	1 medium red bell pepper,
4 cups water	seeded and diced
3 tablespoons extra-virgin olive	2 tablespoons white wine
oil, divided	vinegar
2 medium Roma tomatoes,	5 ounces (142 g) baby arugula
diced	1 cup crumbled feta cheese
2 cloves garlic, peeled and	½ teaspoon salt
minced	½ teaspoon ground black pepper

1. Add pasta, water, and 1 tablespoon oil to the Instant Pot®. Close lid, set steam release to Sealing, press the Manual button, and set time to 4 minutes. When the timer beeps, quick-release the pressure until the float valve drops, open lid, drain pasta, then rinse with cold water. Set aside. 2. In a large bowl, mix remaining 2 tablespoons oil, tomatoes, garlic, bell pepper, vinegar, arugula, and cheese. Stir in pasta and season with salt and pepper. Cover and refrigerate for 2 hours before serving.

Per Serving:

calories: 332 | fat: 12g | protein: 12g | carbs: 44g | fiber: 3g | sodium: 480mg

Chilled Pearl Couscous Salad

Prep time: 15 minutes | Cook time: 10 minutes | Serves 6

3 tablespoons olive oil, divided	¼ cup slivered almonds
1 cup pearl couscous	¼ cup chopped fresh mint
1 cup water	leaves
1 cup orange juice	2 tablespoons lemon juice
1 small cucumber, seeded and	1 teaspoon grated lemon zest
diced	¼ cup crumbled feta cheese
1 small yellow bell pepper,	¼ teaspoon fine sea salt
seeded and diced	1 teaspoon smoked paprika
2 small Roma tomatoes, seeded	1 teaspoon garlic powder
and diced	

1. Press the Sauté button and heat 1 tablespoon oil. Add couscous and cook for 2–4 minutes until couscous is slightly browned. Add water and orange juice. Press the Cancel button. 2. Close lid, set steam release to Sealing, press the Manual button, and set time to 5 minutes. When the timer beeps, let pressure release naturally for 5 minutes. Quick-release any remaining pressure until the float valve drops and open lid. Drain any liquid and set aside to cool for 20 minutes. 3. Combine remaining 2 tablespoons oil, cucumber, bell pepper, tomatoes, almonds, mint, lemon juice, lemon zest, cheese, salt, paprika, and garlic powder in a medium bowl. Add couscous and toss ingredients together. Cover and refrigerate overnight before serving.

Per Serving:

calories: 177 | fat: 11g | protein: 5g | carbs: 12g | fiber: 1g | sodium: 319mg

Toasted Orzo Salad

Prep time: 15 minutes | Cook time: 8 minutes | Serves 6

2 tablespoons light olive oil	1 medium red bell pepper,
1 clove garlic, peeled and	seeded and diced
crushed	¼ cup crumbled feta cheese
2 cups orzo	1 tablespoon extra-virgin olive
3 cups vegetable broth	oil
½ cup sliced black olives	1 tablespoon red wine vinegar
3 scallions, thinly sliced	½ teaspoon ground black pepper
1 medium Roma tomato, seeded	¼ teaspoon salt
and diced	

1. Press the Sauté button on the Instant Pot® and heat light olive oil. Add garlic and orzo and cook, stirring frequently, until orzo is light golden brown, about 5 minutes. Press the Cancel button. 2. Add broth and stir. Close lid, set steam release to Sealing, press the Manual button, and set time to 3 minutes. When the timer beeps, let pressure release naturally for 5 minutes, then quick-release the remaining pressure until the float valve drops and open lid. 3. Transfer orzo to a medium bowl, then set aside to cool to room temperature, about 30 minutes. Add olives, scallions, tomato, bell pepper, feta, extra-virgin olive oil, vinegar, black pepper, and salt, and stir until combined. Serve at room temperature or refrigerate for at least 2 hours.

Per Serving:

calories: 120 | fat: 4g | protein: 4g | carbs: 17g | fiber: 1g | sodium: 586mg

Pasta with Marinated Artichokes and Spinach

Prep time: 10 minutes | Cook time: 5 minutes | Serves 6

1 pound (454 g) whole-wheat	artichoke hearts
spaghetti, broken in half	2 tablespoons chopped fresh
3½ cups water	oregano
4 tablespoons extra-virgin olive	2 tablespoons chopped fresh
oil, divided	flat-leaf parsley
¼ teaspoon salt	1 teaspoon ground black pepper
2 cups baby spinach	½ cup grated Parmesan cheese
1 cup drained marinated	

1. Add pasta, water, 2 tablespoons oil, and salt to the Instant Pot®. Close lid, set steam release to Sealing, press the Manual button, and set time to 5 minutes. 2. When the timer beeps, quick-release the pressure until the float valve drops and open lid. Drain off any excess liquid. Stir in remaining 2 tablespoons oil and spinach. Toss until spinach is wilted. Stir in artichokes, oregano, and parsley until well mixed. Sprinkle with pepper and cheese, and serve immediately.

Per Serving:

calories: 414 | fat: 16g | protein: 16g | carbs: 56g | fiber: 9g | sodium: 467mg

Chapter **14**

Staples, Sauces, Dips, and Dressings

Harissa Spice Mix

Prep time: 5 minutes | Cook time: 0 minutes | Makes about 7 tablespoons

2 tablespoons ground cumin	1 teaspoon garlic powder
4 teaspoons paprika	1 teaspoon ground caraway
4 teaspoons ground turmeric	seeds
2 teaspoons ground coriander	½ teaspoon cayenne powder
2 teaspoons chili powder	

1. Place all of the ingredients in a jar. Seal and shake well to combine. Store in a sealed jar at room temperature for up to 6 months.

Per Serving:
1 tablespoon: calories: 21 | fat: 1g | protein: 1g | carbs: 4g | fiber: 2g | sodium: 27mg

Olive Mint Vinaigrette

Prep time: 5 minutes | Cook time: 0 minutes | Makes ½ cup

¼ cup white wine vinegar	¼ cup extra-virgin olive oil
¼ teaspoon honey	¼ cup olives, pitted and minced
¼ teaspoon kosher salt	2 tablespoons fresh mint,
¼ teaspoon freshly ground black	minced
pepper	

1. In a bowl, whisk together the vinegar, honey, salt, and black pepper. Add the olive oil and whisk well. Add the olives and mint, and mix well. Store any leftovers in the refrigerator in an airtight container for up to 5 days.

Per Serving:
2 tablespoons: calories: 135 | fat: 15g | protein: 0g | carbs: 1g | fiber: 0g | sodium: 135mg

Skinny Cider Dressing

Prep time: 5 minutes | Cook time: 0 minutes | Serves 2

2 tablespoons apple cider	⅓ lemon, zested
vinegar	Salt
⅓ lemon, juiced	Freshly ground black pepper

1. In a jar, combine the vinegar, lemon juice, and zest. Season with salt and pepper, cover, and shake well.

Per Serving:
calories: 2 | fat: 0g | protein: 0g | carbs: 1g | fiber: 0g | sodium: 0mg

Italian Dressing

Prep time: 5 minutes | Cook time: 0 minutes | Serves 12

¼ cup red wine vinegar	1 teaspoon dried Italian
½ cup extra-virgin olive oil	seasoning
¼ teaspoon salt	1 teaspoon Dijon mustard
¼ teaspoon freshly ground black	1 garlic clove, minced
pepper	

1. In a small jar, combine the vinegar, olive oil, salt, pepper, Italian seasoning, mustard, and garlic. Close with a tight-fitting lid and shake vigorously for 1 minute. 2. Refrigerate for up to 1 week.

Per Serving:
calories: 82 | fat: 9g | protein: 0g | carbs: 0g | fiber: 0g | sodium: 71mg

Cucumber Yogurt Dip

Prep time: 5 minutes | Cook time: 0 minutes | Serves 2 to 3

1 cup plain, unsweetened, full-fat Greek yogurt	lemon juice
½ cup cucumber, peeled,	1 tablespoon chopped fresh mint
seeded, and diced	1 small garlic clove, minced
1 tablespoon freshly squeezed	Salt and freshly ground black
	pepper, to taste

1. In a food processor, combine the yogurt, cucumber, lemon juice, mint, and garlic. Pulse several times to combine, leaving noticeable cucumber chunks. 2. Taste and season with salt and pepper.

Per Serving:
calories: 55 | fat: 3g | protein: 3g | carbs: 5g | fiber: 0g | sodium: 38mg

Herbed Oil

Prep time: 5 minutes | Cook time: 0 minutes | Serves 2

½ cup extra-virgin olive oil	leaves
1 teaspoon dried basil	2 teaspoons dried oregano
1 teaspoon dried parsley	⅛ teaspoon salt
1 teaspoon fresh rosemary	

1. Pour the oil into a small bowl and stir in the basil, parsley, rosemary, oregano, and salt while whisking the oil with a fork.

Per Serving:
calories: 486 | fat: 54g | protein: 1g | carbs: 2g | fiber: 1g | sodium: 78mg

Tzatziki

Prep time: 10 minutes | Cook time: 0 minutes | Serves 4

1 large cucumber, peeled and grated (about 2 cups)	1 tablespoon fresh lemon juice
1 cup plain Greek yogurt	½ teaspoon kosher salt, or to
2 to 3 garlic cloves, minced	taste
1 tablespoon tahini (sesame	Chopped fresh parsley or dill,
paste)	for garnish (optional)

1. In a medium bowl, combine the cucumber, yogurt, garlic, tahini, lemon juice, and salt. Stir until well combined. Cover and chill until ready to serve. 2. Right before serving, sprinkle with chopped fresh parsley, if desired.

Per Serving:
calories: 71 | fat: 4g | protein: 3g | carbs: 6g | fiber: 1g | sodium: 325mg

Basic Brown-Onion Masala

Prep time: 20 minutes | Cook time: 6½ hours | Makes 4 cups

2 tablespoons rapeseed oil	Handful fresh coriander stalks,
6 onions, finely diced	finely chopped
8 garlic cloves, finely chopped	3 fresh green chiles, finely
1¾ pounds (794 g) canned plum	chopped
tomatoes	1 teaspoon chili powder
3-inch piece fresh ginger, grated	1 teaspoon ground cumin seeds
1 teaspoon salt	1 cup hot water
1½ teaspoons turmeric	2 teaspoons garam masala

1. Preheat the slow cooker on high (or to the sauté setting, if you have it). Then add the oil and let it heat. Add the onions and cook for a few minutes until they start to brown. Make sure you brown the onions well so you get a deep, flavorsome base. 2. Add the garlic and continue to cook on high for about 10 minutes. 3. Add the tomatoes, ginger, salt, turmeric, coriander stalks, chopped chiles, chili powder, cumin seeds, and water. 4. Cover the slow cooker and cook on low for 6 hours. 5. Remove the lid and stir. Let the masala cook for another 30 minutes uncovered to reduce a little. 6. Add the garam masala after the masala has cooked. 7. Use right away, or freeze it in small tubs or freezer bags. Just defrost what you need, when you need it.

Per Serving:
calories: 286 | fat: 8g | protein: 7g | carbs: 52g | fiber: 8g | sodium: 656mg

Crunchy Yogurt Dip

Prep time: 5 minutes | Cook time: 0 minutes | Serves 2 to 3

1 cup plain, unsweetened, full-fat Greek yogurt	lemon juice
	1 tablespoon chopped fresh mint
½ cup cucumber, peeled, seeded, and diced	1 small garlic clove, minced
	Salt
1 tablespoon freshly squeezed	Freshly ground black pepper

1. In a food processor, combine the yogurt, cucumber, lemon juice, mint, and garlic. Pulse several times to combine, leaving noticeable cucumber chunks. 2. Taste and season with salt and pepper.

Per Serving:
calories: 128 | fat: 6g | protein: 11g | carbs: 7g | fiber: 0g | sodium: 47mg

Pepper Sauce

Prep time: 10 minutes | Cook time: 20 minutes | Makes 4 cups

2 red hot fresh chiles, seeded	2 garlic cloves, peeled
2 dried chiles	2 cups water
½ small yellow onion, roughly chopped	2 cups white vinegar

1. In a medium saucepan, combine the fresh and dried chiles, onion, garlic, and water. Bring to a simmer and cook for 20 minutes, or until tender. Transfer to a food processor or blender. 2. Add the vinegar and blend until smooth.

Per Serving:
1 cup: calories: 41 | fat: 0g | protein: 1g | carbs: 5g | fiber: 1g | sodium: 11mg

White Bean Dip with Garlic and Herbs

Prep time: 10 minutes | Cook time: 30 minutes | Serves 16

1 cup dried white beans, rinsed and drained	oregano
	1 tablespoon chopped fresh
3 cloves garlic, peeled and crushed	tarragon
	1 teaspoon chopped fresh thyme
8 cups water	leaves
¼ cup extra-virgin olive oil	1 teaspoon grated lemon zest
¼ cup chopped fresh flat-leaf parsley	¼ teaspoon salt
	¼ teaspoon ground black pepper
1 tablespoon chopped fresh	

1. Place beans and garlic in the Instant Pot® and stir well. Add water, close lid, set steam release to Sealing, press the Manual button, and set time to 30 minutes. 2. When the timer beeps, let pressure release naturally, about 20 minutes. Open lid and check that beans are tender. Press the Cancel button, drain off excess water, and transfer beans and garlic to a food processor with olive oil. Pulse until mixture is smooth with some small chunks. Add parsley, oregano, tarragon, thyme, lemon zest, salt, and pepper, and pulse 3–5 times to mix. Transfer to a storage container and refrigerate for 4.hours or overnight. Serve cold or at room temperature.

Per Serving:
calories: 47 | fat: 3g | protein: 1g | carbs: 3g | fiber: 1g | sodium: 38mg

White Bean Hummus

Prep time: 10 minutes | Cook time: 30 minutes | Serves 12

⅔ cup dried white beans, rinsed and drained	¼ cup olive oil
	1 tablespoon lemon juice
3 cloves garlic, peeled and crushed	½ teaspoon salt

1. Place beans and garlic in the Instant Pot® and stir well. Add enough cold water to cover ingredients. Close lid, set steam release to Sealing, press the Manual button, and set time to 30 minutes. 2. When the timer beeps, let pressure release naturally, about 20 minutes. Press the Cancel button and open lid. Use a fork to check that beans are tender. Drain off excess water and transfer beans to a food processor. 3. Add oil, lemon juice, and salt to the processor and pulse until mixture is smooth with some small chunks. Transfer to a storage container and refrigerate for at least 4 hours. Serve cold or at room temperature. Store in the refrigerator for up to one week.

Per Serving:
calories: 57 | fat: 5g | protein: 1g | carbs: 3g | fiber: 1g | sodium: 99mg

Chermoula

Prep time: 10 minutes | Cook time: 0 minutes | Makes about 1½ cups

2¼ cups fresh cilantro leaves
8 garlic cloves, minced
1½ teaspoons ground cumin
1½ teaspoons paprika

½ teaspoon cayenne pepper
½ teaspoon table salt
6 tablespoons lemon juice (2 lemons)
¾ cup extra-virgin olive oil

1. Pulse cilantro, garlic, cumin, paprika, cayenne, and salt in food processor until cilantro is coarsely chopped, about 10 pulses. Add lemon juice and pulse briefly to combine. Transfer mixture to medium bowl and slowly whisk in oil until incorporated and mixture is emulsified. Cover and let sit at room temperature for at least 30 minutes to allow flavors to meld. (Sauce can be refrigerated for up to 2 days; bring to room temperature before serving.)

Per Serving:

¼ cup: calories: 253 | fat: 27g | protein: 1g | carbs: 3g | fiber: 1g | sodium: 199mg

Peanut Sauce

Prep time: 5 minutes | Cook time: 0 minutes | Serves 4

⅓ cup peanut butter
¼ cup hot water
2 tablespoons soy sauce
2 tablespoons rice vinegar

Juice of 1 lime
1 teaspoon minced fresh ginger
1 teaspoon minced garlic
1 teaspoon black pepper

1. In a blender container, combine the peanut butter, hot water, soy sauce, vinegar, lime juice, ginger, garlic, and pepper. Blend until smooth.
2. Use immediately or store in an airtight container in the refrigerator for a week or more.

Per Serving:

calories: 408 | fat: 33g | protein: 16g | carbs: 18g | fiber: 5g | sodium: 2525mg

Green Olive Tapenade with Harissa

Prep time: 5 minutes | Cook time: 0 minutes | Makes about 1½ cups

1 cup pitted, cured green olives
1 clove garlic, minced
1 tablespoon harissa

1 tablespoon lemon juice
1 tablespoon chopped fresh parsley
¼ cup olive oil, or more to taste

1. Finely chop the olives (or pulse them in a food processor until they resemble a chunky paste). 2. Add the garlic, harissa, lemon juice, parsley, and olive oil and stir or pulse to combine well.

Per Serving:

¼ cup: calories: 215 | fat: 23g | protein: 1g | carbs: 5g | fiber: 2g | sodium: 453mg

Appendix 1:

Measurement Conversion Chart

VOLUME EQUIVALENTS(DRY)

US STANDARD	METRIC (APPROXIMATE)
1/8 teaspoon	0.5 mL
1/4 teaspoon	1 mL
1/2 teaspoon	2 mL
3/4 teaspoon	4 mL
1 teaspoon	5 mL
1 tablespoon	15 mL
1/4 cup	59 mL
1/2 cup	118 mL
3/4 cup	177 mL
1 cup	235 mL
2 cups	475 mL
3 cups	700 mL
4 cups	1 L

VOLUME EQUIVALENTS(LIQUID)

US STANDARD	US STANDARD (OUNCES)	METRIC (APPROXIMATE)
2 tablespoons	1 fl.oz.	30 mL
1/4 cup	2 fl.oz.	60 mL
1/2 cup	4 fl.oz.	120 mL
1 cup	8 fl.oz.	240 mL
1 1/2 cup	12 fl.oz.	355 mL
2 cups or 1 pint	16 fl.oz.	475 mL
4 cups or 1 quart	32 fl.oz.	1 L
1 gallon	128 fl.oz.	4 L

TEMPERATURES EQUIVALENTS

FAHRENHEIT(F)	CELSIUS(C) (APPROXIMATE)
225 °F	107 °C
250 °F	120 °C
275 °F	135 °C
300 °F	150 °C
325 °F	160 °C
350 °F	180 °C
375 °F	190 °C
400 °F	205 °C
425 °F	220 °C
450 °F	235 °C
475 °F	245 °C
500 °F	260 °C

WEIGHT EQUIVALENTS

US STANDARD	METRIC (APPROXIMATE)
1 ounce	28 g
2 ounces	57 g
5 ounces	142 g
10 ounces	284 g
15 ounces	425 g
16 ounces (1 pound)	455 g
1.5 pounds	680 g
2 pounds	907 g

Appendix 2:

The Dirty Dozen and Clean Fifteen

The Environmental Working Group (EWG) is a nonprofit, nonpartisan organization dedicated to protecting human health and the environment Its mission is to empower people to live healthier lives in a healthier environment. This organization publishes an annual list of the twelve kinds of produce, in sequence, that have the highest amount of pesticide residue-the Dirty Dozen-as well as a list of the fifteen kinds ofproduce that have the least amount of pesticide residue-the Clean Fifteen.

THE DIRTY DOZEN	THE CLEAN FIFTEEN
• The 2016 Dirty Dozen includes the following produce. These are considered among the year's most important produce to buy organic:	• The least critical to buy organically are the Clean Fifteen list. The following are on the 2016 list:

Strawberries	Spinach	Avocados	Papayas
Apples	Tomatoes	Corn	Kiw
Nectarines	Bell peppers	Pineapples	Eggplant
Peaches	Cherry tomatoes	Cabbage	Honeydew
Celery	Cucumbers	Sweet peas	Grapefruit
Grapes	Kale/collard greens	Onions	Cantaloupe
Cherries	Hot peppers	Asparagus	Cauliflower
		Mangos	

• *The Dirty Dozen list contains two additional itemskale/collard greens and hot peppers-because they tend to contain trace levels of highly hazardous pesticides.*	• *Some of the sweet corn sold in the United States are made from genetically engineered (GE) seedstock. Buy organic varieties of these crops to avoid GE produce.*

Appendix 3:

Recipe Index

Made in United States
Troutdale, OR
02/01/2024